Third Edition

The Landlord's Handbook

A Complete Guide to Managing Small Investment Properties

Daniel Goodwin, Richard Rusdorf, and Barbara McNichol

Dearborn™
Trade Publishing
A **Kaplan Professional** Company

Vice President and Publisher: Cynthia A. Zigmund
Acquisitions Editor: Mary B. Good
Senior Managing Editor: Jack Kiburz
Interior Design: Lucy Jenkins
Cover Design: DePinto Graphic Design
Typesetting: the dotted i

Published by Dearborn Trade Publishing
A Kaplan Professional Company

Library of Congress Cataloging-in-Publication Data

Goodwin, Daniel.
    The landlord's handbook : a complete guide to managing small investment properties /
Daniel Goodwin, Richard Rusdorf, Barbara McNichol.— 3rd ed.
      p.   cm.
    Includes bibliographical references and index.
    ISBN 0-7931-7959-9 (pbk.)
    1. Real estate management.   2. Rental housing.   3. Residential real estate—Management.
4. Commercial real estate—Management.   5. Landlords.   6. Landlord and tenant.
I. Rusdorf, Richard.   II. McNichol, Barbara.   III. Title.
HD1394 .G656 2004
333.33′85′068—dc22

                                                                                        2003020323

C o n t e n t s

Many people helped put this book together. We especially would like to thank the staff, officers, and support personnel of The Inland Group for graciously providing us the benefit of their knowledge: Sharen Mangiameli (marketing and leases), Darren Jordan (collections), Lori Ann Ogolini (taxes), Tom Henderson (accounting), Doug Blume (maintenance), and Delores Friedman (insurance).

We are grateful for the legal review and suggestions of Andrew Hull, Phoenix, Arizona, and the review by Scott Henderson, Boulder, Colorado, a professional property manager and consultant to landlords. We are grateful to landlord coach Nancy Spivey, who contributed the Foreword to this book, and to all the landlords profiled on these pages. Thanks to Sherry Sterling for her editorial assistance.

Daniel L. Goodwin, chairman and CEO of The Inland Real Estate Group, has over 30 years of experience in purchasing, selling, financing, and managing more than $3 billion worth of income-producing residential properties plus more than 2,000 real estate transactions nationwide.

Richard F. Rusdorf, CPCC, has more than 28 years of experience in property management, marketing, finance, development, and sales. A former real estate broker and Certified Property Manager, Rich is a past president of the Chicago chapter of the Institute of Real Estate Management. He works as a Certified Personal Coach and lives near San Francisco, California.

Barbara McNichol is a professional writer-editor specializing in real estate and business books. She and her husband have ventured into the landlord world with one condominium in Boulder, Colorado (so far).

N A N C Y   S P I V E Y ,
L *a n d l o r d* **C** *o a c h*

It is amazing—so many ways we can end up in the role of landlord.

Some of us find ourselves with a property that we decide to rent rather than sell when we move into a new home. Others buy a vacation home that we rent out most of the year. Still others just set out to produce monthly cash flow and/or a solid retirement for ourselves by owning and renting property, and some even venture into commercial properties. However you ended up being a landlord, you can be a successful one with some work, lots of knowledge, and a conscious attitude about the opportunities and rewards.

I was asked to write the foreword to *The Landlord's Handbook* because I am a landlord and also a coach, speaker, and trainer. I work closely with both experienced landlords and those just starting to pursue a landlording career. I grew up in a family of landlords: my grandfather and grandmother were landlords, and my uncle was and still is a landlord. Now I am carrying on the family tradition.

I saw the good, the bad, and the ugly side of landlording while growing up. I heard all the nightmare stories and saw the benefits and growth that one can achieve as a landlord. Indeed, many of the richest people in America have been landlords—or still are!

My experience as a landlord has provided me with cash flow, appreciation in property, learning experiences, and great opportunities to positively influence the lives of others. Now, as a landlord trained in the profession of coaching, I also have a great opportunity to help other landlords by working with them through training, speaking, and one-on-one coaching. I am a member of the Georgia Real Estate Investors Association, in which I am an instructor for its Institute of Education. I also belong to the International Coach Federation and the National Speakers Association–Georgia Chapter.

IT'S ABOUT MORE THAN MAKING MONEY

Landlords' experiences can be described in many ways. They can be fun and rewarding. They can also be stressful and tiring. Like anything in life, landlording comes with good and bad. That's why it's important to have the knowledge you need to make the right decisions as a landlord. You likely have more knowledge from your other jobs, dealings, and experiences that will contribute to your success as a landlord than you realize. With a little reading and practice, you can be a pro at the job of being a landlord!

When coaching landlords, I find it's important to help individuals form a clear vision of being a landlord. Typically, making money is a part of the vision. But what aspects of landlording (besides the money) might bring you fulfillment? How can you work toward a vision and/or a mission that will enhance your life as a landlord and positively impact others' lives, neighborhoods, and more?

When you become a landlord, you have a responsibility to do more than make money—one that's greater than making money.

You have an opportunity to offer families enjoyable homes and provide them education, improve neighborhoods by improving your own properties, and improve cities by your positive input in a neighborhood. The seeds that you plant can continue to grow well beyond your seasons here on earth.

FAMILY OF SEVEN THAT COULDN'T PAY RENT

I bought a property a few years ago that came with tenants already living there. Unfortunately, I soon found out those tenants couldn't pay the rent. Everyone I talked with suggested evicting them. Seven people lived in my new rental house: five children, the mother, and the grandmother. The father had left and gone back to Mexico.

I learned there was no place for the family to go. I even checked into shelters in Atlanta, but none were large enough to take all of the children. I didn't want them to be separated nor did I want to evict them, but I did want to cover my expenses and realize a positive cash flow.

How could I handle this situation? Being an eternal optimist, I saw opportunity and possibility. I began my research to find out what options existed. After spending much time talking to local officials, I learned that this family was eligible for public housing. The family had no idea how to get into the public housing program, so I walked with them each step of the way—even asking a friend to help me pick them up and visit the appropriate organizations.

These efforts made it possible for this family to stay together, move into a pleasant new apartment, and pay only $75 a month for rent and utilities. I'll admit that evicting them would have cost me a lot less time and money, but I have my values, heart, and mind to consider. I look back on what could have been a horrific situation and feel great pride and fulfillment about the person I was able to be and what I could contribute through my role as a landlord.

CHOOSE THE KIND OF LANDLORD YOU WANT TO BE

Being a landlord puts you in the position of dealing with people, money, property, and lives. You may have seen images of landlords as guys always grumbling, being cheap, and making all the money for themselves.

You have a choice of the kind of landlord you want to be—and of how you'll handle situations that arise out of the role. The best advice is to remember the Golden Rule: Do unto others as you would have them do unto you.

If you're still feeling "stuck" on the decision about becoming a landlord, I challenge you to consider the following questions:

- *What will being a landlord provide in your life?* This could be extra income, retirement funds, and so on.
- *What can you give back as a landlord?* You can provide nice homes for families, enhance neighborhoods, and the like.
- *What would stop you from becoming a landlord?* Possibly fear, stories you've heard, or the belief that you don't have the necessary experience could deter you.
- *How can you get around the obstacles that could stand in the way of being a successful landlord?* Having confidence is a big factor in overcoming fears and potential obstacles in handling the jobs required of landlords. Understanding the rules and regulations—the "in and outs" of the job—and learning what to do can greatly enhance your confidence as a landlord.
- *What do you expect from the experience?* You've heard that "life is often a self-fulfilling prophecy." Well, being a landlord may prove the truth of this saying as you almost always get exactly what you expect. That means you must manage your expectations and those of your tenants.
- *What do you expect from your tenants?* Setting expectations and communicating them up front can make all the difference in your experience as a landlord. Set expectations for yourself and for your tenants, and create the mental picture that you want to see as a landlord.

BEST WAY TO GET READY FOR LANDLORDING

The Landlord's Handbook is one of the best books I've seen for landlords, covering the broad range of knowledge you need.

From tenants to taxes, the handbook covers the information you need to be successful. Whether you are just starting out or have a lot of experience, this book is a valuable resource! I wish I'd had it when I first became a landlord.

Thankfully, you do have this book. It will help you be the successful landlord you are capable of becoming.

Happy landlording!

Nancy Spivey is the president of Transformation Consultants, Inc. Along with being a landlord and real estate investor, she is a professional business coach, speaker, and trainer. Nancy works with businesspeople who want to start a business or take their business to the next level as well as with people who want a more fulfilling life personally and professionally. Many of her clients are landlords and/or real estate investors.

Nancy has experience in the corporate world and as a business owner. A planner and visionary, she sees trends and knows how to embrace change and implement plans to create growth. Her passion is to help others realize successes they never imagined possible. (Look in Landlord Consultants/Coaches Resources for Nancy's contact information.)

1

MANAGING INCOME-PRODUCING PROPERTIES
An Overview

Jacque Carbone has found her niche in duplexes.

When she was a single mom working full time, she realized she could make ends meet more easily if she owned a duplex—living in one side herself and using the rent from the other to pay her mortgage. "By doing that, I lived nearly rent free for ten years and didn't have to have a roommate," she says. She was fortunate that her dad helped her finance and build her first duplex in an historic area of Lafayette, Colorado.

Working with an architect, they decided to add a lot of custom touches not normally available in rental properties, including wood floors, privacy fences, a washer-dryer, a fireplace, a garage, a deck, and even a lawn and rock garden. "Over time, these custom touches have helped us market to upscale renters for an amount of rent higher than that of most duplexes in this community." The strategy has paid off. During a time when apartment complexes are offering three months' free rent, the "turn" on her duplex was only two weeks. "A new school opened a few blocks away from our duplex, so we attracted teachers as renters. We also allow dogs, and people are willing to pay more because of that. But forget about cats. We just can't get cat hair and smells out of the carpets!"

Jacque scrutinizes prospective canine tenants just as carefully as human ones. "I want to make sure the dogs in our duplexes are friendly and people can walk by them safely."

A few years after building her first duplex, Jacque built a second one next door. Now she and her husband live in one side of it and rent out the other. Except for buying, renting, and selling a single-family home in central Denver at the beginning of her landlord career, Jacque's property ventures have been close to home—both by design and personal preference.

With her side-by-side duplexes, this gregarious entrepreneur has, in effect, created a mini-community. Her tenants get to know each other through get-togethers that Jacque hosts. She lets them know they can borrow her lawnmower and expects them to keep up the yards. She likes to brief them on how to prevent situations that can cause damage. As an example, she says, "One tenant didn't know what Colorado winters were like and left a garden hose turned on—in January." It caused a pipe to crack in the house, and she had a large plumbing bill to pay.

Jacque has applied a few shortcuts over her years of landlording—such as putting up commercial-grade wallpaper in hallways and bedrooms so the walls don't have to be repainted and videotaping units before tenants move in and after they move out—important evidence in case problems crop up.

About day-to-day management, she says, "My husband is the numbers guy who takes care of the bookkeeping. He and my dad do some of the fix-up work and landscaping. I'm the one who deals with tenants—I love the people side of this business." Jacque always conducts background and credit checks, calls applicants' job references and at least three personal references—"and their parents don't count! We have to be diligent about checking references, especially because they're our neighbors. And even then, we can get burned."

Early on, Jacque brought a consultant into her business—a professional property manager in Boulder named Scott Henderson (Personalized Management Services, http://www.persmgt.com). "Before knowing Scott, I did a number of things wrong, such as, for example, not charging a deposit for having a dog. I keep working with Scott because he stays on top of the laws and rules required by the county, and he reviews my contracts and notices. He coaches me through ways to work with my tenants, too. He can be the 'heavy' if I need him to be, including serving papers on someone who hasn't paid rent."

She's pleased with the rewards of being a landlord—tax breaks, flexibile hours, people contact, and regular income. "Landlording has also provided peace of mind over the years . . . just as it did in the beginning, when I knew my mortgage would be covered by the rent coming in. Because of it, I'm able to have a more stable financial future than any 401(k) plan could ever provide," she says.

MANAGING PROFITABLE INVESTMENT PROPERTY

George Benton lives in a one-bedroom condominium ideally located along Chicago's North Lake Shore Drive. Since he bought the condo, George has changed jobs and now works in a Chicago suburb. He would like to live closer to work in a larger home with a fenced backyard for his collie. He doesn't want to sell his downtown condominium, however, because he considers it a good long-term investment, so he manages the rental details.

Nancy Oates and Bill Wellbrook are successful entrepreneurs in South Bend, Indiana. Several years ago, they developed an insurance service that caters to the specific needs of senior citizens. To supplement their income, they are renovating a turn-of-the-century six-flat along South Bend's Lincoln Way East, which will become rental property.

The Hasbrouck, Kiel, and Lippert families of Dallas, Texas, organized the HKL Investment Club several years ago. The club's investments have proven profitable. Because they now want to conserve profits, HKL is planning to purchase a 40-unit, five-story apartment building on Rodeo Boulevard.

What do these people have in common? Like you, they currently own, or are planning to purchase, small income-producing properties. And, like you, what they need is a practical handbook, specifically designed for the do-it-yourself landlord. Most real estate books on the shelves deal mainly with acquiring property and structuring real estate deals. Generally, these books don't give people like you—average real estate investors—practical techniques and suggestions that help you manage your investment property more profitably.

This book has been written to share property management expertise with you in clear, everyday language. Based on the experiences of successful property owners and managers, *The Landlord's Handbook* clearly explains the importance of attracting and keeping good tenants by using good management and marketing techniques. It discusses what you need to know about leases, collections, insurance, maintenance, taxes, and accounting. Most important, it shows you how to form business relationships with your tenants based on mutual respect.

The techniques, forms, and worksheets were developed, and are used by, successful real estate investors and managers across the United States.

Real estate has always been considered a good investment. But the combination of tax reform, low mortgage rates, and poor stock market performance has made small income-producing properties one of the best investments over time. Real estate—both residential and commercial—stands the tests of time and cyclical economies.

Owning and operating small investment properties have made many people financially independent—and can work well for you too. As a real estate investor, you benefit from pride of ownership coupled with a hedge against inflation that serves to protect your real estate assets from losing value.

As a manager of rental properties, your two chief concerns are these:

1. Maintain your property
2. Increase its value

Regardless of your specific goals for your properties, *effective management* is the key to achieving them.

Simply owning rental property will not guarantee financial independence, because properties don't generate cash flow by themselves. To make money, you need to know good property management techniques. Specifically, you need to know:

- How to keep good tenants
- How to collect rents on time
- How to maintain properties
- How to build a team of support people
- How to deal with all kinds of people

OWNING A HOME VERSUS MANAGING RENTAL PROPERTY

To some extent, owning your home has prepared you for owning other buildings, but managing rental property is not the same as managing a home. For example, decorating schemes—especially colorful ones—could be a detriment when trying to rent an apartment, office, or house if bright colors clash with a prospective tenant's furniture and personal taste. For example, carpeting and wall treatments should be in neutral colors and made from durable materials that are easy to clean and maintain.

How you deal with kitchen appliances, for example, may be different for rental properties compared with home use. You may choose to buy an oven that has added features for your own home, but a tenant who doesn't cook much wouldn't want to pay a premium for having it. Also, as a property manager you should be aware of how depreciation works (see Chapter 12); you might therefore choose a water heater or furnace for a rental property different from one you would choose for your own use.

YOU DON'T NEED AN MBA

Some would-be investors think property management requires a master's degree in management. They've heard horror tales of tenant complaints, problems with collecting rent, mechanical equipment failures, apartment vacancies, and so on. They suspect that unless they have formal training, managing rental property could be a nightmarish experience.

Certainly, property management can be a headache if you don't know what you are doing. To maximize your investment property, you focus on making money while keeping expenses in check. If you let tenants run the property down, if you fail to get regular rent increases, or if you mismanage cash flow, you could sacrifice making a profit. Worse, you could even decrease the value of your asset.

Even though attending managerial and real estate courses can be helpful, this book offers you proven methods for dealing with a variety of residential and commercial properties and many types of tenants. All examples are based on actual experience, so you're learning from people who have "been there and done that."

USING YOUR MANAGEMENT SKILLS IN A NEW SETTING

If you work in corporate management or operate your own business, you already have many of the necessary skills for small property management—marketing, maintenance, accounting, customer relations, and managing time and people. It's possible that you take these skills for granted as part of your daily business routine. However, the same marketing and management skills can be transferred to other business situations, including your role as property manager.

Marketing

Just as good grocery store management, for example, requires attracting regular customers, good property management requires attracting good renters. To bring customers into the grocery store, the manager uses numerous marketing tools, including newspaper advertising, special promotions, and so on. The property manager advertises rental vacancies and highlights special features of the property (new carpeting, off-street parking, prime location, etc.).

Maintenance

Conducting regular maintenance is equally important to the grocery store owner and the property owner. The grocery store manager may not be the one to operate the floor scrubber or wash down the checkout counters, but he or she will make sure these jobs are done because customers prefer shopping in a clean environment.

The property manager also needs to actively monitor the maintenance of structures, common areas, landscaping, parking areas, and so on.

Accounting

At the end of the business day, the grocery store manager tallies receipts for each department and prepares bank deposits. These accounting numbers are totaled weekly or monthly against costs of inventory, spoilage, overhead, and other variables to monitor the store's profitability. Similar bookkeeping and accounting skills are required for property management to make sure rental receipts cover costs while also producing a profit. Anyone who knows how to balance a checkbook can quickly learn the accounting procedures used to control the income and expenses required for property management.

Customer Relations

The grocery store manager needs to have a balanced combination of diplomacy and judgment when dealing with customers. For example, if an irate customer demands a refund for one rotten orange found in a five-pound bag, a smart manager will replace that $2.99 bag of oranges or refund the purchase price to keep that customer buying oranges and other products in the store. It's clearly a good investment in customer relations.

Diplomacy and judgment are also crucial in good property management. For example, an irate tenant may insist that he or she needs a new dead bolt lock because the door to the apartment is too difficult to open. A smart property manager will promptly and cheerfully apply a little carbon to the keys and locks. This will probably solve the problem, and the cost in time and materials is about the same as that for the five-pound bag of oranges.

Managing Time and People

Properly done, the management of small rental properties can be a rewarding experience. Property management certainly doesn't have to be a full-time job. Obviously, the amount of time you'll need to manage your rental property depends on your knowledge and resources as well as on the size of your portfolio.

Once you've mastered the techniques offered in *The Landlord's Handbook*, you should be able to manage a single condominium unit in 30 minutes a month, whereas a typical four-flat or office building might require about four hours of your time each month. Most of this time will be spent dealing with people, so how well you deal with people is one key to effective management.

Putting Together a Support Team

When you put together a reliable team that supports your landlording business, experts will be available when you need them. From each of your team members, you want honesty, flexibility, and dependability, so choose well from people in your community. Ideally, they're easy to do business with and expect fees that are reasonable.

Be sure your team includes an attorney who knows landlord-tenant laws in your area; an accountant with experience in real estate and knowledge of the tax laws; an insurance agent familiar with rental properties; a loan representative or broker who specializes in rental property investments; a real estate agent who can help you locate good investment properties; and a contractor or repair person who does quality work for a fair price. You can often locate good people for your real estate team by asking for referrals and taking time to qualify them.

HOW *THE LANDLORD'S HANDBOOK* CAN HELP

The information and forms in *The Landlord's Handbook* provide valuable tools to help you increase your cash flow and create financial independence. This book walks you through the important management tasks involved from the day you hand over the keys to a new tenant through to the day you take them back.

As a new investor and manager, you have to determine the proper rental rate for your property based on local market conditions. We show you how to determine rental rates, how to find tenants, and how to convince them that your rental property meets their specific needs.

Lease applications and rental agreements can be complicated, but this handbook simplifies them and even supplies sample applications, leases, and riders to cover special situations. Terminology and contents are defined along with discussions of prohibited transactions, security deposits, lease distribution, and important caveats. You'll also learn about inspections, lease renewals and subletting, and reletting agreements.

Other important aspects of property management include rent collections, maintenance, different types of required insurance, property taxes, and accounting. You'll find that each of these is thoroughly addressed here along with sample forms and guidelines.

2

MANAGING TENANTS

Jeff Young's foray into the world of landlording was a fluke. "I was dragged kicking and screaming through the door of opportunity" is how he expresses it. Now he's helping others walk through that door with confidence.

While living in a Phoenix condo in the mid-1990s, Jeff realized the importance of moving closer to his son's school. After looking at several alternatives, he decided becoming a landlord was his least objectionable option. Soon after, he remarried and bought a home with his new wife. The couple rented out both of their homes, which made a total of three rental properties to manage.

"One big mistake I made as a landlord," Jeff recalls, "was accepting an out-of-state check for a rental deposit and first month's rent. That was a big no-no. Not only did the check bounce, but it was written on an account that didn't even exist." Ouch!

Deciding it was time to learn from other landlords further down the path, Jeff contacted the Arizona Multihousing Association (AMA) (http://www.azama.org). The AMA had a networking group for small, independent owners like himself, but he found out it was inactive. Jeff could see value in having such a group and took a lead in helping AMA form the Independent Rental Owners Council (IROC). Through its programs and networking, the IROC group supports individuals who own fewer than 20 rental units and derive their primary income from sources other than real estate.

"We set a date for our first lunch, and to promote it I wrote a column in the AMA newsletter," he says. Three people came to that first lunch in 1998. By 2003, the membership of IROC had grown to 250, with an average of 75 to 100 attending each monthly meeting. "This group got a boost in numbers when the stock market took a multiyear swoon. People began seeing real estate as a good investment and wanted to attach themselves to our group to learn more," Jeff says.

A professional financial planner and investment advisor, Jeff advocates that an owner-landlord becomes familiar with the law, sets up a limited liability company (LLC), and buys an umbrella insurance policy for his or her own protection. "Most important of all, landlords need to know the applicable state laws that govern rental properties and become familiar with antidiscrimination laws.

"In my presentations to landlords, I say that if you invest in stocks, the worst that can happen is you lose money. But when you're in real estate, the scenario could be much worse—even going to prison in some cases—if you break the law. Complying with the law comes before everything else."

Jeff also recommends setting specific procedures when renting properties. Here are some that he follows: He checks applicants' employment histories and looks for income that's three times the amount of rent requested. He doesn't accept tenants who work out of their homes if their income histories are unstable. He calls previous, as well as current, landlords and pays special attention to what they say as "current landlords might not speak candidly enough because they want these tenants out."

In summing up his advice to new landlords, Jeff says, "Buy smart, know the law, take good care of your tenants, and be sure to associate with experienced owners and/or managers." As he found out, these experienced landlords can be found through a local multihousing group. And if no such group exists, follow Jeff's lead and start one!

THE LANDLORD-TENANT RELATIONSHIP

Many people believe that landlords and tenants are natural enemies. Landlords are sometimes seen as heartless money-grubbers who would trade their mothers for a rent increase, or they are regarded as overworked, underpaid drudges who are slaves to their properties and tenants. Tenants are frequently seen as ne'er-do-wells who make unreasonable demands, destroy property, and refuse to pay the rent.

There is some truth in these stereotypes: bad landlords and bad tenants do exist. But the landlord-tenant relationship is basically a business relationship. If you learn to manage rental property efficiently—and that includes choosing good tenants—then landlord-tenant transactions can be rewarding for everyone involved.

It is well worth learning to deal with tenants in a rational, fair, and businesslike way. When a property is badly managed, it becomes an active drain on all your valued resources: the physical property itself, your time, your energy, and your money.

Landlords and tenants often have differences of opinion about their mutual responsibilities. Tenants may have the perception that landlords should do everything in their power to make tenants happy. You certainly want your tenants to be satisfied with their living or business spaces, but you are not obligated to provide them a garden paradise unless that's what you are specifically marketing. If you know your basic obligations as a landlord, you will be less likely to resent a tenant's legitimate request and will be able to assertively and confidently refuse an unreasonable demand.

Most of your obligations are governed and limited by the expressed conditions contained in a lease or rental agreement. With or without a written lease, the business of owning and leasing rental property is also subject to state and local municipal statutes and ordinances.

Across the country, local and state governments are beginning to take stronger positions in regard to landlord-tenant relationships. Residential tenant groups are presenting their cases to city councils everywhere and demanding more favorable treatment from landlords. Landlord-tenant ordinances contain the obligations of both parties. Most states in the United States have adopted the Uniform Residential Landlord and Tenant Act (some have been amended), and the entire residential rental industry may soon operate under laws of this type. (To review your state's landlord laws, go to http://www.mrlandlord.com/laws and click on the link that takes you to the appropriate state.) Note: The terms *landlord* and *owner* are interchangeable, as both refer to the lessor.

LANDLORD OBLIGATIONS

Landlords must adhere to three widely recognized obligations: (1) make themselves known; (2) maintain habitable premises; and (3) honor express warranties. Let's examine each of your obligations as a landlord.

Making Yourself Known

An owner (or other person who is authorized to enter into a rental agreement on the owner's behalf) should disclose to the tenant, in writing, at or before the beginning of the lease:

- The name and address of the owner or agent of the premises
- The person authorized to manage the premises

Tenants need to know where to send payments, and both tenant and landlord or agent need to know where to receive and document notices and demands.

If tenants are not told who has authority to respond to their requests, they may be able to file a complaint with the local housing authority, withhold rent, or take other measures to keep their units habitable. Further, the owner may face substantial fines.

In many states, an owner must disclose the insurance agent or carrier for the property. In case of damage resulting from a fire or another form of emergency, tenants know whom to call if the owner or agent is unavailable.

Maintaining Habitable Premises

At all times during a tenancy, owners must maintain the premises in a "habitable" condition. (Note: For commercial properties, signed leases spell out landlord and tenant responsibilities, whereas residential properties are covered by statutes.) A residential dwelling unit is considered habitable if the minimum standards listed below are maintained:

- Effective weather protection is provided, including unbroken windows and doors.
- Plumbing facilities are in good working order.
- The unit has a water supply connected to a sewage system. If the water supply is under the control of the resident, it must be capable of producing hot and cold running water; if under the control of the owner, it must produce hot and cold running water furnished to appropriate fixtures.
- Heating units and, if provided, air-conditioning and ventilation systems are in good working order. If these are under the control of the resident, they are capable of producing heat (or cooling and ventilation); if under the control of the owner, they produce heat (or cooling and ventilation) in the fixtures provided. Minimum temperatures for heat are usually established by municipal code. (A good rule of thumb is having a heating system capable of maintaining a minimum of 70°F at all times in the unit, regardless of how cold it gets outside.)
- Gas or electrical appliances supplied by the landlord must be in good working order and properly installed with appropriate gas piping and electrical wiring systems according to building codes, and they must be maintained in good working order.
- The building, grounds, and areas under the control of the owner must be in a clean, sanitary, and safe condition, free from all accumulation of debris, filth, rubbish, garbage, rodents, and vermin.

- Adequate and appropriate receptacles for garbage and rubbish must be provided. If these are under the control of the landlord, they must be kept in clean condition and in good repair.
- Floors, stairways, railings, and common areas are in good repair.
- Floors, walls, and ceilings are in good repair and in safe condition.
- Elevators are maintained in good repair and safe condition.

Generally, landlords are not held responsible if interruptions in service, breakdown of equipment, or disrepairs are caused by the following:

- Actions of the tenant or members of the tenant's household, guests, or other persons on the premises with the tenant's consent, or other tenants
- The tenant's unreasonable refusal of, or other interference with, entry of the owner or the owner's workers or contractors into the premises for purposes of correcting any defective conditions
- A lack of reasonable opportunity for the owner to correct defective conditions
- Conditions beyond the owner's reasonable control, including strikes, lockouts, and unavailability of essential utilities, materials, or services
- The owner's not having actual knowledge or notice of such defective conditions

Any exclusion or modification of any part, or all, of these obligations must be in writing and separately signed by the party against whose interest the modification works. That is the legal way of saying that if the modification appears in the rental agreement, it must also be typed or printed in a conspicuous place. This means that if you and a tenant have an agreement that the tenant will maintain part or all of the property, the agreement must be specifically spelled out in writing. The tenant should sign an acknowledgment of the agreement.

Honoring Express Warranties

If you make a promise to a tenant about the condition of a specific dwelling unit or business space, or of the overall premises, services or repairs, or replacements to be made, and this promise is part of the reason the tenant signed the lease, you have created an *express warranty*. Such a promise is binding whether it was oral or written.

An express warranty may be created even without a specific intention to make one. It is unnecessary to use such formal words as *warrant* or *guarantee* to create an express warranty. Statements such as "We plan to replace the dishwasher in a few months" or "We wash the outside of the windows three times a year" or "You never have to worry about security around here; this is a safe building" all create express warranties. You might be held liable if someone did have a security problem, or if you washed windows only twice, and so on. It's best to avoid making statements that create express warranties.

On the other hand, giving your opinion of the relative value of the dwelling unit, premises, or services does not create a warranty. For example, you could say, "We have the best maintenance crew around" or "I think my property is the best building on the block" or "The view from this apartment is beautiful" without creating a warranty.

If you think you may have created an express warranty, it would be wise to consult your attorney for guidance in this matter.

ADDITIONAL SERVICES

Tenants expect to receive all of the services and amenities your property offers for their rental dollar. They rightfully expect you to live up to your basic obligations as listed above. But many properties also offer additional services, such as a swimming pool, snow removal, and so on.

Before the tenants move in, outline exactly what additional services you provide, such as snow removal, landscaping, garbage removal, utilities, and so on. Then see that these services are provided consistently.

Closing the swimming pool for repairs on the hottest day of the year or failing to provide snow removal after a blizzard, for example, are good ways to ruin a landlord-tenant relationship. Tenants tend to remember these things when it comes time to renew their leases.

LIABILITIES OF OWNERSHIP

Landlords are generally responsible for maintaining the premises and performing the basic services required and can be held liable for damages caused by negligence. In most cases, these liabilities remain with the owners until a property is sold.

However, in some cases, liability continues after a sale transaction. Unless otherwise agreed, an owner who sells his or her property subject to an existing lease and assigns the lease in a good-faith sale to a bona fide purchaser is relieved of liability for events occurring subsequent to written notice to the resident of the sale and assignment. The new owner becomes liable to the resident for events occurring after this notice and for money to which the resident is entitled from a security deposit or prepaid rent.

If you've retained a manager under a management contract, this person, unless otherwise agreed, is also relieved of liability for events occurring after written notice to the resident of the termination of the manager's contract.

SECURITY AND CRIME PREVENTION

You can help yourself in several ways to become more knowledgeable about securing your property and working toward creating a safer environment for your residents. It may require you to attend a seminar or two from time to time, but the time you spend in these classes is well worth your effort.

Landlords can also do a lot to protect themselves through the signed lease agreement. For example, you can put tenants on notice that crime will not be tolerated by stating it in the lease or in an addendum as in Figure 2.1. Doing this may make it easier in court to prove that tenants have agreed to this requirement and can be evicted if, for example, they allow guests to have illegal substances while on the premises.

One program, called the Crime Free Multi-Housing Program (CFMHP), is being offered in more than 1,400 cities around the world. This rapidly growing program helps residents, owners, and managers of apartments keep drugs and other illegal activity off their property. It was developed at the Mesa, Arizona, Police Department in 1992 and has been implemented in 40 U.S. states, 4 Canadian provinces, and in Japan, Finland, England, and Puerto Rico.

Attendees learn about identifying illegal activities, addressing community concerns, and educating residents about crime prevention. Benefits range from increasing property values to developing better relations among residents in the neighborhood and surrounding neighborhoods.

The program consists of eight hours of training by a local police agency. After the training, the police inspect your property from the viewpoint of security. Residents are invited to crime prevention meetings and are encouraged to form a community Block Watch, a program through which neighbors protectively look out for each other.

Part of the program includes receiving a sample Crime Free Lease Addendum (Figure 2.1) that residents sign to indicate their agreement not to engage in any illegal activity. If they violate the addendum, the law allows the landlord to serve them with a 24-hour eviction notice.

FIGURE 2.1 *Crime Free Lease Addendum (Arizona Version)*

In consideration of the execution or renewal of a lease of the dwelling unit identified in the lease, Owner and Resident agree as follows:

Resident, any members of the resident's household or a guest or other persons affiliated with the resident:

Shall not engage in criminal activity, including drug-related criminal activity, on or near the said premises. "Drug-related criminal activity" means the illegal manufacture, sale, distribution, use, or possession with intent to manufacture, sell, distribute, or use an illegal or controlled substance (as defined in Section 102 of the Controlled Substance Act [21 U.S.C.802]).

Shall not engage in any act intended to facilitate criminal activity.

Shall not permit the dwelling unit to be used for, or to facilitate criminal activity, regardless of whether the individual engaging in such activity is a member of the household, or a guest.

Shall not engage in the unlawful manufacturing, selling, using, storing, keeping, or giving of an illegal or controlled substance as defined in A.R.S. 13-3451, at any locations, whether on or near the dwelling unit premises.

Shall not engage in any illegal activity, including prostitution as defined in A.R.S. 13-3211, *criminal street gang activity* as defined in A.R.S. 13-105 and A.R.S. 13-2308, *threatening or intimidating* as prohibited in A.R.S.13-1202, *assault* as prohibited in A.R.S. 13-1203, including but not limited to *the unlawful discharge of a weapon,* on or near the dwelling unit premises, or *any breach of the lease agreement that otherwise jeopardizes the health, safety, and welfare of the landlord, his agent, or other tenant, or involving imminent or actual serious property damage,* as defined in A.R.S. 33-1368.

VIOLATION OF THE ABOVE PROVISIONS SHALL BE A MATERIAL AND IRREPARABLE VIOLATION OF THE LEASE AND GOOD CAUSE FOR IMMEDIATE TERMINATION OF TENANCY. A single violation of any of the provisions of this added addendum shall be deemed a serious violation, and a material and irreparable non-compliance. It is understood that a single violation shall be good cause for immediate termination of the lease under A.R.S. 33-1377, as provided in A.R.S. 33-1368. Unless otherwise provided by law, proof of violation shall not require a criminal conviction, but shall be by a preponderance of the evidence.

In case of conflict between the provisions of this addendum and any other provisions of the lease, the provisions of this addendum shall govern.

This LEASE ADDENDUM is incorporated into the lease executed or renewed this day between Owner and Resident.

_____ Date: _____
Resident Signature

_____ Date: _____
Property Manager/Owner's Signature

_____
Property Name/Location

Source: International Crime Free Association. Used by permission. This form is available at http://www.crime-free-association.org/multi-housing.htm.

To find out if such a program is offered in your community, contact your local police department or local chapter of the National Apartment Association. Also go to http://www.crime-free-association.org/multi-housing.htm for information on Crime Free Mobile-Housing, Crime Free Condominiums, Crime Free Storage Lockers, and Crime Free Hotels Motels.

Another security program is called FAX NET 1. When a crime happens that could affect anybody in a community, law enforcement sends FAX NET 1 a one-page alert, and FAX NET 1 faxes that alert to anyone in the community that crime could impact next. For information about FAX NET 1 in Glendale, Arizona, call 602-320-3071; send a fax to 602-953-5921; e-mail at: peggy@faxnet1.org; or view its Web site at http://www.faxnet1.org.

TENANT OBLIGATIONS

Tenants are also bound by the lease document and laws governing rental apartments. Unfortunately, most tenants are not knowledgeable about, or made aware of, their obligations, a problem solved by thoroughly communicating these responsibilities before a tenant moves in.

Standard Tenant Responsibilities

Of the most widely recognized tenant obligations, the following are those required in most states:

- Must maintain the dwelling unit, furnishings, fixtures, and appliances in a clean, sanitary, and safe condition
- Must dispose of all rubbish, garbage, and other waste in a clean, sanitary manner in the refuse facilities
- Must use in a reasonable manner all electrical, plumbing, sanitary, ventilating, air-conditioning, and other facilities and appliances, including elevators
- Must not place in the dwelling unit or premises any furniture, plants, animals, or any other thing that harbors insects, rodents, or other pests
- Must not destroy, deface, damage, impair, or remove any part of the dwelling unit or premises or facilities, equipment, or furnishings, except as necessary when hazardous conditions exist that immediately affect the tenant's health or safety
- Must not make alterations, additions, or improvements to the dwelling unit without the owner's prior consent

Tenant Restrictions for Residential Properties

Unless otherwise agreed, a tenant must occupy the premises solely for residential purposes. Residents must respect the fact that someone else owns the property, and they must respect the rights of other tenants. A resident and the resident's guests must conduct themselves in a manner that (1) will not disturb other tenants' peaceful enjoyment of the premises; (2) is not illegal; and (3) will not injure the reputation of the building or its residents.

Tenant Restrictions for Commercial Properties

A big difference between residential and commercial property rentals concerns defaults. If a commercial tenant is in default on rent payments, the landlord can lock out the tenant without notice. This is not true for residential properties. Refer to the Landlord-Tenant Act in your state for full clarification.

Landlord's Right of Access

In most states, tenants cannot unreasonably withhold consent for an owner to enter into the property in order to do the following:

- Inspect the premises
- Make necessary or agreed-on repairs, decorations, alterations, or improvements
- Supply necessary or agreed-on services
- Exhibit the property to prospective or actual purchasers, mortgagees, residents, workers, and contractors

Common courtesy dictates that owners should not abuse this right nor use it to harass tenants. In the event of an apparent or actual emergency, the owner may enter the property at any time without notice.

A lease may state that at any time within 90 days prior to the end of the lease term, the owner may, as often as necessary and on reasonable notice, show the property for rent between the hours of 7 AM and 8 PM. In some states (for example, Oklahoma and Texas), you must have this right stated within the lease, whereas in other states the right is granted to you by statute. At other times the owner should enter only after notice of not less than 48 hours and only between the hours of 7 AM and 8 PM.

Of course, you need to have a key to get into a unit. The owner should be provided with, and retain in a safe place, all keys necessary for access to the dwelling unit. If a tenant changes the lock to his or her unit, you should insist on obtaining a new key.

A landlord has no other right of access except the following:

- Pursuant to a court order
- During the absence of the tenant in excess of 14 days (states vary on the exact number of days)
- To remedy hazardous conditions
- When the tenant has abandoned or surrendered the premises

Starting Out Right

From the moment you meet prospective tenants until the day you refund their security deposit on termination of the lease, you are faced with maintaining good relations. The kind of relationship you develop with your tenants dictates how much peace of mind and profit you derive from your investment property.

Your first meeting with a prospective tenant is crucial to the success of the landlord-tenant relationship. You want your tenants to respect you and the property, while at the same time keeping your relationship on a strictly business level. The image you want to project is one of a professional property owner who is congenial, friendly, and welcoming. Above all, you want to maintain control of the relationship at all times.

Remember that you own the property and people want to rent from you. If you let them think they are doing you a favor by renting your space, you may find yourself the underdog in the relationship. Of course, they are your customers, and you should thank them for renting your place. You can certainly be appreciative. But remember, you're in business and you must exercise control over who rents your property.

In maintaining positive relationships with all your tenants, keep your communications with everyone on a strictly professional business level. You can be sympathetic to tenants' problems, but don't let these problems interfere with your sound judgment or become personal. Landlords have been labeled villains throughout history, and you don't need to aggravate a situation by playing that role.

If you take pride in your property, you'll want your tenants to treat your property with respect. The way to have this respect is to create a positive image in tenants' minds. Let them know how you feel about the property. In the case of residential properties, tell them you want them to make it their home. It is in your best interest if tenants share your pride and maintain the property as if it were their own.

Keeping Good Tenants

Just about every business involves working with people, and being a landlord is no exception. Smart property owners recognize the importance of the human factor in a successful business. If all you had to deal with was leaky plumbing, electrical wiring, and recordkeeping, the job would be simple.

But all businesses need customers, and in the landlord business your customers are your tenants. Successful businesses manage to keep their customers satisfied; when you lose customers in the rental business, you must replace them with others as soon as possible. And when the old customers were especially good, it may not always be possible to replace them with equally good ones. Thus, it is much better to keep your good existing customers than to constantly seek new ones.

Tenant turnover is costly. National surveys estimate that a landlord can lose an amount equal to two months' rent (usually more months for commercial properties) every time a tenant moves out. This amount is based on the possibilities of losing money from the following:

- Cleaning and adapting the premises for new tenants
- Advertising
- Processing paperwork
- Repairing damage to common area walls, doors, halls, and so on
- Showing vacant properties to prospective tenants
- Covering costs when vacancies occur
- Paying commissions to referral services

As an owner, you won't be able to eliminate turnover completely, but you can minimize it by maintaining a good relationship with your tenants. These points of action will help you develop these desired relationships:

- Show a little interest in your tenants' lifestyle and needs during the initial rental interview.
- Follow through on your promises about repairs and decorating. Don't offer something you can't deliver.
- Give residents your work and home phone numbers to use in case of emergencies. Provide them with a list of other important phone numbers for emergency repairs or services.

- Respond promptly to requests for service. Even if you cannot meet their demands, let them know where you stand on the issue. Communication is the key to maintaining good relationships.
- Let your tenants know in advance what you expect from them and what they can expect from you on such issues as rent payment due dates, lease provisions, pets, complaints, services, and so on.
- Respect their privacy and their right to peaceful possession of their home during their lease period. (*Peaceful possession* is a legal term that means the right to use the premises without harassment or interruption.)
- If circumstances force you to enter an apartment when the tenants are not at home and without prior notice, always leave a note stating that you were there and why. You would not like someone coming into your home during your absence and neither do your residents. In general, make it your personal policy to never enter a tenant's space without giving at least 48 hours' notice.

Dealing with Tenant Complaints

Handle complaints quickly and discreetly. If one tenant complains about another, your best response is to ascertain as many facts as possible. Contact the other tenant to find out if there is any validity to the allegation. If it's a matter of loud, disturbing noises, for example, you can politely ask the offending person to be more courteous to his or her neighbors. Most tenants will handle this type of problem without contacting the owner, but if a resident does contact you, don't try to avoid getting involved by telling the person to handle it on his or her own. Having to deal with customer complaints comes with the territory of being a landlord.

If you encounter difficulty with one tenant, don't allow it to escalate to a level that might involve others. Never discuss the situation with noninvolved residents, and, of course, don't spread gossip.

If a tenant complaint is valid and the complained-about person doesn't respond to your requests to correct the situation, your next step is to send the person a Lease Rules and Regulations Violation Letter (Figure 2.2) advising him or her of the lease provision. This letter should also state your legal options if the problem persists.

Maintenance complaints should be handled as quickly as possible. If a repair or replacement cannot be completed in a few days, you must tell the tenants when you expect it to be done. This eases any anxiety and tension between you and your tenants.

FIGURE 2.2 *Sample Lease Rules and Regulations Violation Letter*

Date:

Dear _____:

    We have been informed that there have been complaints about an unusual amount of noise coming from your apartment. This is in violation of paragraph _____ of your lease.

    We realize it is often difficult to keep sounds in an apartment at a level that is not disturbing to neighbors. However, we would greatly appreciate your cooperation in this matter. In particular, please make every effort to play your stereo equipment at a reasonable volume after 10:00 pm. [Or refer to the particular complaint that was made.]

    We trust that there will be no more complaints about noise. However, be aware that if the disturbances continue, we will seek remedies as provided by law.

    If you have any questions, please call. Thank you for your consideration in this matter.

Very truly yours,

Handling Claims and Disputes

There will be times when you and your tenants won't be able to agree on matters concerning physical conditions or operating policies and procedures. In extreme cases, you may have to serve a termination notice or even carry out an eviction. In such cases, it is wise to consult a lawyer. Following are a number of general guidelines.

Legal counsel. It is wise to consult with an attorney before initiating any action against a tenant that could result in canceling or enforcing a lease. If a resident is not in compliance with the lease or is the source of complaints from neighbors, a letter written on your attorney's stationery usually persuades the tenant to correct the problem. Even if the letter is not effective, you'll have the documentation necessary to proceed with an eviction.

When it comes to who is right and who is wrong, do not assume that common sense will apply. If you are not absolutely sure of the applicable law for a situation, always check with your attorney. For information about the Landlord-Tenant Act in your state, go to http://www.mrlandlord.com/laws.

Most states prevent a manager from acting as an agent for an owner to represent the owner in court without being accompanied by an attorney unless the owner actually appears in court.

The following are *general guidelines* in the adjustment of claims or disputes:

- Both you and your tenant, on reasonable notice to the other and for the purpose of ascertaining the facts and preserving evidence, should have the right to inspect the dwelling unit and common area premises.

- You and your tenant may agree at the time of any claim or dispute to allow a third-party inspection or survey to determine the conformity or condition of the dwelling unit or premises, and may agree that the findings shall be binding in any subsequent litigation or adjustment.
- If arbitration by a third party is unavailable or impractical, it may be possible, if the dispute involves monetary damages, for one or the other party to file a suit in small claims court.
- You may elect to voluntarily vacate a tenant's lease; that is, you might allow the tenant to terminate the lease early if you cannot reach a compromise or satisfactorily settle a dispute.

As an example, one particular tenant registered a strong complaint, stating that her kitchen faucet did not have cold water. Normally, you would expect a complaint about hot water, but in this case the tenant expected to have ice-cold water running from the tap.

Because the water was supplied to the building from the city and went directly into the apartments, little could be done to make the tenant's water colder than anyone else's. She persisted, and it became obvious that nothing could be done to satisfy her in this matter, which left two possibilities. The first was to force her to honor the lease and stay in the apartment; the second was to cancel her lease. Because the rental market was strong and the apartment could be easily rerented, a decision was made to let the tenant move out under the condition that she would pay rent until another tenant was found, which, as it turned out, took less than a month.

Most states allow a form of *constructive eviction,* which occurs when a tenant voluntarily vacates a property because of a defect in the condition of the unit—for example, a leaking roof, no heat, no hot water, and so on. For a constructive eviction to be valid, the tenant must actually move out. If you sue the tenant for breaking the lease and the tenant's defense is that you did not cure a problem you were properly notified of, the judge may rule in favor of the tenant, finding that it was a constructive eviction.

If a tenant is in violation of the lease other than not paying the rent and you haven't been able to settle the dispute, you may have to proceed with a termination notice.

Termination Notice

When a tenant is breaking the rules and regulations outlined in the lease and the owner's communications, either verbally or in writing, do not result in cooperation, it may be necessary to begin eviction proceedings. In such a case, a Notice of Termination is used. This kind of form applies to all types of lease violations other than nonpayment of rent and includes unauthorized pets, overoccupancy, or excessive noise.

The Notice of Termination form must be filled out correctly. The chances of winning a case in court for this type of eviction are less than those suing for rent because the lease violations must be well documented. It is important to quote the actual paragraph or clause in the lease that the resident is breaking. Do not simply use the lease paragraph number.

In some states, the law dictates that for a month-to-month tenancy, you must allow a full calendar month and not merely 30 days for eviction. For example, if the notice is served on July 15, the effective date in this space must be the end of the following month, or August 31. Other states, Oklahoma for example, allow you to terminate a tenancy at 30 days, even if that is in the middle of the month.

Deliver the original Notice of Termination to the tenant and keep a copy. The Affidavit of Service section is self-explanatory. Be sure to have the document notarized. Note that in many states you must deliver a termination notice to a tenant or occupant older than 12 years of age. Certain states (for example, Kansas) recognize a notice that was posted or taped on the outside of the property door.

EVICTIONS

Eviction is certainly an unpleasant process that no one wants to be involved in. It is not easy for the landlord, and of course the tenant is not looking forward to it. But unfortunately, evictions are a normal, if infrequent, part of managing property. The more you know about them, the more comfortable you will be and the more efficiently you will handle the situation.

There are two reasons why you would need to evict someone:

1. Nonpayment of rent
2. Noncompliance of a lease provision

Some general forms for dealing with an eviction are covered in Chapter 8.

Eviction procedures vary slightly from state to state. It is best to consult with your attorney prior to initiating any action. Usually some legal fees can be assessed, and you may be able to recover your out-of-pocket expenses as well.

Keep in mind the fair housing laws that must be obeyed when evicting someone. Although you may not think you are discriminating against a particular tenant, it may appear so in the eyes of the law when compared with how you treat another tenant.

According to an article in the April 1997 edition of *Apartment News*, written by attorney Andrew Hull of Phoenix, Arizona, "If you evict one resident for non-payment of rent but, after a court judgment, let the individual sign a repayment agreement and stay, you should do the same for all tenants in a similar situation.

"A landlord should consider establishing strict policies regarding tenant evictions, with an eye toward fair housing concerns. You cannot treat tenants differently because of race, color, religion, sex, family status, physical, or mental disability."

3

MARKETING PROPERTIES

Paul Burrous owns and operates a wood restoration business in San Rafael, California, and came into the landlord business quite by accident. He now owns one sixplex and a single-family home on the same property not far from where he lives.

Paul bought this property because his wife, a mortgage broker, was working with a property owner who was going through a divorce and needed to sell his property quickly. Putting only 10 percent down, they bought her client's sixplex with a house on the same property at a deep discount. They've been renting the house and units consistently for five years.

"We haven't had to market or advertise in four years because we've been able to keep good tenants. Fortunately, most are from the same ethnic group, so when one family moves out, often one of our tenants has already lined up a cousin or friend to move in."

Paul's philosophy is to rent the units at about $100 below market rates—which is about $1,200 a month in this northern California community. "The tenants realize it's a comparatively good deal and don't tend to demand as much because of it," Paul says.

He also has an on-site assistant landlord—a tenant who has been living there for four years. For a reduced rent ($900 instead of $1,200), this tenant fields small problems and helps collect rents. Paul handles most maintenance issues himself and keeps his accounting "rudimentary," as he calls it. "I put data on Quicken (a software program), which creates the statements I need. Then I turn them over to my CPA, who prepares the necessary documents. I'm lucky; all told, I spend four or five hours a month taking care of this property."

Has landlording always been smooth sailing for Paul? "At times I have to mediate small disputes, like when one tenant scratched another tenant's car. But for the most part, I've been blessed with good tenants."

MARKETING TASKS

In marketing rental properties, your task is to present the unit in such a way that a prospect will want to rent and an existing tenant will want to renew. You can become quite effective at marketing your units without going back to school to earn a marketing degree. All it takes is a little knowledge and some time to sell your product.

The process of marketing entails six elements:

1. Understanding the marketplace and determining a rental rate
2. Finding and selecting good tenants
3. Qualifying prospects
4. Advertising the product
5. Selling the product
6. Following up on leads

UNDERSTANDING THE MARKETPLACE

How you market your property depends on the demand for properties in your neighborhood. Market conditions change every six months or so. A strong market with very few vacancies in your neighborhood indicates a seller's market, in which you'll be able to rent at a good price with a minimum amount of effort. But if the market is soft, with many vacancies in the area (a buyer's market), you'll have to be more creative in your approach.

For example, in a buyer's market you may have to place larger ads with additional selling points about what makes your property appealing; and it might be necessary to advertise in more than one newspaper. You may also have to offer a discount or rent concession.

Determining a Rental Rate

Before you embark on a search for a tenant, you must first determine how much rent to charge. If you buy a property that has existing tenants, you won't have to face the problem of determining rents immediately, but you will have to calculate how much to increase the rent when it comes time to renew the leases. A detailed discussion of renewal increases is contained in Chapter 6.

Determining how much rent to charge is based on two key factors:

1. Return on investment (yield)
2. Market analysis

Return on Investment (Yield)

First, you have to look at the math involved in owning the property. You want to generate enough income to cover expenses, debt payments, taxes and insurance, and profit. If you project annual operating expenses per unit to be $1,200, your mortgage and taxes are $2,400, and you want an annual 8 percent profit on your initial $15,000 down payment, you will have to generate an income of $4,800 to break even (not taking into account income tax savings through depreciation, and so on—see Chapter 12).

$1,200 Annual operating expenses
+ $2,400 Annual mortgage, principal, and taxes
= $3,600 Total outlay of cash
+ $1,200 Return on investment (profit or ROI)
= $4,800 Income to be generated
$4,800 divided by 12 months equals $400 per month
Monthly rent = $400 (yield amount)

Make every effort to purchase a property whose size, amenities, condition, and location warrant a rental rate close to your desired yield. The first year or two of operating a rental property may produce a negative cash flow in which total income does not equal expenses, but the deficiency and losses are made up through tax savings. Each year, as increases in rents outpace increases in expenses, the investment gets closer to producing a positive cash return and your desired yield.

Market Analysis

In addition to using the income/expense approach, you also have to consider what the market will bear, the law of supply and demand. Market rent is determined by comparing what similar properties in comparable locations are getting and then making adjustments for local vacancy factors. It isn't difficult to find out current market rents. Some time spent responding to For Rent advertisements, visiting other properties, and reading your local newspaper's classified section will give you a fair idea of what other properties are charging.

You don't have to know absolutely everything about every property, but you should be thoroughly familiar with your competition. How much are other properties renting for in the same area? Compare your property with competing properties and adjust for the major differences. For example, are your rooms larger or smaller? Does your unit have a balcony or patio? How close is your property to schools, shopping, and major transportation routes? You must be thoroughly familiar with each of the competing properties and the features of each. With this knowledge, you'll be able to set an accurate rental rate and be ready to respond to prospects' questions as to why your rent may be higher or lower than other properties in the immediate area.

If similar one-bedroom properties offering similar amenities in your vicinity are renting for $750 a month, you'll have a hard time trying to get $1,000. On the other hand, if your property has more desirable qualities or is better situated, you may be able to command $800 to $850. If the vacancy rate in the neighborhood is low with few properties similar to yours available, then you're in a position to raise the rent in accordance with specific demand. On the other hand, if your properties are smaller or lower in quality than the competition, you'll have to adjust your rent downward; but again, this adjustment may be offset by a low vacancy rate; and you may be able to get the higher rent if you offer a longer lease.

Rental rates vary greatly from city to city, from neighborhood to neighborhood, and from street to street. They even vary substantially between high and low floors and according to views in a high-rise building. Because too many factors affect rents to allow scientifically arriving at an optimum figure, the approach most owners take is ascertaining the general market rent for the area and then setting a price that is somewhat higher, reducing it slightly if they encounter too much resistance. This may not be scientific, but it does take into consideration competition and the merchandising and sales ability of the landlord.

FINDING AND SELECTING GOOD TENANTS

It is difficult to precisely describe an ideal tenant; nonetheless, good tenants have at least five things in common:

1. They pay their rent on time.
2. They care for the property as if it were their own.
3. They are stable and tend to renew their leases.
4. They will leave the premises in as good condition as they found it or better.
5. They don't cause problems for their neighbors.

Therefore, you want a responsible tenant who is and has been steadily employed, earning enough income to pay the rent. Your first choice would not be someone with a long history of credit problems, although a bad credit history by itself may not be indicative of a bad tenant. Couples with newborn infants often make good tenants. These young families may not be able to buy a house, yet they are upwardly mobile and will want to make your property a home they can be proud to show off to their family and friends. Moreover, they usually move to a larger unit in your building in a year or two.

The elderly also make good tenants. They often have fixed incomes and don't move frequently.

Contrary to popular belief, people who have pets, especially cats, can be good tenants as long as a pet is well trained. A pet owner won't want to move because of the difficulty of finding a building that accepts pets. Sometimes these people have been turned down by so many buildings that they are willing to pay a premium and will maintain a good relationship with the landlord for the privilege of living in a unit that accepts pets (see Figure 4.8).

Through experience, you'll learn how to distinguish good tenants from bad ones, but you will still make an occasional mistake. Consider that the success ratio of people picking marriage partners is only 50 percent. If more than 60 percent of your tenants turn out to be good, you are far ahead of the game.

Tenant screening companies. For added protection or convenience, you may want to consider using a credit reporting or tenant screening company to run credit, character, and criminal checks. One such company, Tenant Screening Center, Inc. (800-523-2381, info@tsci.com, http://www.tsci.com), runs a comprehensive national credit reporting business; its fees range from $20 for a minireport to $45 for a full report.

Another national company is Rent Grow (800-736-8476, support@rentgrow .com, http://www.rentgrow.com). In addition to providing credit reporting services, it also specializes in fair housing compliance, including the rules and regulations governing fair housing in each state.

To obtain further recommendations for finding a good tenant screening company, contact the National Property Association (703-518-6141, http://www.naahq .org). The people there will give you the name and number of the closest affiliated association in your area that should be able to provide a good recommendation.

It's a common practice to ask applicants for their previous landlord's address and phone number. If they refuse to provide this information or have not rented before, you'll have to weigh the risks against other factors. It is also common to request a letter from the prospect's employer verifying employment and income.

FAIR HOUSING AND DISCRIMINATION

Cases of high-dollar awards for discrimination against handicapped prospects prompt us to focus attention on the appropriate means of serving prospective tenants who are disabled. The Federal Housing Act of 1988, coupled with legislation in most states, makes it illegal to discriminate against the handicapped. The ADA (Americans with Disabilities Act) requires that all public accommodations be accessible to the disabled. Property communities must make every reasonable effort to have facilities accessible to disabled persons regardless of when the community was built.

Physically challenged individuals must be able to park and enter the property without facing any physical barriers. Wheelchair users need minimum standards just to enter a property. Even if the costs of modifying an existing property are prohibitive, the property owner is required by law to "reasonably accommodate" the disabled.

You must be an equal opportunity landlord. Throughout your discussions and interviews with prospective tenants, remember to adhere to anti-discrimination laws, particularly the Civil Rights Act of 1968, which prohibits discrimination in seven protected categories:

1. Race
2. Color
3. Religion
4. Sex
5. National origin
6. Family status
7. Physical or mental disabilities

Do not volunteer information or comment about the race, religion, color, nationality, sex, family status, or handicaps of tenants, even when asked about it directly or indirectly by a prospect. If prospects ask you questions that you cannot answer because of fair housing laws, tell them that it is your policy to consider any qualified applicants, and that it is against fair housing laws for you to answer questions about protected categories of your current tenant population.

Do not make recommendations about specific locations and/or buildings that you think the tenant may like because of a potential discriminatory factor. For example, it is discriminatory to recommend that a family with children be on the first floor or in a special building with other families.

A few states and municipalities have enacted laws prohibiting adults-only rental policies. Such policies are still permissible in some states (for example, Florida, Arizona, and Texas). In other states, a requirement by owners that prospective tenants shall have no children under the age of 14 is prohibited. Any owner who attempts to enforce such requirements in a state that prohibits it shall be subject to remedies as set forth by law. Before instituting an adults-only policy, check with your local real estate board to make sure it is legal in your state.

You can contact the U.S. Department of Housing and Urban Development (HUD) (202-708-1112, http://www.hud.gov or local HUD offices) to get updated information on fair housing or discrimination issues.

QUALIFYING THE PROSPECT

Qualifying prospects is both about marketing your product to a specific customer and about determining if a customer is right for your product. A qualifying conversation is used to establish a rapport with prospects and put them at ease and at the same time inquire about their background and needs. This information helps you in marketing your property. (To learn how to determine if a prospective tenant is "income-qualified" to rent your property, see Chapter 4.)

Begin qualifying prospective tenants over the telephone when they respond to your advertising. In this preliminary interview, find out as much as you can about their lifestyle and property expectations. Strike up a friendly conversation. Ask a lot of questions. The more you know about your prospects' needs and desires, the easier it will be to match them with a property. One way to get prospects to elaborate on what they like is to ask them what they don't like about their present living quarters. Based on their answers, you can point out the particular advantages of your property.

Some important questions to ask include these:

- When do you need the property?
- What kind of property are you looking for?
- Do you have a pet? If so, what kind?
- How far do you (and other tenants) commute to work?
- What features of property living are important: large rooms, large kitchen, balcony or patio, privacy, quiet, high or low floor in a high-rise, and so on?
- What is wrong, if anything, with your present dwelling unit?
- Why do you want or need to move?
- How many people will occupy the property?

With answers to these questions, you can determine whether to go on to subsequent steps. For instance, if you have only a one-bedroom property available, there is no reason to attempt to rent that property to prospects with large families. It is up to you to identify what the prospects need. If you don't have a suitable property available, you can offer to put the prospects on a waiting list.

The prospects have been qualified when the following details are worked out and/or requirements fulfilled:

- A property of the appropriate type and size is available.
- The prospects are of legal age to sign contracts.
- The prospects are employed or otherwise earning a qualifying income.
- The prospects have the appropriate family size for the particular unit.
- The prospects are moving out of their present accommodations legally.

All, or most, of this information can be obtained during your initial conversation.

ADVERTISING THE PROPERTY

Several ways are available to reach prospective suitable tenants, all involving some form of advertising. You may have the best property in the world, but it will not rent itself. You must make your property's availability known.

Property Rental Agencies

If you don't have the time to advertise and show your units, you can use a property rental agency or referral service, even though you should still learn a little about what types of advertising to use. These companies work on a contingency basis with many different owners; they screen all prospective tenants, completing all the groundwork, showing the unit as many times as it takes, completing the negotiations, and then presenting you with a signed lease.

Their fees are usually based on a percentage of the rent, which varies between 50 percent and 100 percent of one month's rent. For example, suppose you retain an agency to rent a vacant property for October 1 at a rental of $800 a month. You agree to pay a 50 percent commission for a bona fide signed lease. The agency will locate, qualify, and execute a lease with a suitable tenant, usually collecting the first month's rent and a security deposit equal to a month's rent. In most cases, the agency deducts its fee from these funds and gives you the balance along with the signed documents. In this example, the fee would be $400. Some agencies add miscellaneous fees for advertising, but this is not a common practice; the agency's commission should cover its out-of-pocket expenses.

Using a property referral service can save you time. One drawback, however, is that professional rental agencies work for many different owners simultaneously and thus offer prospective tenants a wide variety of units. Because of the large volume and selection of properties they represent, it may take longer to rent yours if it's a lot less desirable than others in an agency's portfolio.

To find a property rental agency, look in the local Yellow Pages in your area; some firms don't accept clients that own fewer than 50 units. If you decide to use an agency, be sure to get at least three bids and always ask for references. It is doubtful that any company will give you a guarantee that your vacant properties will rent, but you can ask for a company's track record and inquire how long it takes it on average to rent units similar to yours.

Types of Advertisements

Your first order of business is to consider a written ad. You can advertise in the classified section of your local newspaper or in a property rental guide magazine. You can put fliers or signs around the property building or complex. Keep in mind when considering the timing of an ad that prospective tenants usually start looking for a property two to three months before they need it.

Property rental magazines. We have all seen them in grocery and convenience stores—the property rental guides or magazines that list dozens and dozens of properties throughout a region. Now they are as close as your computer, too, as more and more listing companies work through Internet connections. See the Resources section for a list of both current real estate magazines and Web sites that assist landlords in renting their properties.

Newspapers. Almost all prospective tenants look at newspaper ads. A good newspaper ad should include all the information necessary to attract promising prospects, including these items:

- Location
- Monthly rent
- Property size
- Major amenities
- Contact name and phone number

If the property is currently occupied, you should also mention the availability date. Emphasize important selling features, such as good views, a high floor in a high-rise building, backyards, patios, playgrounds, nearby shopping, schools, and transportation.

All advertising is highly competitive. And this is true even more so on the classified page, where there are literally hundreds of ads vying for the reader's attention. In order to get the message across, you want your ad to do the following:

- Gain the reader's attention.
- Hold the reader's interest.
- Stimulate a desire for your property.
- Persuade the reader to act on your rental.

To be successful, it is important to remember that the property you are writing about cannot be all things to all people. For your ad to get action, you must direct your advertising to a specific market. Before you write the ad, always ask yourself: Who is a likely customer for this property?

To pinpoint the market, you must consider the demographics of potential renters. Be sure to determine (1) renters' household income, (2) size of their household, and (3) the age, occupation, and education of your target market. Then write your ad for that particular group. An effective ad answers the question: How does the property fulfill a potential renter's needs?

The sample ads in Figure 3.1 are examples of effective copy that would produce the desired results.

Fliers. Professional-looking fliers can be designed on computers or typed on regular typewriters and reproduced inexpensively. Because a flier provides more space than an ad, you can include more information, such as a floor plan or a photo of the property. You can distribute fliers throughout the neighborhood (where permitted by law) and, with permission, in grocery stores, churches, coin laundries, and other establishments where there are bulletin boards. Fliers can also be distributed to tenants of other property buildings in the area—not with the intent to solicit your competitions' tenants directly but rather to make them aware of a property available in your building just in case someone has a friend or relative who needs one.

Note: The U.S. Postal Service prohibits placing fliers inside mailboxes unless they are stamped.

Signs. Because most people have a preconceived notion about the neighborhood where they wish to live, one of the most effective and cost-efficient means

FIGURE 3.1 *Sample Newspaper Ads*

EVANSTON 8825 ALBANY DELUXE 6 LARGE RMS $886 Across from Lincoln Schl. Near beach, shops, subway, commuter train. 555-3456 June 1 555-7890	**6 ROOMS**—2nd flr, heated, 2 blocks west of Dan Ryan on 105th St. No pets. $875 + sec. Days 555-2686 or Eves. 555-4974	**HYDE PARK**—7500 E. 54th Pl. 1st fl., 4 rms, decor., $635. Avail. now. Excellent transp. 555-4192
GARDEN PROPERTY 31/2 rms, stove & frig. Utilities incl. 8100 W./7600 N. $550 + 2 mos. sec. 555-1136	Newly renovated Victorian. 2 BR, owner occ. Walk to train. Immediately avail. $950/mo. **555-2093**	Near Irving & Western. 2 bdrms, 2nd flr, 2-flat. Available May 1. Cable. Will decorate & carpet. Htd. No pets. $825/ mo. + dep. 555-2144 afternoons & eves.
Lrg. 4-rm, 1 BR in English Tudor bldg. Very classy, very bright. Walk-in closets & more. No pets please. Managed by owner. Avail. 5/1. 5543 N. Washington (4300W). $725. Eves. 555-3765	**HARVEY**—2 bedrooms. Apt newly dec. Tenants pay util. $700 + 1 mo. sec. Sect. 8 welcome. 731-2049	**SKOKIE**—Spacious Garden Apt., near train, all utilities paid. $920 mo. Call 555-4467
	HAMPTON/MILWAUKEE 6 rms, clean, quiet, stv./refg., firepl. $835 mo., htd. 555-7878	2 blks from Jeff. Pk. terminal. 2-br apt. Oak flrs. 2nd flr of quiet bldg. No pets. Nonsmoker pref. $900 + sec. 555-5167
NEWLY REMOD.—Near 63rd & Ashland. 5 rms, 3 bdrms., living room, large cabinet kitchen, tile bath. $750 + utilities. 644-4441	Avail. May 1—Kimball/ Sawyer. 2-Flat, 5 Rms, 2 Br. Mod. Kit. $875 + sec. 555-6110	DesPlaines—HUGE dlx. 1 BR. Quiet 4-unit bldg. New dec., appls. Pkg., ht incl. Near train. $825. 555-3004

of advertising is a sign. Prospective tenants often drive or walk around the area where they wish to live, and a simple sign advertising your property is the least expensive way to attract a customer.

A small handwritten or typed sign (Figure 3.2) can be taped on the door of the building highlighting basic rental information in a neat, legible manner.

A larger and more expensive, professionally painted, permanent-portable wooden or metal sign on the building or in the front of the property can also be used. Frequently, the placement, size, and type of sign are regulated by zoning codes. To play it safe, visit your local city zoning department and ask about sign regulations before putting up your sign. Temporary signs are usually exempt from zoning regulations.

Because of its larger size and overall appearance, a wooden or metal sign attracts more attention than a paper sign and should state only the types of units

FIGURE 3.2 *Sample Doorway Sign*

P R O P E R T I E S
F O R   R E N T
in This Building

Floor	Rooms	Rental
2nd	3½	$825 month
	Sunny, one-bedroom, parquet floors, fully applianced kitchen, one month security deposit. Utilities not included.	

Apply to: Mr. J. Neits
555-1616 Days
555-1212 Evenings

available and a contact phone number. Depending on the street traffic pattern, the sign can be either double-sided or single-faced in an appropriate size to allow easy readability from the street.

Depending on the number of units you own, a sign may be installed permanently subject to local sign codes. If there are no vacancies at one particular property, the sign can still be useful—serving as a referral to other locations where you may have vacancies. Or it can invite prospective tenants to be on a waiting list.

A sign should always be fresh, clean, and professional looking. A poorly lettered, weather-beaten sign gives a poor first impression.

The Internet. The authors have been actively using the Internet for several years, and we have seen it become one of the most useful tools to reach an audience. "Surfing the Net" has become a popular pastime as well as an easy way to find lots of information about relocating within a city or in a different city. Don't overlook its potential as a marketing tool to advertise your product. Several companies have sophisticated Web pages advertising hundreds of properties in almost every major city in the United States and will list your units for a small fee.

Most of the people who use the Internet to search for housing want relocation information. But the data are also reviewed as well by locals who want to save time by scanning the Internet. Because it's growing faster than we can write, it is safe to say that this is an effective marketing tool for your rental properties. A prospective tenant can access information about your property electronically, view photos or a video of the unit and the surrounding neighborhood, then click a button for more information, or, better still, begin the rental application process. Many renters are using this technology to define their searches and save time before calling landlords or visiting properties. This means you might advertise your properties over the Internet in some way (through your own Web site, a newspaper's Web site, a property manager's Web site, etc.).

Referrals. Your most effective, and certainly least expensive, method of finding new tenants is through referrals from existing tenants. If people like where they live, they are prone to tell others about the positive aspects. In fact, over the long run your best source for valuable new leads is probably other satisfied tenants. Most tenants make referrals voluntarily, but if you want to help motivate them to bring you possible referrals, you can offer a referral fee of anywhere between 25 to 50 percent of a month's rent.

SELLING THE PRODUCT

Once you have located a prospective tenant, you must sell your product to him or her. This is a complex task. It involves preparing the property for showing, doing preliminary interviews to determine the prospect's needs, and making a good first impression when greeting the prospect in person. You then have to present your property in the best possible light, handle objections diplomatically, and, finally, ask for the closing.

Preparing the Property

Before letting prospective tenants see your building or properties, first make certain that the property is sparkling clean, freshly painted, and in good operating condition. First impressions are lasting ones. Do *not* show a property if it's not ready to be seen. Many people lack imagination and cannot easily envision a filthy property cleaned up and looking good in the future. As an owner, you may be able to "see it" in your mind, but rest assured they won't. If, while you are showing the unit, you have to say such things as, "We are going to paint" or "We are going to replace the carpeting" or "We will be fixing the entryway," you will be making your marketing job a lot harder. For more information on this subject, refer to Chapter 10: "Maintenance."

Greeting the Prospective Tenant

A prospective tenant is any person who either calls or walks in to inquire about a property. Every prospect should be treated as a future tenant who will provide the income to sustain your business. See Figures 3.3 and 3.4 for detailed reviews of effective presentation techniques.

Convincing the Prospect

Once you have qualified your prospective renters, you must then persuade or convince them that you have the best property available. Following are a few useful techniques to help convince prospects to rent.

Talk to prospects, showing a genuine interest. People sometimes rent a property even if it's not as perfectly suited to their needs as others they have seen. Why? Because the rental agent or owner gave them a warm, welcome feeling and showed sincerity when talking to them. On the other hand, if you leave your prospects feeling cold and unwelcome or treat them with indifference, they may not rent even if the property is perfect and the rent lower than other options they've looked at. Your personal and professional image is all-important in making or breaking a potential rental. This is another way of saying the dwelling unit will not "rent itself," no matter how perfect or appealing it is.

Ask questions about your prospects' lifestyle and gear your presentation to what they say. Appeal to both their intellect and emotions; it is on both of these levels that they will make a decision. Remember, prospects see only walls, floors,

FIGURE 3.3 *How to Greet a Prospect*

These are ten things you should do when greeting a prospect:

1. Stand up and greet the person as soon as he or she enters the room.
2. Introduce yourself, ask for names, and shake hands.
3. Ask, "How may I help you?"
4. Find out what the person is interested in and then *listen*.
5. Talk about how the property or properties meet the prospect's stated needs and offer to show each one.
6. Show your prospect the properties.
7. Ask if any property is suitable and then *listen*. Ask specifically what he or she wants and then *listen*.
8. Ask if the prospect would like to reserve one of the properties by filling out an application and stating a move-in date.
9. Ask for a deposit.
10. Thank your prospect for visiting.

FIGURE 3.4 *Checklist of Presentation Techniques*

- ❏ Did I introduce myself?
- ❏ Did I ask their names?
- ❏ Did I offer them chairs and cold drinks/coffee?
- ❏ Did I ask about their family size?
- ❏ Did I ask when they expected to move?
- ❏ Did I ask why they are moving and how long they expect to stay in their new rental property?
- ❏ Did I ask what type of property and facilities they are looking for?
- ❏ Did I discuss the number of vacant properties available?
- ❏ Did I ask where they are working?
- ❏ Did I point out the convenience and accessibility of this property complex?
- ❏ Did I discuss advantages of the neighborhood: shopping, schools, recreational facilities?
- ❏ Did I exhibit a "spic and span," completely prepared property?
- ❏ Did I describe property benefits and offer proof of those benefits? (Example: "After you move into this property, it will feel just like your own home because the rooms are unusually spacious.")
- ❏ Did I build enthusiasm by eliciting "yes" (positive) responses?
- ❏ Did I attempt to close the sale?
- ❏ Did I offer an application to be completed?
- ❏ Did I ask for a deposit?
- ❏ Did I use a persuasive close by offering options? (Example: "Would you prefer to leave your deposit by cash or check?")
- ❏ Did I continue to try and "sell" even after they indicated uncertainty?
- ❏ Did I try to close a second time after reviewing the key benefits?
- ❏ Did I appear sincere and interested in their needs?

and ceilings. You must create an image, allowing them to envision and desire the property and the community as their home. As an example, instead of making obvious statements such as "This is the living room" or "This is the kitchen," let the prospects make these observations while you point out the benefits of your unit. You can say, "Doesn't this view give you a peaceful feeling?" or "The neutral color of the carpet will go well with your furniture."

Accentuate the positive. Offset negative aspects with positive comments. You can anticipate getting objections and hesitations. If you have studied the marketplace, you will know all about your competition. Be prepared. That enables you to emphasize your property's strong points.

If there are many vacant properties in the area, don't point this out to the prospects. Good salespeople demonstrate that their product is in great demand, thereby creating a sense of urgency that helps finalize the sale. Most prospects want to be sold, and they only get confused if the salesperson points out dozens of other alternatives. They want you to help them make up their minds. That's your role.

If the available property doesn't show well because it's dirty or needs decorating, show your prospects a similar unit in good condition if you have one. Point out how it meets their exact needs as discovered in your conversations with them. Then, even if your prospect doesn't insist, make every effort to show the actual unit before the prospect signs a lease. This will avoid having an unhappy tenant who fell in love with some aspect of the shown unit that the actual unit lacks.

In fact, certain states require the actual property be shown to prospective tenants, but this can be handled after they have decided to rent. In these jurisdictions, failure to show the actual unit can result in a cancellation, possibly requiring you to return all moneys collected. Quite a few properties have been rented by showing only a model unit. The actual property quite often may not have been built yet. Remember that lease provisions should permit access to occupied units; thus you can show an occupied property as a model.

Handling Objections

Prospects often point out their objections about the property—either a legitimate concern or an attempt to gain a rent reduction or other concession. Whatever the underlying reason, they always expect a response.

Learn how to respond positively, avoiding anything that resembles an apology, a defensive statement, or a leaning toward agreeing to a concession. For example, if someone comments, "The kitchen is very small," your positive response could be, "Yes, it is; cleaning it will be a snap, and look at the spacious, well-lit dining room you have."

Following is a list of some common objections with suggested responses.

The rent is too high. This statement doesn't always mean the prospect can't afford it. Point out that the rent is comparable to similar units in the area. The amount of rent you are asking is adjusted to the market for the type of property and amenities offered. You can control the rental rate, however, and you may lower it for other considerations (but don't be hasty to volunteer it).

The view is bad. Some so-called bad views are privacy views. Not everybody is looking for the spectacular scenic skyline view. The amount of rent for the unit has been adjusted accordingly. You may not be able to change the view, but you can suggest a variety of window treatments to offset a poor view.

The rooms are too small. Mention that efficient room sizes are good for energy savings. You cannot make the rooms bigger, but you may be able to counter the objection if you have large closets or other amenities such as storage lockers, a bike room, and so on.

The property is dirty. Never show your property if it's dirty. If you must show an occupied property that is dirty, explain that it will be cleaned and redecorated. This is the type of objection you can take action on.

The closets are too small. Point out to your prospects that smaller closets take up less square footage space, allowing for more living space. It's difficult to add more closet space, but you can suggest having the closets more efficiently reorganized by using new shelving and rods specifically designed for this purpose.

The kitchen is too small. Smaller kitchens are usually step-saver kitchens with less floor area and cabinetry to clean. Although you usually can't make the kitchen larger, you can point out the larger living room, bedroom, or bathroom and show how the kitchen layout is efficient. If the kitchen is very small, let the prospects enter it first; don't walk into it and ask them to come in after you.

We don't like an electric stove. Electric stoves are modern and usually trouble free. More benefits: Electric cooking is cleaner and creates less odor; cooking vapor residue doesn't build up; gas fumes can sometimes fade clothes, furniture, and drapes and get things dirty.

An all-electric property is expensive. Many all-electric heating and cooling systems provide individually controlled thermostats located in the property, allowing the tenants to selectively control the temperature in each room. Electric systems are controlled by the tenants, and they pay only for what they use. When utilities are included in the rent, the landlord must charge more to offset these costs, and the tenants then pay not only for what they use but partially also for what their neighbors use. You may not be able to change the system, but you can point out energy-saving tips in the use of the heating and air-conditioning units. In tenant-heated buildings, tenants often forget that their electric bill includes electricity for lights, appliances, a microwave, a stove, and so on. The portion of the electric bill spent on electric heat is usually less than it appears.

If it's an apartment building, there is no lobby door attendant. A small building with a few units does not warrant hiring a door attendant. A large condominium property in which you own and rent out an investment unit may benefit from having an attendant to help maintain privacy. Providing 24-hour coverage can cost a building up to $125,000 per year, an expense added into the assessments that forces the landlord to increase the rent. Attendants don't provide security and serve only as a convenience to tenants. If you think having the entrance staffed is necessary, you can suggest it to the board of directors of your condominium association.

The carpet is the wrong color. Carpeting cannot usually be replaced to suit each new tenant's color choice. Instead, suggest using an area rug. Explain that once furniture is put in place, there will not be much perimeter carpet showing.

The carpeting is old. Carpets are replaced periodically as the result of tears or bad stains. New carpeting would increase the monthly rent if replaced unnecessarily. If a prospect insists on having a serviceable carpet replaced, however, suggest putting it in if the prospect agrees to pay for it amortized over the lease period. Tenants must agree to pay any outstanding balance should they terminate their lease early. Be sure to write any agreements into the lease.

The appliances are old (or the wrong color). Appliances should be replaced if they aren't in good working order, but appliances can't be replaced to suit each new tenant's color choice. Suggest that the prospects either pay for new appliances or amortize their purchase over the lease period.

There is no parking garage. Properties with garages cost more to rent than those without. In some cases, street parking is available. You have no control over this factor, but you can provide information about public garages or parking lots in the area. Tenants in downtown areas often use public transportation, and many don't own cars.

There is no balcony or patio. Tenants seldom use their balconies or patios, which frequently serve only as storage areas for bicycles and miscellaneous debris. You can't add a balcony, but you can provide information on where public storage facilities are, and you may suggest sunbathing at the pool, rooftop sundeck, or nearest public facility. Suggest that tenants barbecue in the park or nearby picnic grounds.

We don't like the layout of rooms. You can't change the floor plan, but you can point out the advantages of your floor plan. As an example, if the bedrooms are side by side down the hall from the living room, point out how this arrangement is suited for entertaining by allowing privacy and quiet in the sleeping areas. If the bedrooms are on opposite sides of the living room, point out how this facilitates privacy between roommates or parents and children.

We don't like hardwood floors. Mention that they are easy to keep clean and don't create dust, so tenants won't have to purchase a vacuum cleaner. You can offer to carpet the floor for additional rent, but suggest an area rug as an option.

There is no swimming pool. Properties with pools usually demand higher rents than those without. Tell the prospects the locations of the nearest public pools and/or beaches and even give them directions.

There is no security. The word *security* should never be used because you really should not be responsible for tenants' security. You are providing a place to live for a fair rent. State that a building has controlled access (not "security doors"). Do not say you have security guards but that the building is controlled. Security is the responsibility of the tenants themselves. Whatever security that management provides covers the building and the surrounding property—not the tenants. You can suggest that they install additional locking devices on their entry doors or windows, but tell them you need copies of all keys.

There are no storage facilities. Properties without separate storage facilities usually have larger closets. If lack of storage space is a common objection, you could provide information about the closest self-storage facility.

There are not enough bathrooms. This is another situation you cannot change, although you might point out that previous tenants lived there satisfactorily with the existing bath arrangement.

The rooms need decorating. The property will be decorated insofar as being cleaned, painted, carpet cleaned, and the like. Make tenants aware that they can decorate the place themselves within the boundaries of the lease or your management policies.

The property needs repairs. If you must show a property in need of repairs, explain that the owner will have all repairs completed before move-in. Sometimes you can allow the tenant to do the repairs in exchange for a rent deduction, but this is generally not a good practice.

There is no dishwasher. Point out that many people prefer washing dishes by hand because they feel they get them much cleaner. Also, running a dishwasher increases the electric bill. Depending on kitchen size and layout, there might be room to install either a double sink or a compact-sized dishwasher, or the tenants may want to use their own portable unit.

There is no health club. When a complex offers a health club, the rents are higher and all tenants pay for it whether they use it or not. Provide information on the nearest available facility, and try to obtain a promotional introductory membership to the nearest local health club for your new tenants.

Remember that it is the prospects who will be paying the rent and not you, so don't let your personal opinions of the property influence a customer's decision. Just because you may not like some aspect of the property doesn't mean prospects have the same objection. Do not let prospective tenants wander around a property unit unattended; always remain at a discreet distance yet close enough to hear and observe any negative comments that may arise.

Familiarize yourself with the surrounding community and be prepared to answer questions about schools, shopping, commuting, local laws, and nearby services.

Ask for the Sale

Many people in the property management business are excellent at greeting and qualifying prospects and showing properties, yet their efforts result in few actual rentals. That's because they fail to ask for the sale.

Be sure to ask for a signature on the application and a security deposit while the prospects are still with you. Discourage people from saying, "We want to think about it" or "We'll be back." It is worth being a little pushy at this point. Indicate that your units rent quickly so if they hesitate in making a decision, they may lose the opportunity to rent the property. Press to get a commitment, a deposit, and a signature.

FOLLOW UP

Because not every prospect agrees to rent the first time she or he walks through a property, it doesn't mean you have lost the prospect or should give up. Keeping in touch with prospects can be productive over time. Assuming that you have kept the prospect's address and phone number, for example, you can send a postcard the day after the prospect visits the property. The card should be handwritten, and the wording should politely encourage further questions and visits.

Take time to telephone your prospects 24 hours after showing the unit. Be prepared to give them some new piece of information that wasn't covered previously. Be enthusiastic. Impress prospects with your desire to see them living in your property soon.

For more ideas on marketing, consult an expert (see Landlord Consultants/ Coaches in Resources section) or locate a wealth of information on Web sites geared for landlords (see Web sites in Resources section).

4

APPLICATIONS, LEASES, AND RENTAL AGREEMENTS

Eileen and Tim Goode quietly started their landlord business when they bought their second home, keeping their first home in Colorado as a rental. Four years later, they found a good buy on a single-family home in a nearby community. During the mid-1990s, at the peak of the high-tech boom, the rental income from this house provided good cash flow in an "up" economy.

In 2001, an attractive job opportunity in Madison, Wisconsin, opened for Tim. He had attended university there and his parents live in nearby Lacrosse. But the idea of managing two rental properties from a distance didn't appeal to the Goodes. So they researched the requirements of the Internal Revenue Code's Section 1031 tax-free exchanges, took half a year to sell their rental houses as well as their primary home in Colorado, then hustled to locate desirable properties in Wisconsin before the required 45-day "identification" phase slipped by.

"Those were crazy days, trying to make sound investment decisions in a short window of time," says Eileen, who'd gained enough experience to buy and sell some of their properties without a real estate agent. Looking back, she and Tim regard their $30,000 savings in commission fees as her salary for the months they were in transition.

To help determine which properties would be good investments, Tim, a computer programmer, designed a spreadsheet to help them crunch the numbers and evaluate such factors as cash flow and return on investment (ROI). Through this analysis, they instantly identified which properties to pass on.

About dealing with all these transactions in a short period, Eileen said, "We learned that we prefer to do the research and contract work ourselves, write in contingencies, and get a lawyer to look over the paperwork at the end. I've gained a keen sense of satisfaction in becoming self-sufficient with managing our own investment properties," Eileen said.

By the end of their transition time, the Goodes succeeded in turning their two Colorado rental properties into five units in Wisconsin—two duplexes and one single-family house—plus selling the home they lived in and buying another in their new community.

During this hectic time, Eileen found it especially helpful to join the state's apartment association. She read a number of books about real estate investing and continues to glean more information about the Wisconsin market while holding a part-time job.

"I found the most useful tool to be the association's handbook, which includes leases, forms, and other paperwork for landlords. I can also e-mail questions to the association's consultant about such procedures as collecting security deposits, and I receive a response quickly."

After placing ads in rental magazines and on bulletin boards at off-campus housing and supermarkets, the Goodes determined the best way to advertise is through the Sunday pull-out section of the *Madison Capital Times*. Early on, as a way to avoid tenant headaches, they made a decision not to rent to undergraduate students nor accept Section 8 low-income housing vouchers. "We're renting to people with lower incomes in Wisconsin than we did in Colorado. But even in a slow market, we're confident there are enough working people to pay the going rents here."

The best advice they'd give to new landlords? Do your analysis, work the numbers, and have cash reserves from the beginning in case of unexpected major repairs.

"In our experience, landlords can be successful by finding solid deals that have a combination of good cash flow and probable appreciation. We've benefited from low interest rates, and we know we'll have to work harder to make the numbers work as rates go up. Given all the variables, we're happy with the choices we've made," Eileen said.

APPLICATION FOR LEASE (RENTAL AGREEMENT)

When prospects apply to rent a property, have them fill out an Application for Lease shown in Figure 4.1, in your presence. Never take an application over the telephone. You should always meet the prospects and discuss the lease terms in person. You want to be sure that they understand and agree to the rules and regulations that pertain to the property before they sign a lease. Also, this is the time to ask for their security deposit and credit check funds.

A married couple can fill out a joint application using only one form, but roommates or cotenants should fill out individual applications. Check the credit and verify employment for all joint tenants, including a husband and wife if they are listed together on the lease as being jointly and severally responsible.

When the prospective tenants have completed and signed the form, review the application for any incomplete or missing information. Question the prospects to obtain such information and record a brief explanation in any blanks where the information cannot be provided or completed. It's a common practice

FIGURE 4.1 *Application for Lease*

☐ NEW RENTAL:	**MID-AMERICA MANAGEMENT CORP.**
☐ PRERENT FOR:	
☐ RELET FROM:	**APPLICATION FOR LEASE**
☐ ROOMMATE WITH:	
☐ BUYOUT/CANCELLATION:	
☐ CO-SIGNER:	

Employee ID#_____
CIC #_____

BLDG #_____ UNIT #_____

REFERRED BY _____

TERMS OF LEASE:

From:_____ To:_____
Move in Date:_____
Rent:_____ / Addl. Rent_____
Sec. Dep.:_____
Additional Sec. Dep.:_____
Pet Fee:_____
Address:_____ Apt. #_____
Concession:_____
Bedrooms: 0 1 2 3 (circle one)

S/D Pd: _____	S/D Recd: _____
C/C Pd: _____	C/C Recd: _____
Rent Pd: _____	Rent Recd: _____
Bal. Due: _____	Date: _____
Riders: _____	By: _____
COMPLEX	MAIN OFFICE

APPLICANT:_____ SPOUSE:_____
SS #_____ SS #_____
DRIV. LIC. #_____ DRIV. LIC. #_____

PLEASE DO NOT WRITE ABOVE THIS LINE

APPLICANT

Name_____ Age_____ Date of Birth_____

Current Address_____ City_____ State_____ Zip Code_____ Phone (____)_____

Landlord Name_____ Phone (____)_____ How Long_____/Monthly Rent_____ Date Verified_____

Previous Address_____ City_____ State_____ Zip Code_____ Phone (____)_____

Landlord Name_____ Phone (____)_____ How Long?_____

Current Employer_____ Person to Contact_____

Employment Address_____ City_____ Phone (____)_____ Date Verified_____

Position_____ Years Service_____ Weekly Gross Earnings_____

Previous Employer_____ Person to Contact_____

Previous Empl. Address_____ City_____ Phone (____)_____

Position_____ Years Service_____ Weekly Gross Earnings_____

Additional Income $_____ Explain_____

SPOUSE

Name_____ Age_____ Date of Birth_____

Current Employer_____ Person to Contact_____

Employment Address_____ City_____ Phone (____)_____

Position_____ Years Service_____ Weekly Gross Earnings_____

Additional Income $_____ Explain_____

MISCELLANEOUS

How Many People Will Occupy This Apartment?_____

Do You Have Any Pets? ____Yes ____No If yes, type_____ Weight_____

In Emergency Notify_____ Relationship_____

Address_____ City_____ State_____ Phone (____)_____

Car Make(s)_____ Year(s)_____ License No.(s)_____ Finance By_____

Were you convicted of a felony within the last ten years or have you been in prison for a felony conviction within the last ten years? _____yes _____no

This application is not intended to create or extend a duty or obligation of the owner and property manager to protect against criminal conduct against tenants, guests and their property.

Date Approved:_____ Manager's Signature:_____

Date Resident Notified:_____ Person Contacted:_____ By:_____

FAIR HOUSING STATEMENT: Mid-America Management Corp. is an equal-opportunity housing manager. It is the policy of Mid-America Management Corp. for it and its employees and agents not to discriminate on the basis of race, color, religion, national origin, ancestry, physical or mental disability, familial status, age, marital status, sex or unfavorable discharge from military service in the offering of rental apartments or in the terms, conditions or privileges of rental. You have the right to be offered and to choose any rental apartment that we have available that meets yourbudgetary requirements. We will offer any available rental apartment to you, subject to our standard confirmation of your credit history, income and housing references. If you believe that you have been treated unfairly or discriminated against by any employee or agent of Mid-America Management Corp., please contact the compliance officer at (630) 574-2400.

I represent to you that I have read this entire application and that all of the above information hereon is true and correct. I further represent that my rental and credit records are in good standing with no judgements or liens against me. If any of the above information is false, I hereby agree that my entire deposit may be forfeited to you. I also agree that if I am accepted and fail to complete this transaction by signing your lease, my entire deposit will be forfeited to you. I understand that this application is subject to your approval, and if my application is not accepted, my deposit will be returned in full. I understand that my credit check fee is nonrefundable and hereby authorize you to obtain a consumer credit report regarding myself. I also understand that this is not a lease and should my application be accepted, I agree to sign your lease form currently in use. If for any reason whatsoever you are unable to make the apartment which is the subject of this application available at the beginning of the lease term, I hereby waive any and all rights to seek to recover any damages whatsoever against you, including without limitation, actual, punitive or consequential damages.

_____ _____
APPLICANT RECEIVED BY

_____ _____
APPLICANT DATE

4301 REV. 09/01 ORIGINAL

to ask applicants for their previous landlord's address and phone number. If they refuse to provide this information or haven't rented before, you'll have to weigh the risks against other factors.

At the time of signing the rental application, explain to the applicants that they will receive a refund of the security deposit if the application is not accepted but that the entire deposit will be forfeited if they cancel. When an applicant submits a security deposit and is later rejected, he or she should expect to wait a few days for a refund unless the payment was in cash or a canceled check is submitted. This time is required to ensure that the check or money order is backed by sufficient funds.

Some landlords ask for a *preliminary* deposit when a prospective tenant applies to rent a property. Says Scott Henderson, who manages several properties in Colorado, "I have an interim lease that says the applicants can rent the property pending approval of their background and credit checks. They pay a preliminary deposit, usually $250. Once they're approved, this preliminary deposit becomes part of their security deposit. If they don't sign our ten-page lease for whatever reason, they don't get the preliminary deposit back. This policy serves to get rid of 'tire kickers'—people who aren't really serious applicants."

APPROVING THE APPLICATION

Tell applicants that you will verify income and other items listed on the application, after which you will contact them as soon as possible. It is imperative that prospective tenants be notified immediately of acceptance or rejection. Get a telephone number where the prospects can be reached or where you may leave a message. If the process of verification takes too long, the tenants may find other suitable housing.

Income Requirements

Check an applicant's income against the rule of thumb that is standard in the industry: rent should not exceed 30 percent of a renter's annual income. If the applicant earns less than that amount, you may want to request a double security deposit, if permitted by law (see "Double Deposit Clause" in this chapter), or you might ask the prospect to have a qualified cosigner fill out an application and sign the lease also. If the rent exceeds 30 percent of the applicant's income, you can reject that person or demand to have the lease put in a qualified cosigner's name with the prospect listed as an additional tenant.

Verifying Employment and Other Sources of Income

If you want to do this work yourself instead of using a tenant screening company (see Chapter 3), you can use the information a prospect has provided on the Application for Lease (see Figure 4.1) to call his or her current employer and explain why you want to verify employment. If the employer insists you make the request in writing, ask to speak to the "person to contact" named by the prospect on the application. If you can't get verification over the telephone, you will have to send the employer a verification request letter or fax. You may want to ask prospects to expedite a prompt response from their employers to speed up the approval process.

If the employer reports lower gross earnings than an applicant indicated, use the 30 percent rule to be sure the applicant still qualifies for the property. If the employer won't verify any information, ask the applicant to provide a letter, on company stationery, verifying length of employment and amount of income.

If the applicant is self-employed, you can request copies of his or her latest tax returns that would show gross earnings. In lieu of this, a prospect can provide a financial statement verified by a bank. A letter of reference or recommendation from an officer of a banking or other financial institution is a reasonable request. Although such a letter won't demonstrate an applicant's credit history, it may give you a better idea of his or her general overall creditworthiness. Your primary goal is to ascertain that the prospect earns enough income to qualify for the property.

RENTAL AGREEMENTS AND LEASE FORMS

A lease is the primary legal document used by landlords. It specifies the terms of the rental agreement binding the owner and the tenant. A lease is a contract between an owner of real property and a tenant for the possession and use of lands and improvements in return for payment in rent. It defines the formal relationship between the landlord and tenant. In addition to what common sense and state laws dictate about tenant-landlord obligations, the lease spells out specific agreements that bind both parties.

Oral Leases

Oral leases are generally not recommended unless you want to have month-to-month tenants. It is extremely important to use a written lease, and plenty of good standard forms are available.

Years ago, it may have been to a landlord's advantage not to give a tenant a written lease. The tenant was then at the mercy of the landlord, who could raise rents at will and give short termination notices. The problems are that oral leases run on a month-to-month basis, can't be substantiated, and may not always be enforceable. A written lease is a binding contract on both parties and is usually upheld in court in case of a dispute.

Commercially Available Lease Forms

Many good preprinted lease forms are available. Some of the best are offered through local Realtor® associations, the Peachtree Business Products (800-241-4623, http://www.pbp1.com), and local chapters of the National Property Association (703-518-6141, http://www.naahq.org). These organizations keep their forms updated to reflect current landlord-tenant laws.

If you cannot find what you want through one of the above organizations, go to a local stationery store. Forms purchased in a local store must be carefully reviewed to see that they are up-to-date and will work for you. Also, go to the Resources section in this book for more sources.

Owners and tenants may add to a preprinted lease form any terms and conditions that are not prohibited by state or local ordinances or other rules of law. Additions to a lease document may include additional rent, additional terms of agreement, additional rules and regulations, lease riders, and other provisions governing the rights and obligations of the parties. You'll find explanations of these additions in various sections that follow.

TERMS AND CONDITIONS OF LEASES

The following brief summary discusses the terms and conditions of most standard property rental agreements (leases). Riders to a lease and additional lease clauses are discussed later in this chapter.

Filling Out the Lease

Many states indicate in their statutes that all blank spaces on a lease must be completed or the lease may be voidable. You may already be familiar with some of the basic lease language and definitions, but pay special attention to the following areas in which you will insert specific details concerning your property and prospective tenants. *Note:* Some of the forms presented as figures in this book can be adapted for your personal use, but this is not true of lease forms. Always purchase and use original blank leases.

Lessor is you, the landlord.

Lessee is the tenant. Enter the full names of all occupants 18 years or older on the lease. If there is a cosigner, his or her name is added under the occupant's name and the word *cosigner* should appear.

The date the lease begins is the date the tenant starts paying rent, which could be a date different from the actual move-in date. This happens when, for example, you offer a concession such as one month's free rent (see prorated or free rent programs later in this chapter).

Make the date the lease ends the last day of a month.

Unless the rental agreement fixes a definite term, the tenancy is week-to-week in the case of a tenant who pays weekly rent but month-to-month in all other cases.

Monthly *rent* is the dollar amount the tenant will pay for rent of the unit each month. Additional monthly payments for a parking space, garage, pet, furniture rental, or other applicable charges can be reflected on the appropriate lease clause or rider.

The *security deposit* is normally equal to one or two months' rent, though some landlords charge a flat fee. You may require additional deposits for pets, furniture rental, or extra security. In soft rental markets, a smaller security deposit might serve as an added inducement to a potential renter. There is no legal requirement to charge a security deposit, however, you may be required to pay interest on the security deposit depending on local laws.

Premises refer to the complete address of the property being leased.

The special provisions section of the lease is for documentation of any additional riders to the lease, such as pet, garage, and furniture riders, or of any special provisions that require additional security deposits.

PROHIBITED PROVISIONS IN RENTAL AGREEMENTS

Many states have restrictions on the language and agreements in leases. For example, in Illinois (see Figure 4.2) the following provisions would be prohibited:

- An agreement to waive or forgo any rights or remedies granted by law
- A provision that authorizes any person to confess judgment on a claim arising out of the rental agreement
- An agreement to exculpate or limit any liability of the other party arising as a result of the other party's willful misconduct or negligence; or to indemnify the other party for that liability or the cost connected therewith

FIGURE 4.2 *Chicago Apartment Lease*

UNIVERSITY PRINTING COMPANY CHICAGO, IL	NO. 15C–TH (Tenant Heated)	REV 1998	©CHICAGO ASSOCIATION OF REALTORS® COPYRIGHT 1998 ALL RIGHTS RESERVED
NOT FURNISHED	**CHICAGO APARTMENT LEASE**		

DATE OF LEASE	TERM OF LEASE		MONTHLY RENT	SECURITY DEPOSIT*
	BEGINNING	ENDING		

ADDITIONAL CHARGES AND FEES

Late Charge $_____	Returned Check Charge $_____	Reletting Charge $_____	Parking Fee $_____	Laundry Room Fee $_____
Social Security No. _____ - _____ - _____		Storage Fee $_____	_____ $_____	_____ $_____

IF NONE, WRITE "NONE." Paragraph 5 of Lease Agreements and Covenants then INAPPLICABLE.

TENANT

TENANT　●

APARTMENT　●

BUILDING　●

CITY　●

LESSOR (Owner or agent authorized to manage the Apartment and to act for or on behalf of the Owner for the purpose of service of process and for the purpose of receiving and receipting for notices and demands.)

NAME　●

ADDRESS　●

CITY　●

PHONE　●　(　　　)

In consideration of the mutual agreements and covenants set forth below and on the reverse side hereof (the same being fully included as part of this Lease) Lessor hereby leases to Tenant and Tenant hereby leases from Lessor for use in accordance with paragraph 8 hereof the Apartment designated above, together with the fixtures and accessories belonging thereto, for the above Term. All parties listed above as Lessor and Tenant are herein referred to individually and collectively as Lessor and Tenant respectively.

5-12-100　Building Code Violations

Tenant is hereby notified that, during the 12 month period prior to the date of execution of this Lease, the following code violations have been cited for the Apartment and or the Building and the following notices have been received from the City of Chicago or any utility provider regarding termination of utility services (If none write "none"; if enforcement litigation is pending, also state the case number):

ADDITIONAL AGREEMENTS AND COVENANTS (including DECORATING AND REPAIRS), if any.

HEATING COST DISCLOSURE (for Tenant Heated Apartments)

(For all properties to which the Heating Cost Disclosure Ordinance (Chicago, IL Municipal Code CH. 193.21) is applicable). Effective 1/1/88.

1. The cost of heating the Apartment shall be the responsibility of Tenant.
2. Tenant acknowledges that Tenant was provided with heating cost information prior to any written or verbal agreement to enter into this lease and prior to any exchange of money. The projected average monthly cost of heat utility service (based on energy consumption during the most recent Annual Period by continuous occupancy by one or more occupants, current or estimated rates and normal weather) for the Apartment is $_____.
3. A copy of the Heating Cost Disclosure Form as required by the City of Chicago Department of Consumer Services is attached to this lease.
4. By execution of this Lease, Tenant confirms and acknowledges that Tenant has received the Heating Cost Disclosure Form.

FIGURE 4.2   *Chicago Apartment Lease, continued*

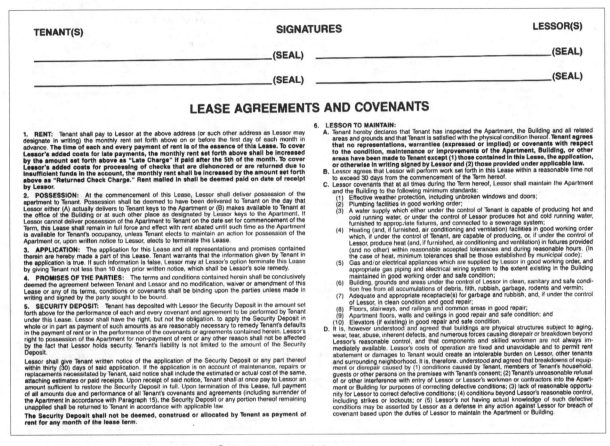

Source: Chicago Association of REALTORS®. Used with permission.

- An agreement to waive attorney's fees as provided by state or local ordinance, or to pay the attorney's fees of the other party except as may be required by law
- A provision that the rental agreement shall be terminated if there are, or shall be, any children under the age of 14 years in the tenant's family

If any of the above provisions are included in a rental agreement, the provision would be unenforceable while the rest of the lease would remain valid, provided there is a clause that states this provision.

If a party is injured by a prohibited provision in a rental agreement initiated by the other party and such injury results in damages, the injured party may bring suit to recover actual damages and reasonable attorney's fees. If the inclusion was deliberate and with knowledge, an additional monetary amount may be awarded.

FIGURE 4.3 *Apartment Lease*

New Lease ☐ $ ___________ Transfer Lease ☐
Renewal Lease ☐ $ ___________ Replacement Lease ☐
Lease Extension ☐ $ ___________ Relet/Rerent ☐

APARTMENT LEASE

S.C. NO. ______________ **BLDG.** ______________ **UNIT** ______________

LEASE TERM		MONTHLY RENT	REQUIRED SECURITY DEPOSIT	OTHER REQUIRED RENT**	REQUIRED PET DEPOSIT**	OTHER REQUIRED DEPOSIT
Begins	Ends					

LESSOR: MID-AMERICA MANAGEMENT CORP.
Managing Agent
2901 Butterfield Road
Oak Brook, Illinois 60523

LESSEE: NAME
NAME
NAME

****See Rider attached hereto and made a part hereof.**

PREMISES: ADDRESS ______________________________ **APT. NO.** ______________

Special Provisions:

Lessor and Lessee have read and herby agree to all the covenants, conditions and provisions contained in this lease on the face of this page, the reverse side of this page and in any Rider(s) attached hereto (any such Rider(s) are specifically incorportED into this Lease and made part of this Lease).

______________________________ (Seal)
Lessee
______________________________ (Seal)
Lessee
______________________________ (Seal)
Lessee
Dated: ______________________, 20 ________

MID-AMERICA MANAGEMENT CORP., Managing Agent
By ______________________________ (Seal)
____
Dated: ______________________, 20 ________

GUARANTEE

On this ______________________, for and in consideration of good and valuable consideration, the receipt and sufficiency of which is hereby acknowledged, the undersigned Guarantor hereby guarantees the payment of rent and performance by Lessee, Lessee's heirs, executors, administrators, successors, or assigns of all covenants and agreements of this Lease.

____
Guarantor (print name)

______________________________ (Seal)
Guarantor (signature)

Fair Housing Statement: Mid-America Management Corp. is an equal-opportunity housing manager. It is the policy of Mid-America Management Corp. for it and its employees and agents not to discriminate on the basis of race, color, religion, national origin, ancestry, physical or mental disability, familial status, age, marital status, sex or unfavorable discharge from military service in the offering of rental apartments or in the terms, conditions or privileges of rental. You have the right to be offered and to choose any rental apartment that we have available that meets your budgetary requirements. We will offer any available rental apartment to you, subject to our standard confirmation of your credit history, income and housing references. If you believe that you have been treated unfairly or discriminated against by any employee of agent of Mid-America Management Corp., please contact the compliance office at (630) 574-2400.

In consideration of the execution or renewal of this lease, Lessee and Lessor agree as follows:

A. Lessee, any member of the Lessee's household or a guest or visitor shall not engage in criminal activity, including drug-related criminal activity, with or without Lessee's knowledge, on or near the Premises. "Drug-related criminal activity" means the illegal manufacture, sale, distribution, use, or possession with intent to manufacture, sell, distribute, or use of a controlled substance (as defined in Illinois Compiled Statutes Chapter 720).

B. Lessee, any member of the Lessee's household or a guest or visitor shall not engage in any act intended to facilitate criminal activity, including drug-related criminal activity, with or without Lessee's knowledge, on or near the Premises.

C. Lessee, any member of the Lessee's household or a guest or visitor will not permit the Premises to be used for or to facilitate criminal activity, including drug-related criminal activity regardless of whether the individual engaging in such activity is a member of the household, a guest or a visitor.

D. Lessee, any member of the Lessee's household or a guest or visitor will not engage in the manufacture, sale, or distribution of illegal drugs at any locations, whether on or near the Premises or otherwise.

E. Lessee, any member of the Lessee's household or a guest or visitor shall not engage in acts of violence or threats of violence, including but not limited to the unlawful discharge of firearms with or without Lessee's knowledge on or near the Premises.

F. VIOLATION OF THE ABOVE PROVISIONS SHALL BE A MATERIAL VIOLATION OF THE LEASE AND GOOD CAUSE FOR TERMINATION OF TENANCY. A single violation of any of the above provisions shall be deemed a serious violation and material non-compliance with the lease. It is understood and agreed that a single violation shall be good cause for termination of the lease. Unless otherwise provided by law, proof of violation shall not require criminal conviction, but shall be by a preponderance of the evidence.

G. In the case of conflict between any of the above provisions and any other provisions of the lease, the above provisions shall govern.

Lessor, in consideration of the covenants, conditions and agreements herein contained on the part of the parties hereto, hereby leases the Premises to the Lessee to be occupied as a private dwelling for the use of Lessee and other persons as stated in the lease application, and to no other person, and for no other purpose for the above stated Lease Term. In consideration thereof, Lessee agrees to pay Lessor the above stated Monthly Rent, in advance throughout the Lease Term, and without notice or demand on the FIRST DAY of each calendar month of the Lease Term at the Lessor's address as set forth above or wherever designated in writing by Lessor from time to time. It is agreed by the parties hereto that the time of each and all such payments is the essence of this agreement. Lessee acknowledges and consents that Lessor reports Lessee's payment activity to credit reporting agencies.

1. SECURITY DEPOSIT. Lessee shall deposit with Lessor the above-described deposit to secure the faithful and timely performance of each and every covenant and provision of this lease, and covenants to maintain said entire security deposit with the Lessor until the termination of this lease. Provided Lessee has satisfied and complied with all the conditions of the release of security deposit as set forth on the reverse side of this lease, said deposit will be returned to Lessee after the termination of this lease in accordance with applicable law; it being understood that Lessee will remain liable for any loss or damage sustained by Lessor arising out of Lessee's failure to fully and faithfully perform hereunder. Lessee agrees that the security deposit shall not be considered an advance payment of rent and that Lessee shall at no time apply said deposit to payment of any rent becoming due hereunder. Should Lessee violate this paragraph by using the security deposit as the last month's rent, Lessee herein agrees to a special handling charge of $50.00 in addition to damages, if any, said charge to be deemed so much additional rent due and payable to Lessor immediately without notice or demand.

2. SPECIAL CONDITIONS. It is mutually agreed that in the event the rent payment is not made on the **FIRST DAY** of each calendar month of the Lease Term, a charge of two dollars ($2.00) per day for each day overdue shall become due and payable, which charge shall constitute so much additional rent hereunder, payable on demand. Lessee herein agrees to a $10.00 per day charge should he violate any restriction against pets, which charge shall constitute so much additional rent hereunder, payable on demand. Lessor shall have the right, but not the obligation, to apply any payment received from Lessee towards the payment of any additional rent or charges that remain unpaid at the time of receipt of such payment, and the balance of Lessee's payment, if any, shall then be applied towards current monthly rent due hereunder. The Premises, the building in which the Premises are situated, the facilities and public areas shall be used by Lessee at his own risk. Drinking of alcoholic beverages in public places is strictly prohibited. No person other than the person(s) signing this lease and other persons described in Lessee's lease application may occupy or live in said Premises without the prior written consent of Lessor. Lessee warrants and represents to Lessor that all information in the lease application for this lease is true. In the event any of the information supplied by the Lessee in the lease application is false or inaccurate, or misleading, this lease and any renewal thereof, shall be deemed to be materially breached by Lessee at its inception, and at the Lessor's option, the Lessee's occupancy shall be deemed a forcible entry and detainer.

3. CONDITIONS OF PREMISES. Lessee has examined the Premises before signing this lease, and is satisfied with the physical condition thereof, and his signing shall be conclusive evidence of this acknowledgement except as otherwise specified herein. Lessee agrees that no representation or warranty as to condition or repair has been made by Lessor or Lessor's Agent except as contained herein, and that no promise to decorate, alter, repair or improve the Premises has been made by Lessor or Lessor's Agent, either before or at the signing hereof. Lessee also acknowledges that no representation or warranty as to security at the Premises or at the building or apartment complex of which the Premises are a part has been made by Lessor.

4. NO ASSIGNMENT OR SUBLETTING. Lessee shall not sublet the Premises or any part thereof, nor assign this lease, nor permit to take place by any act or default of himself or any person, any transfer by operation of Law of Lessee's interest created hereby; nor offer the Premises or any portion thereof for lease or sublease.

5. USE OF PREMISES. No part of the Premises shall be used or occupied for a boarding or lodging house, for rooming or school purposes, to give instructions of any kind, for any trade, business or entertainment, for any purpose that will increase the rate of insurance thereon, nor shall there be kept on or used in or around the Premises or in any place contiguous thereto any flammable fluids or explosives. Neither Lessee nor any other person with or without Lessee's permission shall commit or permit any unlawful or immoral practice, nor any act, nor any practice that will injure the reputation of the Premises or the building of which the Premises are a part, or that disturbs other tenants or occupants of the building, or any other building within the apartment complex of which the Premises are a part, or that violates any local ordinance applicable to the Premises, or that is injurious to the Premises, the building or the apartment complex of which the Premises are a part, or the operation thereof. Lessee shall be fully responsible for the conduct of all persons residing with, or visiting Lessee. Lessor has the right to bar individuals from the Premises, or the apartment complex of which the Premises are a part. Lessee must inform his guests of the terms of this lease, and all rules and regulations as contained herein. If any of the terms of this lease or any of the rules or regulations are violated by Lessee's guests, they may be barred and/or arrested for criminal trespass.

6. RADIOS, TV, ETC. Lessee, any other person permitted to occupy the Premises, or any guest of Lessee, shall not operate any audio or visual equipment, radios, televisions, musical instruments, citizens band radios or other equipment or device on the Premises, or in or on any part of the apartment complex of which the Premises are a part, which disturbs an occupant or occupants of any building in the apartment complex of which the Premises are a part.

7. UPKEEP. Neither the Lessee nor any other person permitted to occupy the Premises nor any guests of Lessee shall suffer or commit any waste in or about the Premises or in or about the building of which the Premises are a part, and shall keep the Premises, together with the fixtures therein and appurtenances, in a clean, sightly, and sanitary condition and in good repair and free from vermin, rodents, and insects, all at his own expense, and shall yield the same back to Lessor upon termination of the lease or of Lessee's right of possession, by expiration of the Lease Term or in any other manner, in the same condition as at the

FIGURE 4.3 *Apartment Lease, continued*

date of the signing hereof, except as repaired or altered by Lessor and except loss from reasonable wear and tear. If however, the Premises shall not be kept by the Lessee as aforesaid, Lessor may enter the same, himself or by his agents, and put the same in good condition, and Lessee agrees to pay Lessor in addition to the rent hereby reserved, the expense of Lessor in so doing, the amount of which such expense shall be due from Lessee to Lessor on the first day of the month following that in which such expense may be incurred, as so much additional rent. Lessee hereby assumes full and complete liability and responsibility for any and all loss, costs or damages, including, but not limited to, fire damage, resulting from Lessee's negligent or intentional acts or any other act or omission of Lessee, anyone acting on Lessee's behalf, or any other person permitted to occupy the Premises, or any invitee of Lessee. Lessee will carry liability insurance to insure Lessor for all of the aforementioned negligent or intentional acts and omissions. In no instance, including, but not limited to, the payment of rent, shall Lessee or Lessee's agents or invitees, be considered an insured, as a co-insured or an additional insured, or otherwise under Lessor's property or casualty insurance policies or under Lessor's self-funded risk management programs, if any. Lessee also agrees to see to it that none of the foregoing persons violate any of the terms or provisions of this lease or the rules and regulations that are a part hereof or cause damage or disrepair to any part of the Premises, the building of which the Premises is a part, or any property on or adjacent thereto.

8. ACCESS. Lessee agrees to give the Lessor or persons designated by Lessor, free access to the Premises, at all reasonable times, to inspect, alter or repair the Premises, or exhibit the Premises for sale or for rent or to exterminate vermin, rodents and insects from the Premises or to permit the Lessor to display a "For Rent" sign in any window during any sixty (60) day period prior to the expiration of the Lease Term and agrees not to move or remove such a sign. For each breach of this paragraph, the Lessee agrees to pay the Lessor twice the amount of one month's rent as liquidated damages for such action, the same constituting so much additional rent hereunder, payable upon demand.

9. SECURITY. At its election Lessor, its agents and employees may, but is not obligated, to retain an independent contractor to provide protective services for the proper security and safeguard of the property of which the Premises are a part. Where Lessor has elected to furnish such security service, it is expressly understood and agreed that security personnel, in rendering any of the services provided or otherwise, shall not under any circumstances whatsoever be considered employees of Lessor. It is further understood and agreed that the providing of said security confers neither rights upon Lessee nor corresponding obligations upon Lessor. Lessor may withdraw said service at any time without notice to Lessee. This provision is not a basis of the bargain and Lessee is not responsible for any proportionate share of any costs and expenses incurred by Lessor in providing security. Lessee acknowledges that no representations have been expressed or implied by Lessor regarding the security or safety of the Lessee or Lessee's property.

10. NO SIGNS, ETC. Without Lessor's prior written consent, Lessee shall not cause or permit the display of any sign or advertising material upon or about the Premises or the building of which it is a part.

11. NO ALTERATIONS. Lessee shall make no alterations or additions without the prior written consent of Lessor. All alterations and additions shall remain as part of the Premises, unless the Lessor shall otherwise elect, including without limitation, locks, bolts, antennas, carpeting and all fixtures.

12. NO INSTALLATION WITHOUT PERMISSION. Lessee shall not install in, on, or about the Premises, nor attach to or affix to any interior or exterior part of the building of which the Premises are a part including without limitation, any air conditioning unit, dishwasher, humidifier, dehumidifier, laundry equipment, refrigerator, satellite dish and/or antenna or any other mechanical device or appliance of any kind or nature in whole or in part, without the prior written consent of Lessor or Lessor's agent, and any such consent shall be wholly and solely upon the terms and conditions specified in such consent, if given.

13. HEAT AND UTILITIES. Lessor agrees, if the building is equipped for the purpose and there is no separate system or meter servicing the Premises, to furnish, during the Lease Term, sufficient heat to comply with the minimum requirements set forth in the applicable laws of the municipality in which the Premises are situated, gas, electricity and/or water. The cost of said utilities will be paid by Lessor unless otherwise provided herein or by Rider hereto. Lessor shall not be held liable for any injury or damage whatsoever which may arise or accrue from its failure to furnish any of the above items, regardless of the cause of such failure, all claims for such injury or damage being hereby expressly waived by Lessee. In the event the Premises are equipped with a self-contained furnace system and/or are separately metered for gas, hot water for heat, electricity and/or water, Lessee covenants and agrees to be responsible for all charges for same and/or establish and maintain in its own name accounts with the appropriate utilities and timely make all required deposits and utility payments for such items; and the Lessee further covenants and agrees to operate the system at a temperature sufficient to prevent damage to Premises or any portion of the building in which the Premises are located; and Lessee further covenants and agrees to be fully liable and responsible for any damage to the Premises and/or the building resulting due to a breach of this paragraph. Lessor shall also have the right, but not the obligation, to make any such utility payments when due and pay any arrearages of such payments, which amount shall immediately become due to Lessor from Lessee as additional rent hereunder. Lessor shall also have the right to apply payments received from Lessee first to payment of additional rent under this paragraph, and then to monthly rent and other amounts due from Lessee under this lease. Lessee hereby indemnifies and holds Lessor and the owner of the Premises harmless from and against any and all claims of nonpayment for utility services, including, without limitation, all amounts paid by Lessor in satisfaction of such claims and all costs, expenses and attorney's fees which may be incurred.

14. FIRE AND CASUALTY. In case the Premises shall be rendered untenable by fire, explosion or other casualty. Lessor may, at its option, either repair the Premises within sixty (60) days or make available to the Lessee another apartment of Lessor's choice which is comparable to the Premises, in which case all the terms and conditions of this lease shall apply to the new apartment or Lessor shall have the right to terminate this lease. Lessor's exercise of any of the foregoing options shall not in any way be deemed to waive or to limit the liability of Lessee for certain of its acts or the acts of the Lessee's agents or invitees as set forth in paragraph 7 hereof, including, but not limited to, liability of Lessee for loss or damage caused by fire.

15. SURRENDER OF PREMISES. At termination of this lease or of Lessee's right of possession by lapse of time or otherwise. Lessee shall yield immediate possession of the Premises to Lessor, and deliver all keys to Lessor or its agent at the place where rent is payable.

16. RIGHTS AND REMEDIES. If Lessee permits the Premises to remain vacant or unoccupied without payment of rent due for a period of ten (10) days, or otherwise abandons the Premises, or in the event of the breach of any covenant or agreement contained in this lease. Lessee's right to the possession of the Premises thereupon shall terminate without notice or demand, and the mere retention of possession thereafter by Lessee shall constitute a forcible detainer, and if the Lessor so elects, but not otherwise, this lease shall thereupon terminate, and upon termination of Lessee's right of possession, as aforesaid whether this lease be terminated or not, Lessee agrees to surrender possession of the Premises immediately. If Lessee permits the Premises to remain vacant or unoccupied without payment of rent due for a period of ten (10) days, or if Lessee shall at any time during the Lease Term or at the termination of this lease or of Lessee's right of possession of the Premises cease to occupy the Premises as and for his actual residence and fails to remove from the Premises any and all articles of personal property therein, whether they be the property of the Lessee or others, then in any such case Lessee hereby grants to Lessor full and complete right to enter the Premises and remove therefrom any such articles of personal property as may be found therein, without any liability to Lessee or others whose property may be left on the Premises. Lessor is also hereby given the right and privilege to remove such articles from the Premises, to store at Lessee's sole risk, or to sell any and all such articles at public or private sale and apply the proceeds of any such sale, after deducting all costs and expenses incurred thereby, to any indebtedness due to Lessor from Lessee. If there is no such indebtedness due and owing to Lessor. Lessor shall hold the net proceeds of any such sale for the Lessee, payable to him upon demand in writing. Neither Lessor nor his agents shall be liable to Lessee for any act of itself, or its agents for the doing of any act or thing or about the exercise of the right herein conferred or for the care or preservation of any such articles.

17. WAIVER OF NOTICES. During the Lease Term and at all times thereafter, Lessee hereby waives all notices of any election by Lessor hereunder, demand for rent or additional rent, notice to quit, demand for possession and any and all notices and demands which shall be required by any statute of this State relating to forcible detainer and entry, or to landlord and tenant or any other statute or law. It is agreed that whenever Lessor does provide any notice or demand upon Lessee, it shall be sufficient to deliver or cause to be delivered to Lessee a written or printed copy thereof or to send a written or printed copy thereof by United States certified mail, postage prepaid, addressed to Lessee at the Premises, in which event the notice or demand shall be deemed to have been served at the time the copy is mailed, or to leave a written or printed copy thereof with some person above the age of twelve (12) years residing on or in possession of the Premises or, if no one answers the door, to affix the same upon any door leading into the Premises, in which event or events the notice or demand shall be deemed to have been served at the time the copy is so delivered, left or affixed.

18. LESSOR'S RIGHTS NOT WAIVED. The acceptance of rent after it falls due or after the knowledge of any breach hereof by Lessee, or the giving of any notice or making any demand, whether according to any statutory provisions or not, or any other act or waiver other than written waiver shall not be construed as a waiver of Lessor's right to act without notice or demand or any other right hereby given Lessor, or as an election not to proceed under the provisions of this lease.

19. ABANDONMENT AND RELETTING. If Lessee shall vacate the Premises or Lessee's right to possession thereof shall be terminated, the Premises or any part thereof may, but need not, be relet by Lessor for such rent and such terms and such period as Lessor may elect without releasing Lessee from any liability hereunder (but Lessor shall not be required to accept or receive any tenant offered by Lessee or by others). Lessee agrees to pay all deficiencies in case of reletting if sufficient sums shall not be received therefrom to satisfy the rent herein provided in addition to the sum necessary to pay all expenses thereof, including, but not limited to, decoration, advertising, repairs, replacements, commissions and Lessor's customary service charge.

20. LEGAL EXPENSES. Lessee shall pay and discharge all costs, expenses, attorney's fees, witness fees and administrative costs, including but not limited to, a processing fee of $50.00 each time a five-day or other statutory notice is served on Lessee and delinquent rent is not paid within the five day (or other applicable) period, which shall be incurred or expended by Lessor due to breach of the covenants and agreements of this lease by Lessee, the same constituting so much additional rent hereunder, payable on demand.

21. LESSEE'S LIABILITY NOT WAIVED. Lessee's obligation to pay rent during the Lease Term or any extension thereof shall continue and shall not be waived, released or terminated by service of a five-day notice, demand for possession, notice of termination of tenancy, the filing of a forcible entry and detainer action, or the entry of a judgment for possession and/or rent in such forcible entry and detainer action, or any other act resulting in the termination of the Lessee's right to possession. The payment or receipt of rent due shall not waive or affect any such notice, demand, suit or judgment or in any manner waive, affect, change, modify or alter any rights or remedies of Lessor, and it is agreed that no act of Lessor or Lessor's agent in apparent acquiescence in or failure to object to, any breach by Lessee of any of the terms, covenants, conditions or agreements in this lease or failure to demand any additional rent or other sums due hereunder from Lessee, shall act as a bar to or waiver of Lessor's right to thereafter insist upon the complete performance of all such terms, covenants, conditions and agreements herein contained or payment of such additional rent or other sums.

22. RULES AND REGULATIONS PART OF LEASE. The rules and regulations contained in this lease are hereby made a part of and incorporated into this lease and Lessee shall observe the same. Failure to keep and observe said rules will constitute a material breach of the terms of this lease in the same manner as if contained herein as covenants, and a failure to observe the same shall be of the same effect. Lessee shall keep and observe such further rules and regulations as may be required by Lessor or its agent from time to time which Lessor may deem necessary for the proper and orderly care of the building of which the Premises are a part.

23. LEASE BINDING ON HEIRS, ETC. All covenants and agreements of this lease shall be binding upon and inure to the benefit of the heirs, executors, administrators, successors and assigns of the Lessor and Lessee, respectively without affecting the restrictions imposed in paragraph 4 hereof.

24. LESSOR'S REMEDIES CUMULATIVE. The rights and remedies of the Lessor under this lease are cumulative, and the use of one or more thereof shall not exclude or waive the right to use any other remedy.

25. INTERPRETATION. The words "Lessor" and "Lessee" used herein include the plural thereof and the necessary changes required to make the provisions hereof apply to corporations or men or women shall be construed as if made. The words "Lessee" when used in this lease shall be construed to be plural if more than one person comprises Lessee and each shall be jointly and severally obligated to perform all of the terms and conditions of Lessee as contained in this lease.

26. INDEPENDENT CONVENANTS. Lessee's covenant to pay rent is and shall be independent of each and every other covenant of this lease. Lessee agrees that Lessee's damages for Lessor's breach shall in no case be deducted from rent nor set off for purposes of determining whether any rent is due in any action brought on the basis of unpaid rent, except as permitted by law.

27. RESIDENT/RENTER INSURANCE. Lessor is not an insurer of Lessee's person or possessions and Lessor does not provide liability insurance for Lessee in connection with the acts or conduct of Lessee or Lessee's agents or invitees which cause damage to the person or property of others. **Lessee agrees that all of Lessee's person and property on the Premises or elsewhere in the building shall be at the risk of Lessee and that Lessee will carry such insurance as Lessee deems necessary therefor,** except for property damage and personal injury caused solely by the negligent acts or omissions of Lessor. Lessee agrees that Lessor, its agents and employees shall **NOT** be liable for any damage to the person or property of the Lessee or any other person occupying or visiting the Premises or building, sustained due to the Premises or building or any part thereof or any appurtenance thereof becoming out of repair (as example and not by way of limitation, damage caused by water, snow, ice, frost, steam, sewage, sewer gas or odors, heating, cooling and ventilating equipment, bursting or leaking pipes, faucets and plumbing fixtures, mechanical breakdown or failure, electrical failure, security services or devices or mailboxes being misused or becoming temporarily out of order, and fire), or due to the happening of any accident in or about the building, or due to any act or neglect of any other tenant or occupant of said building or any other person, or of neighboring property. Lessee understands that Lessee will receive no monthly rent reductions, adjustment, or compensation whatsoever due to repairs or interruptions of service except as provided by law.

28. LEASE SUBORDINATE TO MORTGAGE. This lease is not to be recorded and is subordinate to any present or future mortgages or leases on the land (or any part of it) upon which the building in which

(continued)

FIGURE 4.3 *Apartment Lease, continued*

the Premises are a part is situated or upon the building itself and to all advances upon the security of such leases or mortgages. Lessee shall attorn to and recognize any purchaser at a foreclosure sale of any mortgage or deed of trust or to any such purchaser at a sale exercised in connection with any lender's remedy of power of sale pursuant to any mortgage or deed of trust affecting the Premises or to any transferee who acquires the Premises by deed in lieu of foreclosure, and the successors and/or assigns of such transferee or purchaser.

29. UNCOLLECTIBLE CHECK. In the event any payments required of Lessee hereunder are made by check and such check is returned unpaid to Lessor for any reason whatsoever, the Lessor shall charge Lessee the sum of $25.00 which charge shall constitute so much additional rent hereunder, payable on demand. The Lessor, at its sole discretion, shall have the right, but not the obligation, to refuse to accept personal checks from Lessee, if Lessee had previously had one or more checks returned unpaid for any reason, or is otherwise in default under any of the terms or conditions of this lease.

30. RENEWAL. If Lessor presents a renewal lease to Lessee at least 45 days prior to expiration of this lease. Lessee agrees that within 15 days after receipt thereof he shall either enter into a new lease with Lessor or notify Lessor in writing of his intent to vacate. Should Lessee fail to timely comply, it will be considered that Lessee's intent is to vacate, and Lessor will proceed to re-rent the Premises to another person.

31. FAILURE TO VACATE UPON LEASE EXPIRATION. Lessee covenants and agrees that in the event Lessee fails to vacate the Premises by twelve midnight (C.S.T.) on the last day of the Lease Term (as set forth on the front page of this lease), the Lessee shall be in violation of Lessee's agreement to yield immediate possession of the Premises to Lessor as contained in paragraph 15 above, and shall be deemed a tenant at sufferance and shall pay as liquidated damages an amount equal to double the Monthly Rent for each and every month that Lessee withholds possession. Lessee's liability for said amount shall accrue on the first day of each and every month and shall not be prorated. **This means that even if Lessee withholds possession for one day beyond the Lease Term, Lessee will pay double the entire Monthly Rent.** Should Lessee fail to vacate as provided herein, Lessor shall have available to it all remedies as provided in this Lease including, without limitation, the filing of an eviction action for immediate possession of the Premises. Lessee shall pay all court costs and attorney's fees incurred in prosecuting said action as provided in paragraph 20 above.

32. ENTIRE AGREEMENT. This lease represents the entire agreement of the parties and may not be changed, altered, modified or amended unless same as in writing and is signed by all parties hereto.

33. SEVERABILITY. Wherever possible, each provision of this lease shall be interpreted in such manner as to be effective and valid under applicable law, but if any provision of this lease shall be prohibited or invalid under such law, such provision shall be ineffective only to the extent of such prohibition or invalidity, without invalidating the remainder of such provision or the remaining provisions of this lease. Further, if any provision of this lease conflicts with governing statutory law, the latter shall prevail.

34. CAPTIONS. All captions in this lease are inserted only as a matter of convenience, and in no way define, limit or extend the scope or intent of this lease or any provision hereof.

RULES AND REGULATIONS

Lessor reserves the right to change and/or expand these "Rules and Regulations" from time to time, by written notice to Lessee, which notice may be accomplished by individual notice to Lessee and/or posting in common area of the building in which the Premises are located.

1. No rugs shall be beaten on porches or balconies. No dust, rubbish, litter or anything else shall be swept, thrown, or emptied from any of the windows or upon or from the porches or balconies of the building or into the halls or entryways thereof. Lessee shall not utilize charcoal, gas or electric barbecue grills or similar cooking devices within the Premises or the building in which the Premises are located, on porches, balconies, or patios, or within ten (10) feet of the building in which the Premises are located, or within ten (10) feet of any other building within the apartment complex in which the building is located.

2. Children shall not be permitted to loiter or play on the stairways, halls, basements, laundry areas, porches, or court areas used by the public or other tenants.

3. The sidewalks, entryways, vestibules, halls and stairways outside of the several apartments, shall not be obstructed or used for any other purpose than for ingress and egress to and from the respective rooms or apartment.

4. Lessee shall not cause or permit anything to be hung from the outside windows, porches or balconies or placed on the outside window sills or porches or balconies. No door nor window treatments visible from outside the Premises shall be kept by Lessee in or upon the Premises except such as are both consistent with decor of the building and in good taste, as determined by Lessor in its sole discretion. By way of illustration, not limitation, window coverings would include blinds, curtains and drapes, not paper coverings or bedding sheets.

5. The water shall not be left running for an unreasonable or unnecessary length of time.

6. Lessee shall not interfere in any manner with any part of the heating, lighting, refrigerating or cooling apparatus in or about the Premises or in or about the building containing the same.

7. Laundry work shall be done only in the areas provided for such purposes, Lessee agrees to follow the posted hours of the laundry facility. Washing machines and apparatus shall be used and operated in such areas only, and Lessee may not install such equipment within the Premises without Lessor's prior written consent. The use of water-power washing machines is prohibited, except by prior written consent of Lessor.

8. Lessee shall neither keep nor maintain any dog, cat, bird, reptile, or other animal in the Premises nor permit any occupant of the Premises to do so without first obtaining Lessor's prior written consent. Lessee assumes full responsibility to see that this regulation is observed.

9. Lessee shall not keep nor store nor permit any occupants of the Premises to keep or store any articles of any kind on any part or portion of the building in which Premises are located other than inside the Premises or in a storage room, if such storage room is provided by Lessor.

10. The Lessee shall not alter any lock nor install a new lock or a knocker or other attachment on any door of the Premises without prior written consent of the Lessor. If Lessor's consent is given to Lessee, Lessee agrees to immediately provide Lessor with a key to the new lock or knocker. If a key is not so provided, Lessee shall be responsible for all charges and repairs related to Lessor's entry into the Premises pursuant to this lease.

11. Vehicles which are inoperable, unlicensed, or have expired licenses shall not be parked or stored on the property in which the Premises is a part, and any such vehicle may be towed away at the owner's expense, and without notice. In the event Lessor incurs any expense in connection with the towing of such vehicles, Lessee shall reimburse Lessor for such expense immediately upon demand therefor.

12. The use of garbage receptacles or incinerators shall be in accordance with posted signs, and garbage and refuse shall be kept in small, light parcels or bags and said garbage and refuse must be placed only in garbage receptacles or incinerators unless allowed in writing. Lessee agrees to fully cooperate with Lessor, in complying with all federal, state or municipal laws, acts and ordinances including, but not limited to, those regarding the recycling of waste materials.

13. No furniture filled with liquid or semi-liquid shall be brought in or used on the Premises, unless contained in a proper frame or liner. Lessee shall be responsible and liable for any and all damage to the Premises and/or the building in which the Premises are a part which is caused by such furniture.

14. Parking shall only be permitted in those areas and/or spaces as designated by the Lessor or Lessor's agent. Any vehicles which violate this regulation shall be subject to towing at the owner's expense and without notice. Working on motor vehicles in the parking lots, driveways and other areas of the property is prohibited.

15. Motorized vehicles, including but not limited to motorcycles and motorbikes, shall not at any time be stored in the Premises or any patio area. Such vehicles may be stored only in areas designated by Lessor.

16. Recreational vehicles, boats, trailers of any kind, tow trucks, flat beds, and any form of commercial vehicle are not to be parked anywhere on the grounds of the apartment complex of which the Premises are a part without the express written permission of Lessor and, if Lessor's permission is given, shall be parked in designated areas assigned by Lessor. Violators will be subject to towing at their own expenses.

RELEASE OF SECURITY DEPOSIT IS SUBJECT TO SATISFACTION OF THE FOLLOWING CONDITIONS

1. Full term of lease has expired and all provisions herein complied with.
2. Should Lessee desire to RELET under the provisions of the lease, a "one half month's rent" service charge will be assessed.
   (a) Approval must be obtained from Lessor prior to initiating a relet.
   (b) Notice in writing must be given to management by certified mail prior to initiating a relet.
3. Entire apartment including range, oven, refrigerator, bathroom, closets, cabinets, windows, carpet, balcony, etc. cleaned.
4. No damage to apartment beyond normal wear and tear.
5. No unpaid late charges or delinquent rent.
6. Forwarding address left with management.
7. No indentations or scratches in wood or resilient floor caused by furniture or other means. Floor must be restored to the original condition if tack down or wall-to-wall carpeting was installed by Lessee.
8. No wallcoverings, stickers, scratches, or large holes on walls.
9. All keys including those from mailboxes must be returned.
10. All debris, rubbish, and discards to be placed in proper rubbish containers in designated area.
11. All building-owned carpeting must be professionally cleaned and condition of the carpet after such cleaning is subject to approval of Lessor.

IF THE ABOVE CONDITIONS ARE NOT COMPLIED WITH, LESSEE WILL BE CHARGED THE CURRENT RATES LESSOR IS PAYING TO HAVE ITEMS REPAIRED AND/OR CLEANED

The cost of labor and materials for cleaning, decorating, maintenance, repairs, removals and replacements, where applicable, or rent loss due to necessary repair time, and numerous other charges based on actual damages will be deducted from the security deposit. The following is a schedule of Lessor's current minimum charges for cleaning, decorating and maintenance.

Cleaning		
1. Trash removal		$14.00 per hour
2. Kitchen		
Stove		$30.00
Refrigerator		$20.00
Cabinets & Countertops		$20.00
Floor		$20.00
3. Bathrooms (each)		
Toilets		$7.00
Shower and Tub		$20.00
Medicine Cabinet		$7.00
Vanity		$7.00
Floor		$7.00
4. Closets		$12.00
5. Windows		$7.00
6. Floors		
Vacuum		$7.00
Tile Cleaning	1 Bedroom	$45.00
	2 Bedroom	$55.00
Carpet Cleaning	1 Bedroom	$40.00
	2 Bedroom	$50.00
7. Excessive Cleaning		$14.00 per hour
Decorating		
1. Patching holes 1/2" to 2"		$12.00 each
2. Double Coating		$12.00 each wall
3. Removal of wall coverings		$20.00 per hour
Maintenance		
1. Materials plus labor at		$27.00 per hour
2. Light bulb replacement		$1.75 each

SECURITY DEPOSITS

An owner may, according to a written rental agreement, require a security deposit from the tenant in an amount that generally is not more than two months' rent. However, nothing prevents an owner from requiring prepaid rent in any amount.

If the tenant does prepay rent, the money cannot be applied as security but only to the payment of rent as it becomes due. A security deposit shall not be used nor applied as rent except as provided by law.

Applicants should pay the full, required security deposit at the time of signing the lease and always prior to moving into the property. Avoid taking a partial payment, and don't take your property off the market unless the full security deposit has been paid.

Most provisions in the lease form pertaining to security deposits (see Figure 4.3) provide that the lessor has the right, but not the obligation, to apply the security deposit in payment of any unpaid delinquent rent or other moneys due from the tenant. Some leases also provide that the lessor's right to possession of the property for nonpayment of rent or any other reason is not affected by the fact that the lessor holds a security deposit.

In some states, if you apply a security deposit to the payment of unpaid rent due or to compensate for damages caused by a tenant's noncompliance with the rental agreement, you must notify the tenant within a reasonable period, usually 15 to 20 days. In the case of compensation for damages, include an itemized statement of the damage allegedly caused to the dwelling unit or the premises and the estimated or actual cost for repairing or replacing each item on that statement, with estimates or paid invoices or copies attached. If estimated costs are given on this statement, owners should furnish the tenant with copies of paid invoices within 30 days from the date of the statement. Security deposits may not be used by the owner to repair or replace items due to normal wear and tear.

Tenants have a specified time limit, normally 15 days, after receiving notice that the security deposit has been applied to rent or damages to pay the owner an amount sufficient to restore the security deposit in full.

Security deposit laws in most states dictate that within a certain amount of time of termination of the tenancy (usually 14 to 45 days), owners must refund the security deposit or any portion of it that remains unapplied. Each state differs on the exact number of days; check with your local real estate association to find out how much time you have. Failure to return a security deposit within the legal time limit may result in additional monetary fines.

As an owner, don't withhold any portion of the security deposit because of the tenant's failure to give you advance notice of vacating the dwelling unit (this applies unless the requirement of advance notice is stated on the face of the rental agreement and the tenant fails to give such notice), the dwelling unit is vacant for a subsequent period, and local laws permit such withholdings.

In the event of a sale, lease, or other transfer of the property, owners have to transfer or assign any security deposit funds to the new owner (purchaser, lessee, assignee, mortgagee). When the owner notifies each tenant affected by the transfer, the new owner assumes the obligations concerning security deposits and is bound by law to perform. If a new owner comes into possession of a property and has not in fact received the security deposit moneys, he or she would not be liable to the tenants for the return of the security deposits unless otherwise agreed to in advance.

States have different rules governing the handling of security deposit funds. In Illinois, for example, security deposits for residential properties containing six or more units must be deposited in a bank or savings and loan association chartered by a state or federal agency. Deposits aren't subject to claims of creditors of the owner; and interest paid on the account is paid to the owner. This number of units—six or more—may be reduced in future legislation; other states have no exemption.

Even if your state doesn't require it, security deposit money should be kept in a separate interest-bearing bank account instead of mingling it with your personal funds. Many states require landlords to pay semiannual interest to tenants on the security deposit amount.

If owners fail to comply with a security deposit provision of their state statute, tenants can sue to recover the property or money due them and in some cases can be awarded punitive damages and reasonable attorney's fees.

RESTRICTIONS ON USE

Many leases contain specific rules and regulations that limit the use of a dwelling unit and the common areas in the property building. Common restrictions include prohibiting pets, setting up waterbeds, and cooking on a barbecue; they often govern the use of air conditioners and the replacement of locks. These restrictions are legal in most cases; however, if there is an ambiguity in the meaning of the restriction, the language would be construed in favor of the tenant against the landlord.

Owners can adopt new rules or regulations concerning a tenant's use and occupancy of the premises, but such new rules are generally enforceable against the tenant only if they meet the following criteria:

- Their purpose must be to promote the convenience, safety, or welfare of all the tenants on the premises; preserve the owner's property from abusive use; or make a fair distribution of services and facilities offered to tenants in general.
- They must be reasonable in relation to the purpose for which they are adopted.
- They must apply to all tenants on the premises in a fair manner.
- They must be sufficiently explicit in their prohibition, direction, or limitation to fairly inform a tenant of what the tenant must or must not do to comply.
- They are not for the purpose of evading the obligations of the owner.
- A tenant must be notified of the rules and regulations at the time he or she enters into the rental agreement.

A rule or regulation incorporated after a tenant enters into the rental agreement is enforceable against the tenant only if reasonable notice of its adoption is given to the tenant and doesn't bring about a substantial reduction of the tenant's value in renting the property.

For example, if someone rented an apartment in your complex because you allowed that tenant to keep a pet and you subsequently adopted a new rule prohibiting pets, or if someone rented because your property had a swimming pool that was free and open until 10 PM and then you decided to charge a fee or reduce the hours the pool was open, these changes would be reductions in value to the tenant.

RIDERS AND ADDITIONS TO THE LEASE

The standard property rental agreement covers most, but not all, aspects of the landlord-tenant relationship. You may want to add clauses and riders to the document to cover such matters as garage rent, pets, agreements to extend or cut short the term of the lease, furniture rental, and so on. Clauses are typed onto the lease; riders are separate sheets that are attached to the lease.

Following are some commonly used riders and clauses.

Moisture, Mildew, and Mold Rider

This rider requires the lessee to report to the landlord or property manager any evidence of a water leak or excessive moisture and other stipulations (see Figure 4.4). Lessee also acknowledges receiving the mold and mildew pamphlet produced by the Department of Health.

Lead-Based Paint Disclosure Form

Housing built before 1978 may contain lead-based paint; and lead from paint, paint chips, and dust can pose health hazards if not managed properly. Lead exposure is especially harmful to young children and pregnant women. A federal law effective December 1996 affects rental housing built before 1978. It requires lessors to disclose the presence of known lead-based paint and/or lead-based paint hazards in the dwelling, before the lease takes effect. Lessees must also receive a federally approved pamphlet on preventing lead poisoning.

The Environmental Protection Agency's (EPA's) pamphlets and the Lead-Based Paint Disclosure Form shown in Figure 4.5 must be attached to the lease and signed by both the lessor and the lessee(s).

FIGURE 4.4 *Moisture, Mildew, and Mold Rider to the Lease*

MID-AMERICA MANAGEMENT CORP.
2907 Butterfield Road
Oak Brook, Illinois 60523

BLDG. NO. _____

UNIT NO. _____

__MASTER RIDER__

THIS RIDER is hereby made a part of and incorporated as part of a certain lease agreement dated _____ (ie: starting date of current lease), for an apartment ("The Premises") located at _____ _____ in _____, _____, by and between MID AMERICA MANAGEMENT CORPORATION ("Lessor") and _____ ("Lessee").

THE TERMS AND CONDITIONS OF THIS RIDER SHALL GOVERN OVER
THE TERMS AND CONDITIONS OF THE ATTACHED LEASE AGREEMENT.

MOISTURE, MILDEW AND MOLD RIDER

Humidity, leaks, condensation, water infiltration or flooding in the Premises can cause building materials to become moist or water damaged, which can in turn lead to the presence of mold or mildew. Lessee agrees to immediately (within 24 hours of first discovering) report to the management office any evidence of a water leak or excessive moisture in the Premises. Lessee agrees to provide appropriate climate control, keep the Premises clean, and take other sanitary measures to retard and prevent mold and mildew from accumulating in the Premises. Lessee agrees to clean the Premises regularly and to remove moisture from all windows, walls and other interior surfaces as soon as reasonably possible. Lessee agrees not to obstruct or cover any of the heating, ventilation or air-conditioning systems. Lessee agrees to timely report to Lessor any evidence of mold or mildew-like growth which common household cleaners and wiping do not remove or any areas in the Premises or the building which repeatedly show evidence of mold or mildew. Lessee also agrees to timely report any failure or malfunction in the heating, ventilation or air conditioning system in the Premises, any leaking and any inoperable doors or windows which leak or could cause leaks. Lessee shall be responsible for damage to the Premises and Lessee's property as well as injury to Lessee and/or any other occupants of the Premises and/or the Apartments resulting from Lessee's failure to comply with the terms of this Rider. Lessee agrees to give Lessor or persons designated by Lessor access to the Premises at all reasonable times to inspect, alter or repair the Premises.

Lessee acknowledges that Lessee has received from Lessor the Mold and Mildew pamphlet produced by the Department of Health.

FIGURE 4.5 *Lead-Based Paint Disclosure Form*

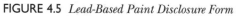

CHICAGO ASSOCIATION OF REALTORS®/MLS

DISCLOSURE FORMAT FOR PRE-1978 HOUSING RENTAL AND LEASES
DISCLOSURE OF INFORMATION
LEAD-BASED PAINT AND/OR LEAD-BASED PAINT HAZARDS

Lead Warning Statement

Housing built before 1978 may contain lead-based paint. Lead from paint, paint chips, and dust can pose health hazards if not managed properly. Lead exposure is especially harmful to young children and pregnant women. Before renting pre-1978 housing, Lessors must disclose the presence of known lead-based paint and/or lead-based paint hazards in the dwelling. Lessees must also receive a federally approved pamphlet on lead poisoning prevention.

Lessor's Disclosure (initial)

_____(a)   Presence of lead-based paint and/or lead-based paint hazards (check one below):

☐ Known lead-based paint and/or lead-based paint hazards are present in the housing (explain):
_____
_____

☐ Lessor has no knowledge of lead-based paint and/or lead-based paint hazards in the housing.

_____(b)   Records and Reports available to the Lessor (check one below):

☐ Lessor has provided the Lessee with all available records and reports pertaining to lead-based paint and/or lead-based hazards in the housing (list documents below):
_____
_____

☐ Lessor has no reports or records pertaining to lead-based paint and/or lead-based paint hazards in the housing.

Lessee's Acknowledgement (initial) (All Lessees should initial)

_____(c)   Lessee has received copies of all information listed above.

_____(d)   Lessee has received the pamphlet *Protect Your Family From Lead in Your Home*.

Agent's Acknowledgement (initial) (Lessor's Agent)

_____(e)   Agent has informed the Lessor of the Lessor's obligations under 42 U.S.C. 4852 d and is aware of his/her/its responsibility to ensure compliance.

Certification of Accuracy

The following parties have reviewed the information above and certify, to the best of their knowledge, that the information they have provided is true and accurate.

Lessor _____ Date / /   Lessor _____ Date / /

Lessee _____ Date / /   Lessee _____ Date / /

Agent _____ Date / /   Agent _____ Date / /

Keep a fully executed copy of this document for three (3) years from the date hereof.

This Disclosure Form should be attached to the Lease.

[62796\hddoc\leadpnt2.dis]

Source: Chicago Association of REALTORS®. Used with permission.

Because some cities and states have their own laws for lead-based paint activities, check with the EPA and/or your state agency to see which laws apply to you. Most state agencies can also provide information on finding a lead abatement firm in your area and on possible sources of financial aid for reducing lead hazards.

Check on the Internet at http://www.epa.gov/epahome/whereyoulive.htm. You can retrieve information about your community by entering your zip code and choosing from available databases. You can also locate EPA regional offices through links on the map as well as linking to related local government environmental offices.

Says property manager Scott Henderson, "I now put the lead-based paint disclosure form as the first page of my lease because the EPA wants the tenants to sign it *before* signing the lease. They also put the date and time on it and on the lease, showing the lead-based paint disclosure form was signed first. I actually have this disclosure signed for every property I rent out, even those built after 1978. I follow this policy consistently."

Security Deposit Agreement

This form (see Figure 4.6, "Security Deposit Agreement") specifies the conditions under which a security deposit will be returned. It should be signed by all parties signing the lease and attached to the lease form. The second page lists charges for various repairs, but you can modify the schedule and prices to suit your specific situation. The amount of the required security deposit should correspond with the amount indicated on the lease.

Garage and Vehicle Riders

If your property has carports, garages, or designated parking spaces available for rent and your tenant elects to lease a space, you should execute a Garage Rider (see Figure 4.7). The form spells out the terms and conditions under which a space is rented.

If you want the garage rental term to coincide with the dates of the property lease, be sure the tenant understands that the garage rental agreement applies to every month covered by the lease.

FIGURE 4.6 *Security Deposit Agreement*

Security Deposit Agreement

Due from _____ (Lessee) $_____ Dollars

as Security Deposit for _____ (Address)

Apartment # _____ in _____, _____ (City/Village, State)

Release of Security Deposit is Subject to the Following Provisions

1. Full term of lease has expired and all provisions herein complied with.
2. Should lessee desire to RERENT (sublet or assign) under the provisions of the lease, a "one-half month's rent" service charge will be assessed.
   a. Approval must be obtained from lessor prior to initiating a rerent or sublet.
   b. Notice in writing must be given to management by certified mail prior to initiating a rerent or sublet.
3. For company transfers, comply with No. 2 above, with notice given on Company letterhead.
4. Entire property including range, oven, refrigerator, bathroom, closets, cabinets, windows, carpet, balcony, etc., cleaned.
5. No damage to property beyond normal wear and tear.
6. No unpaid late charges or delinquent rents.
7. Forwarding address left with management.
8. No indentations or scratches in wood or resilient floor caused by furniture or other means. Floor must be restored to the original condition if tack-down or wall-to-wall carpeting was installed by lessee.
9. No wall coverings, stickers, scratches, or large holes on walls.
10. All keys including those from mailboxes must be returned.
11. All debris, rubbish, and discards to be placed in proper rubbish containers in designated area.
12. All building-owned carpeting must be professionally cleaned.

IF THE PREREQUISITE CONDITIONS ARE NOT COMPLIED WITH, LESSEE WILL BE CHARGED THE CURRENT RATES LESSOR IS PAYING TO HAVE ITEMS REPAIRED AND/OR CLEANED.

The cost of labor and materials for cleaning, repairs, removals, and replacements, where applicable, or rent loss due to necessary repair time, and numerous other charges based on actual damages will be deducted from the security deposit. See reverse side for charges.

Lessor agrees that subject to the conditions listed above, this Security Deposit will be refunded in full.

Lessee agrees that this Security Deposit may NOT be applied as rent and is fully aware of the provision set forth on this agreement. Lessee further agrees that he will be present for final inspection of property.

By: _____   _____ Lessee

Date: _____   _____ Lessee

_____

_____

_____

(continued)

FIGURE 4.6 *Security Deposit Agreement, continued*

	Minimum Charges
Cleaning	
1. Trash removal	$14.00 per hour
2. Kitchen:	
Stove	$30.00
Refrigerator	$20.00
Cabinets and Countertops	$20.00
Floor	$20.00
3. Bathrooms (each)	
Toilet	$7.00
Shower and Tub	$20.00
Medicine Cabinet	$7.00
Vanity	$7.00
Floor	$7.00
4. Closets	$12.00
5. Windows	$7.00
6. Floors	
Vacuum	$7.00
Tile Cleaning 1 Bedroom	$45.00
2 Bedroom	$55.00
Carpet Cleaning 1 Bedroom	$40.00
2 Bedroom	$50.00
7. Excessive Cleaning	$14.00 per hour
Decorating	
1. Patching Holes: 1/2″ to 2″	$12.00 each
2. Double Coating	$12.00 each wall
3. Removal of wall coverings	$20.00 per hour
Maintenance	
1. Materials plus labor at	$27.00 per hour
2. Light bulb replacement	$1.75 each

Pet Rider

If you allow pets on your property and a tenant chooses to keep one, you can use a Pet Agreement (see Figure 4.8), which dictates the terms and conditions of maintaining pets on your property. It has become fairly common to require a pet deposit for each pet; some owners also charge a fixed monthly rent or other non-refundable fees for pets. A pet rider can be executed and made a part of the lease at any time during the lease term.

FIGURE 4.7 *Garage Rider Form*

BLDG. No. _____ UNIT No. _____

MID-AMERICA MANAGEMENT CORP.
2901 Butterfield Road
Oak Brook, Illinois 60523

GARAGE RIDER

THIS RIDER is hereby made a part of and incorporated as part of a certain lease agreement ("Lease") dated _____, 20___, for an apartment located at _____ in _____ ("Premises"), by and between MID-AMERICA MANAGEMENT CORP. as Managing Agent ("Lessor") and _____ _____ _____ ("Lessee").

TO THE EXTENT OF ANY CONFLICT IN TERMS, THE TERMS AND CONDITIONS OF THIS RIDER SHALL GOVERN OVER THE TERMS AND CONDITIONS OF THE AFORESAID LEASE.

In consideration of the deposit of the sum of _____ ($_____) DOLLARS to be paid by Lessee to Lessor upon the execution hereof, the parties hereto agree to the following:

1. Lessor shall permit Lessee to use _____ parking space(s) designated as space number(s) _____ at the Premises for the term of the Lease.
2. Lessee agrees to maintain the space(s) in a clean and sanitary condition at all times.
3. Lessee agrees to utilize the space(s) only for the purpose of parking the assigned vehicle(s).
4. Lessee agrees to remove any vehicle deemed unsightly or in non-working condition by Lessor within five (5) days of notification.
5. Lessee agrees that in the event of any violation of the terms and conditions set forth above, the Lessor shall have the right to make a demand for immediate possession of said space(s). Any refusal of Lessee to comply with such demand by Lessor to return said space(s) shall be material breach of the Lease, and Lessor shall be entitled to retain aforementioned deposit as well be entitled to any and all other remedies provided by law or equity. However, if Lessee returns said space(s) upon such demand, the deposit shall be returned less damages, if any, caused by violation hereof and said Lease shall continue in effect, except that this rider shall be deemed null and void.

IN WITNESS WHEREOF, the Lessor and Lessee have executed this document on the _____ day of _____, 20 _____.

MID-AMERICA MANAGEMENT CORP.
Managing Agent

By: _____   _____
             Agent   LESSEE

                                                 _____
                                               LESSEE

$ _____ **is required deposit for each garage transmitter.**

$ _____ **is the required monthly rental amount.**

4307 3/00

FIGURE 4.8 *Pet Agreement*

PET AGREEMENT

Your imprint & logo here

In the event of a violation of any of the following terms and conditions, the owner/management shall have the right to immediately cancel this agreement and require the pet owner/tenant to immediately remove the pet from the premises. Cancellation of this agreement will not imply a waiver of the tenant's responsibility for any damages.

Tenant's Name _____

Address _____

Owner/Management agrees to waive the pet restrictions of the rental agreement/lease provided that the tenant and pet owner agree to and meet the following terms and conditions:

1. Only the pet/pets listed and described below are authorized under this pet agreement. Additional or other pets must be approved by the owner/management.

2. Pet/pets will not cause: danger, damage, nuisance, noise, health hazard, or soil the apartment/unit, premises, grounds, common areas, walks, parking areas, landscaping or gardens. Tenant agrees to clean up after the pet and agrees to accept full responsibility and liability for any damage, injury, or actions arising from or caused by his/her pets.

3. Tenant agrees to register the pet/pets in accordance with local laws and requirements. Tenant agrees to immunize the pet/pets in accordance with local laws and requirements.

4. Tenant warrants that the pet/pets is housebroken. Tenant warrants that the pet/pets has no history of causing physical harm to persons or property, such as biting, scratching, chewing, etc., and further warrants that the pet/pets has no vicious history or tendencies.

5. The tenant agrees to observe the following regulations:

   Dogs and Cats: Must be controlled at all times. Must be kept on a short leash while in common areas or on the grounds. Barking will not be tolerated in that it is considered to be a nuisance to other tenants. Proper disposal of cat litter (securely bagged) will be done on a frequent basis. Odors arising from cat litter will not be tolerated.

   Birds: Birds will be properly caged. Seeds and droppings will be shielded or caught to prevent accumulation and/or damage to carpeting/floors.

   Fish: Aquariums will not leak and will be cleaned regularly to prevent foul water and/or odors.

   Other Terms: _____

Pet Description:	Kind	Type or Breed:	Color	Name	Age	Weight

Pet Fee/Deposit:

Tenant agrees to pay the following non-refundable pet fee .... $_____

Tenant agrees to pay the following pet deposit .... $_____

Other .... $_____

                              TOTAL $_____

NOTICE: ANY FEE OR DEPOSIT ABOVE SHALL NOT LIMIT THE TENANT'S OBLIGATION

Date _____

Owner/Management Signature _____

Tenant Signature _____

Source: Peachtree Business Products. Used with permission. (To order this form or a catalog, call 800-241-4623.)

Condominium Property and Lease Rider

If you own investment condominiums, you can use a special condominium lease rider attached to a regular property lease. Many condominium associations have rules and special procedures regarding renting units. Contacting the management office or association president provides the information you need. Sometimes an association requires your tenant to sign additional forms and agreements, such as a separate agreement to abide by the condominium's specific rules and regulations. Some associations levy move-in fees, key deposits, and so on; and some owners pass these fees on to the tenant, making sure to collect the money before the tenant moves in. The larger associations usually have a manager who adds the fees to the assessment statement if they are not paid in advance.

You may elect to use a separate Condominium Unit Property Lease shown in Figure 4.9 that has been specifically designed and written for condominiums. This document contains much of the language condominium associations require of an investor-owner in addition to enough blank space to add a clause that allows you to cancel the lease in the event you sell the unit to a buyer who wants to take possession and occupy the unit.

Indicate the rental amount and deposit in the spaces marked "Other required rent" and "Other required deposit" on the lease. If your lease does not contain this blank space, write the information on the top of the form. On the rider, indicate the deposit and the monthly rental amount.

The tenant should also complete the Vehicle Information Form shown in Figure 4.10 listing all pertinent information concerning the vehicles that will use the facility.

Lease Extension Agreement

When renewing a lease, you can do one of two things. One option is to present the tenant with a brand-new lease typed on a regular lease form. If you decide to use a new lease, you should type the words *First Renewal, Second Renewal,* and so on at the top of the form. This will remind you that your tenant has been in occupancy for longer than one year when it comes time to renew the following year.

Another option is to use a Lease Extension Agreement (Figure 4.11) instead of a regular lease form. It may also be used for lease renewals for periods of less than a full year. Indicate the existence of this rider by making a notation on the original lease.

Refer to Chapter 6 for further information on the procedures to follow and the forms to use in executing renewals.

FIGURE 4.9 *Condominium Unit Property Lease*

A 101 — Lease of a Condominium unit. 12-96

Prepared by Arnold Mandell, Esq.
©1987 by **Blumberg**Excelsior, Publisher, NYC 10013

LEASE OF A CONDOMINIUM UNIT

The Landlord and Tenant agree to lease the Unit and Landlord's interest in the Common Elements located in the Condominium at:.. (Premises)

LANDLORD: ....   **TENANT:** ....

....   Address   ....

....   for   ....

....   Notices   ....

Unit (and terrace, if any) ....   Garage space (if any) ....

Bank ....

Lease date	Term	Yearly Rent	$
Broker*	beginning	Monthly Rent	$
	ending	Security	$
	Tenant's Insurance $	Garage Fee	$

Declarant of Condominium: .... (Declarant)
Name of Condominium: .... (Declaration)

1. Lease is subject and subordinate

This Lease is subject and subordinate to (A) the By-Laws, Rules and Regulations and Provisions of the Declaration Establishing a Plan for Condominium Ownership of the Premises and (B) Powers of Attorney granted to the Board of Managers, leases, agreements, mortgages, renewals, modifications, consolidations, replacements and extensions to which the Declaration or the Unit are presently or may in the future be subject. Tenant shall not perform any act, or fail to perform an act, if the performance or failure to perform would be a violation of or default in the Declaration or a document referred to in (B). Tenant shall not exercise any right or privilege under this Lease, the performance of which would be a default in or violation of the Declaration or a document referred to in subdivision (B). Tenant must promptly execute any certificate(s) that Landlord requests to show that this Lease is so subject and subordinate. Tenant authorizes Landlord to sign these certificate(s) for Tenant. Tenant acknowledges that Tenant has had the opportunity to read the Declaration of Condominium Ownership for the Condominium, including the By-Laws. Tenant agrees to observe and be bound by all the terms contained in it which apply to the occupant or user of the Unit or a user of Condominium common areas and facilities. Tenant agrees to observe all of the Rules and Regulations of the Association and Board of Managers.

2. Lender Changes

Landlord may borrow money from a lender who may request an agreement for changes in this Lease. Tenant shall sign the agreement if it does not change the rent or the Term, and does not alter the Unit.

3. Use

The Unit must be used only as a private residence and for no other reason. Only a party signing this Lease and the spouse and children of that party may use the Unit.

4. Rent, added rent

A. The rent payment for each month must be made on the first day of that month at Landlord's address. Landlord need not give notice to pay the rent. Rent must be paid in full and no amount subtracted from it. The first month's rent is to be paid when Tenant signs this Lease. Tenant may be required to pay other charges to Landlord under the terms of this Lease. They are called "added rent". This added rent is payable as rent, together with the next monthly rent due. If Tenant fails to pay the added rent on time, Landlord shall have the same rights against Tenant as if Tenant failed to pay rent. Payment of rent in installments is for Tenant's convenience only. If Tenant defaults, Landlord may give notice to Tenant that Tenant may no longer pay rent in installments. The entire rent for the remaining part of the Term will then be due and payable.

B. This Lease and the obligation of Tenant to pay rent and perform all of the agreements on the part of Tenant to be performed shall not be affected, impaired or excused, nor shall there be any apportionment or abatement of rent for any reason including, but not limited to, damage to the Unit or inability to use the Common Elements.

5. Failure to give possession

Landlord shall not be liable for failure to give Tenant possession of the Unit on the beginning date of the Term. Rent shall be payable as of the beginning of the Term unless Landlord is unable to give possession. Rent shall then be payable as of the date possession is available. Landlord will notify Tenant as to the date possession is available. The ending date of the Term will not change.

6. Security

Tenant has given security to Landlord in the amount stated above. The security has been deposited in the Bank named above and delivery of this Lease is notice of the deposit. If the Bank is not named, Landlord will notify Tenant of the Bank's name and address in which the security is deposited.

If Tenant does not pay rent on time, Landlord may use the security to pay for rent past due. If Tenant fails to perform any other term in this Lease, Landlord may use the security for payment of money Landlord may spend, or damages Landlord suffers because of Tenant's failure. If the Landlord uses the security Tenant shall, upon notice from Landlord, send to Landlord an amount equal to the sum used by Landlord. At all times Landlord is to have the amount of security stated above.

If Tenant fully performs all terms of this Lease, pays rent on time and leaves the Unit in good condition on the last day of the Term, then Landlord will return the security being held.

If Landlord sells or leases the Unit, Landlord may give the security to the buyer or lessee. In that event Tenant will look only to the buyer or lessee for the return of the security. The security is for

*If no broker, insert "None."

Landlord's use as stated in this Section. Landlord may put the security in any place permitted by law. If the law states the security must bear interest, unless the security is used by Landlord as stated Landlord will give Tenant the interest less the sum Landlord is allowed to keep for expenses. If the law does not require security to bear interest, Tenant will not be entitled to it. Landlord need not give Tenant interest on the security if Tenant is not fully performing any term in this Lease.

7. Alterations

Tenant must obtain Landlord's prior written consent to install any panelling, flooring, "built in" decorations, partitions, railings or make alterations or to paint or wallpaper the Unit. Tenant must not change the plumbing, ventilating, air conditioning, electric or heating systems. If consent is given the alterations and installations shall become the property of Landlord when completed and paid for. They shall remain with and as part of the Unit at the end of the Term. Landlord has the right to demand that Tenant remove the alterations and installations before the end of the Term. The demand shall be by notice, given at least 15 days before the end of the Term. Tenant shall comply with the demand at Tenant's own cost. Landlord is not required to do or pay for any work unless stated in this Lease.

If a Mechanic's Lien is filed on the Unit or building for Tenant's failure to pay for alterations or installations in the Unit, Tenant must immediately pay or bond the amount stated in the Lien. Landlord may pay or bond the Lien immediately, if Tenant fails to do so within 20 days after Tenant is given notice about the Lien. Landlord's costs shall be added rent.

8. Repairs

Tenant must take good care of the Unit and all equipment and fixtures in it. Tenant must, at Tenant's cost make all repairs and replacements whenever the need results from Tenant's act or neglect. If Tenant fails to make a needed repair or replacement, Landlord may do it. Landlord's expense will be added rent. Subject to Tenant's obligations under this Lease, Landlord will require the Association (to the extent that the Association is obligated under the terms of the Declaration or other agreement) to maintain the Unit, or repair any damage to it, except where caused in whole or in part by the act, failure to act, or negligence of Tenant, or Tenant's licensees, invitees, guests, contractors or agents. Tenant must give Landlord prompt notice of required repairs or replacements.

9. Fire, accident, defects, damage

Tenant must give Landlord prompt notice of fire, accident, damage or dangerous or defective condition. If the Unit can not be used because of fire or other casualty, Tenant is not required to pay rent for the time the Unit is unusable. If part of the Unit can not be used, Tenant must pay rent for the usable part. Landlord shall have the right to decide which part of the Unit is usable. Landlord need only arrange for the damaged structural parts of the Unit to be repaired. Landlord is not required to arrange for the repair or replacement of any equipment, fixtures, furnishings or decorations. Landlord is not responsible for delays due to settling insurance claims, obtaining estimates, labor and supply problems or any other cause not fully under Landlord's control.

If the fire or other casualty is caused by an act or neglect of Tenant or guest of Tenant, or at the time of the fire or casualty Tenant is in default in any term of this Lease, then all repairs will be

FIGURE 4.9 *Condominium Unit Property Lease, continued*

made at Tenant's expense and Tenant must pay the full rent with no adjustment. The cost of the repairs will be added rent.

If there is more than minor damage to the Unit by fire or other casualty, Landlord may cancel this Lease within 30 days after that fire or casualty by giving notice. The Lease will end 30 days after Landlord's cancellation notice to Tenant. Tenant must deliver the Unit to Landlord on or before the cancellation date in the notice and pay all rent due to the date of the fire or casualty. If the Lease is cancelled Landlord is not required to arrange for the repair of the Unit. The cancellation does not release Tenant of liability in connection with the fire or casualty. This Section, when permitted, is intended to replace the terms of applicable statutory law. Tenant has no right to cancel this Lease due to fire or casualty.

10. Liability

Landlord is not liable for loss, expense, or damage to any person or property, unless due to Landlord's negligence. Landlord is not liable to Tenant if anyone is not permitted or is refused entry into the Building.

Tenant must pay for damages suffered and money spent by Landlord relating to any claim arising from any act or neglect of Tenant. If an action is brought against Landlord arising from Tenant's act or neglect Tenant shall defend Landlord at Tenant's expense with an attorney of Landlord's choice.

Tenant is responsible for all acts of Tenant's family, employees, guests or invitees. Tenant must carry whatever property or liability insurance Landlord may require and will name Landlord as a party insured. The insurance shall be no less than a Tenant's Homeowners Insurance Policy in the minimum amount stated above. Tenant shall deliver a copy of the binder to Landlord prior to taking possession of the Unit.

11. Entry by Landlord

Landlord or parties authorized by Landlord may enter the Unit at reasonable hours to: repair, inspect, exterminate, install or work on systems and cause performance of other work that Landlord decides is necessary. At reasonable hours Landlord may show the Unit to possible buyers, lenders or tenants.

If Landlord enters the Unit, Landlord will try not to disturb Tenant. Landlord may cause to be kept in the Unit all equipment necessary to make repairs or alterations to the Unit or Building. Landlord is not responsible for disturbance or damage to Tenant because of work being performed on or equipment kept in the Unit. Landlord's or the Association's use of the Unit does not give Tenant a claim of eviction. Landlord or those authorized by Landlord may enter the Unit to get to any part of the Building.

Landlord has the right at any time to permit the following people into the Unit: (i) receiver, trustee, assignee for benefit of creditors; or (ii) sheriff, marshall or court officer; and (iii) any person from the fire, police, building, or sanitation departments or other state, city or federal government and (iv) the Association, Board of Managers and any other party permitted or authorized by the Declaration or Management Agreement covering the Unit or Condominium. Landlord has no responsibility for damage or loss as a result of those persons being in the Unit.

12. Construction or demolition

Construction or demolition may be performed in or near the Building. Even if it interferes with Tenant's ventilation, view or enjoyment of the Unit it shall not affect Tenant's obligations in this Lease.

13. Assignment and sublease.

Tenant must not assign this Lease or sublet all or part of the Unit or permit any other person to use the Unit. If Tenant does, Landlord has the right to cancel the Lease as stated in the Default section. Tenant must get Landlord's written permission each time Tenant wants to assign or sublet. Permission to assign or sublet is good only for that assignment or sublease. Tenant remains bound to the terms of this Lease after a permitted assignment or sublet even if Landlord accepts rent from the assignee or subtenant. The amount accepted will be credited toward rent due from Tenant. The assignee or subtenant does not become Landlord's tenant. Tenant is responsible for acts of any person in the Unit.

14. Tenant's certificate

Upon request by Landlord, Tenant shall sign a certificate stating the following; (1) This Lease is in full force and unchanged (or if changed, how it was changed); and (2) Landlord has fully performed all of the terms of this Lease and Tenant has no claim against Landlord; and (3) Tenant is fully performing all the terms of the Lease and will continue to do so; and (4) rent and added rent have been paid to date. The certificate will be addressed to the party Landlord chooses.

15. Condemnation

If all or a part of the Building or Unit is taken or condemned by a legal authority, Landlord may, on notice to Tenant, cancel the Term. If Landlord cancels, Tenant's rights shall end as of the date the authority takes title to the Unit or Building. The cancellation date must not be less than 30 days from the date of the Landlord's cancellation notice. On the cancellation date Tenant must deliver the Unit to Landlord together with all rent due to that date. The entire award for any taking including the portion for fixtures and equipment belongs to Landlord. Tenant gives Landlord any interest Tenant may have to any part of the award. Tenant shall make no claim for the value of the remaining part of the Term.

16. Tenant's duty to obey laws and regulations

Tenant must, at Tenant's expense, promptly comply with all laws, orders, rules, requests, and directions, of all governmental authorities, Landlord's insurers, Board of Fire Underwriters, or similar groups. Notices received by Tenant from any authority or group must be promptly delivered to Landlord. Tenant will not do anything which may increase Landlord's insurance premiums. If Tenant does, Tenant must pay the increase in premium as added rent.

17. Sale of Unit

If the Landlord wants to sell the Unit Landlord shall have the right to end this Lease by giving 30 days notice to Tenant. If Landlord gives Tenant that notice then the Lease will end and Tenant must leave the Unit at the end of the 30 days period in the notice.

18. No liability for property

Neither Landlord, the Association or Board of Managers is liable or responsible for (a) loss, theft, misappropriation or damage to the personal property, or (b) injury caused by the property or its use.

19. Playground, pool, parking and recreation areas

If there is a playground, pool, parking or recreation area, or other common areas, Landlord may give Tenant permission to use it. If Landlord gives permission, Tenant will use the area at Tenant's own risk and must pay all fees Landlord or the Association charges. Landlord is not required to give Tenant permission.

20. Terraces and balconies

The Unit may have a terrace or balcony. The terms of this Lease apply to the terrace or balcony as if part of the Unit. The Landlord may make special rules for the terrace and balcony. Landlord will notify Tenant of such rules.

Tenant must keep the terrace or balcony clean and free from snow, ice, leaves and garbage and keep all screens and drains in good repair. No cooking is allowed on the terrace or balcony. Tenant may not keep plants, or install a fence or any addition on the terrace or balcony. If Tenant does, Landlord has the right to remove and store them at Tenant's expense.

21. Correcting Tenant's defaults

If Tenant fails to correct a default after notice from Landlord, Landlord may correct it at Tenant's expense. Landlord's cost to correct the default shall be added rent.

22. Notices

Any bill, statement or notice must be in writing. If to Tenant, it must be delivered or mailed to the Tenant at the Unit. If to Landlord it must be mailed to Landlord's address. It will be considered delivered on the day mailed or if not mailed, when left at the proper address. A notice must be sent by certified mail. Landlord must notify Tenant if Landlord's address is changed. The signatures of all Tenants in the Unit are required on every notice by Tenant. Notice by Landlord to one named person shall be as though given to all those persons. Each party shall accept notices of the other.

23. Tenant's default

A. Landlord must give Tenant notice of default. The following are defaults and must be cured by Tenant within the time stated:

(1) Failure to pay rent or added rent on time, 3 days.

(2) Failure to move into the Unit within 15 days after the beginning date of the Term, 5 days.

(3) Issuance of a court order under which the Unit may be taken by another party, 5 days.

(4) Failure to perform any term in another lease between Landlord and Tenant (such as a garage lease), 5 days.

(5) Improper conduct by Tenant annoying other tenants, 3 days

(6) Failure to comply with any other term or Rule in the Lease, 5 days.

If Tenant fails to cure in the time stated, Landlord may cancel the Lease by giving Tenant a cancellation notice. The cancellation notice will state the date the Term will end which may be no less than 3 days after the date of the notice. On the cancellation date in the notice the Term of this lease shall end. Tenant must leave the Unit and give Landlord the keys on or before the cancellation date. Tenant continues to be responsible as stated in this Lease.

B. If Tenant's application for the Unit contains any misstatement of fact, Landlord may cancel this Lease. Cancellation shall be by cancellation notice as stated in Paragraph 23. A.

C. If (1) the Lease is cancelled; or (2) rent or added rent is not paid on time; or (3) Tenant vacates the Unit, Landlord may in addition to other remedies take any of the following steps: (a) enter the Unit and remove Tenant and any person or property, and (b) use eviction or other lawsuit method to take back the Unit.

D. If this Lease is cancelled, or Landlord takes back the Unit, the following takes place:

(1) Rent and added rent for the unexpired Term becomes due and payable. Tenant must also pay Landlord's expenses as stated in Paragraph 23. D(3).

(2) Landlord may re-rent the Unit and anything in it. The re-renting may be for any Term. Landlord may charge any rent or no rent and give allowances to the new tenant. Landlord may, at Tenant's expense, do any work Landlord feels is needed to put the Unit in good repair and prepare it for renting. Tenant remains liable and is not released in any manner.

(3) Any rent received by Landlord for the re-renting shall be used first to pay Landlord's expenses and second to pay any amounts Tenant owes under this Lease. Landlord's expenses include the costs of getting possession and re-renting the Unit, including, but not only, reasonable legal fees, brokers fees, cleaning and repairing costs, decorating costs and advertising costs.

(4) From time to time Landlord may bring actions for damages. Delay or failure to bring an action shall not be a waiver of Landlord's rights. Tenant is not entitled to any excess of rents collected over the rent paid by Tenant to Landlord under this Lease.

(5) If Landlord re-rents the Unit combined with other space an adjustment will be made based on square footage. Money received by Landlord from the next tenant, other than the monthly rent, shall be considered as part of the rent paid to Landlord. Landlord is entitled to all of it.

Landlord has no duty to re-rent the Unit. If Landlord does re-rent, the fact that all or part of the next tenant's rent is not

FIGURE 4.9 *Condominium Unit Property Lease, continued*

collected does not affect Tenant's liability. Landlord has no duty to collect the next tenant's rent. Tenant must continue to pay rent, damages, losses and expenses without offset.

E. If Landlord takes possession of the Unit by Court order, or under the Lease, Tenant has no right to return to the Unit.

24. Jury Trial and counterclaims

Landlord and Tenant agree not to use their right to a Trial by Jury in any action or proceeding brought by either against the other, for any matter concerning this Lease or the Unit. The giving up of the right to a Jury Trial is a serious matter. There are rules of law that protect that right and limit the type of action in which a Jury Trial may be given up. Tenant gives up any right to bring a counterclaim or set-off in any action by Landlord against Tenant on any matter directly or indirectly related to this Lease.

25. Bankruptcy, insolvency

If (1) Tenant assigns property for the benefit of creditors, (2) Tenant files a voluntary petition or an involuntary petition is filed against Tenant under any bankruptcy or insolvency law, or (3) a trustee or receiver of Tenant or Tenant's property is appointed, Landlord may give Tenant 30 days notice of cancellation of the Term of this Lease. If any of the above is not fully dismissed within the 30 days, the Term shall end as of the date stated in the notice. Tenant must continue to pay rent, damages, losses and expenses without offset.

26. No Waiver

Landlord's failure to enforce, or insist that Tenant comply with a term in this Lease is not a waiver of Landlord's rights. Acceptance of rent by Landlord is not a waiver of Landlord's rights. The rights and remedies of Landlord are separate and in addition to each other. The choice of one does not prevent Landlord from using another.

27. Illegality

If a term in this Lease is illegal that term will no longer apply. The rest of this Lease remains in full force.

28. Representations, changes in Lease

Tenant has read this Lease. All promises made by the Landlord are in this Lease. There are no others. This Lease may be changed only by an agreement in writing signed by and delivered to each party.

29. Inability to perform

If due to labor trouble, government order, lack of supply, Tenant's act or neglect or any other cause not fully within the Association's reasonable control, the Association, or Board of Managers is delayed or unable to carry out any of their respective obligations, requirements, promises or agreements, if any, this Lease shall not be ended or Tenant's obligations affected in any manner.

30. Limit of recovery against Landlord

Tenant is limited to Landlord's interest in the Unit for payment of a judgment or other court remedy against Landlord.

31. End of Term

At the end of the Term, Tenant must: leave the Unit clean and in good condition, subject to ordinary wear and tear; remove all of Tenant's property and all Tenant's installations and decorations; repair all damages to the Unit and Building caused by moving; and restore the Unit to its condition at the beginning of the Term. If the last day of the Term is on a Saturday, Sunday or State or Federal holiday the term shall end on the prior business day.

32. Space "as is"

Tenant has inspected the Unit and Building. Tenant states that they are in good order and repair and takes the Unit as is. Sizes of rooms stated in brochures or plans of the Building or Unit are approximate and subject to change. This Lease is not affected or Landlord liable if the brochure or plans do not show obstructions or are incorrect in any manner.

33. Quiet enjoyment

Subject to the terms of this Lease, as long as Tenant is not in default Tenant may peaceably and quietly have, hold, and enjoy the Unit for the Term.

34. Landlord's consent

If Tenant requires Landlord's consent to any act and such consent is not given, Tenant's only right is to ask the Court to force Landlord to give consent. Tenant agrees not to make any claim against Landlord for money or subtract any sum from the rent because such consent was not given.

35. Lease binding on

This Lease is binding on Landlord and Tenant and their heirs, distributees, executors, administrators, successors and lawful assigns.

36. Landlord

Landlord means the owner of the Unit. Landlord's obligations end when Landlord's interest in the Unit is transferred. Any acts Landlord may do may be performed by Landlord's agents.

37. Broker

If the name of a Broker appears in the box at the top of the first page of this Lease, Tenant states that this is the only Broker that showed the Unit to Tenant. If a Broker's name does not appear Tenant states that no agent or broker showed Tenant the Unit. Tenant will pay Landlord any money Landlord may spend if either statement is incorrect.

38. Paragraph headings

The paragraph headings are for convenience only.

39. Rules

Tenant must comply with these Rules. Notice of new or changed Rules will be given to Tenant. Landlord, the Association or Board of Managers need not enforce Rules against other tenants. Landlord is not liable to Tenant if another tenant violates these Rules. Tenant receives no rights under these Rules:

(1) The comfort or rights of other tenants must not be interfered with. Annoying sounds, smells and lights are not allowed.

(2) No one is allowed on the roof. Nothing may be placed on or attached to fire escapes, sills, windows or exterior walls of the Unit or in the hallway or public areas. Clothes, linens or rugs may not be aired or dried from the Unit or on terraces.

(3) Tenant must give the Landlord keys to all locks. Locks may not be changed or additional locks installed without Landlord's consent. Doors must be locked at all times. Windows must be locked when Tenant is out. All keys must be returned to Landlord at the end of the Term.

(4) Floors of the Unit must be covered by carpets or rugs. Waterbeds or furniture containing liquid are not allowed in the Unit.

(5) Dogs, cats or other animals or pets are not allowed in the Unit or Building. Feeding of birds or animals from the Unit, terraces or public areas is not permitted.

(6) Garbage disposal rules must be followed. Wash lines, vents and plumbing fixtures must be used for their intended purpose.

(7) Laundry machines, if any, are used at Tenant's risk and cost. Instructions must be followed. Landlord may stop their use at any time.

(8) Moving furniture, fixtures or equipment must be scheduled with Landlord. Tenant must not send Landlord's employees on personal errands.

(9) Improperly parked cars may be removed without notice at Tenant's cost.

(10) Tenant must not allow the cleaning of the windows or other part of the Unit or Building from the outside.

(11) Tenant shall conserve energy.

(12) Tenant may not operate manual elevators. Smoking or carrying lighted pipes, cigarettes or cigars is not permitted in elevators. Messengers and trade people must only use service elevators and service entrances.

(13) The entrances, halls and stairways may only be used to go to or leave the Unit.

(14) Professional tenants must not allow patients to wait in public areas.

(15) Inflammable or dangerous things may not be kept or used in the Unit.

(16) No tour of the Unit or Building may be conducted. Auctions or tag sales are not permitted in Units.

(17) Bicycles, scooters, skate boards or skates may not be kept or used in lobbies, halls or stairways. Carriages and sleds may not be kept in lobbies, halls or stairways.

40. Appliances, etc., included in Lease

The Lease includes only personal property itemized on the annexed schedule called the Personal Property schedule.

41. Definitions

a) "Association" means the Unit Owners Association and/or any organization, whether or not incorporated, whose membership is essentially limited to owners of units in the Condominium or in condominiums located in the vicinity.

b) Words defined in applicable statutes have the meanings therein set forth.

c) "Condominium" — See Heading.

d) "Unit" — See Heading.

e) "Board of Managers" — group of persons selected, authorized and directed to manage and operate a condominium, as provided by the Condominium Act, and the Declaration.

f) "Building" — See Article 1.

g) "Common Charges"—each unit's share of the Common Expenses in accordance with its Common Interest in the Common Elements of the Condominium.

h) "Common Elements"—that which is described in the Declaration.

i) "Common Expenses"—the actual and estimated expenses of operating the Condominium and any reasonable reserve for such purposes, as found and determined by the Board of Managers plus all sums designated Common Expenses, including, but not limited to, real estate taxes, if applicable, by or pursuant to the Condominium Act, or the declaration.

j) "Common Interest"—the proportionate, undivided interest each Unit-owner has in the Common Elements.

k) "Unit-owner"—the person or persons owning 1 or more units in the Condominium in fee simple.

42. Increase in Common Charges and Real Estate Taxes

A. Tenant shall pay to Landlord, as added rent, all increases in Common Charges, Common Expenses and Association dues related to the Unit, which exceed those charges, expenses or dues payable on the date of this Lease.

B. Tenant shall pay to Landlord, as added rent, any increase in the Real Estate Taxes (including all equivalent, and/or use and/or supplemental taxes and taxes assessed against the Unit as a substitute for Real Estate Taxes) above the Real Estate Taxes assessed or imposed against the Unit (including but not limited to increases in assessed value or tax rate) for the fiscal tax year in effect on the commencement date of the Term of this Lease.

43. No Liability

A. Landlord, the Board of Managers, the Association and their respective agents, contractors and employees, shall not be liable for, injury to any person, or for property damage sustained by Tenant, its licensees, invitees, guests, contractors and agents, or by any other person for any reason except for negligence of Landlord, the Board of Managers or the Association.

B. Tenant agrees to protect, indemnify and save harmless Landlord, the Board of Managers and the Association from all losses, costs, or damages suffered by reason of any act or other occurrence which causes injury to any person or property and is related in any way to the use of the Unit.

44. Automobiles

The use or storage of Tenant's or any other person's automobile whether or not parked or being driven in or about the Building

FIGURE 4.9 *Condominium Unit Property Lease, continued*

parking area or garages, if any, shall at all times be at the sole risk of Tenant. Should any employee of the Condominium assist Tenant or take part in the parking, moving or handling of Tenant's or any other person's automobile or other property given to the custody of any employee for any reason whatsoever, that employee is considered the agent of Tenant or such other person and not of Landlord, the Condominium, the Board of Managers or the Association and none of them shall be liable to Tenant or to any other person for the acts or omission of any employee or for the loss of or damage to the automobile or any of its contents.

Any vehicle or personal property belonging to Tenant, which in the opinion of Landlord, the Association or Board of Managers is considered abandoned, shall be removed by Tenant within 1 day after delivery of written notice to Tenant. If Tenant does not remove it, Landlord or the Association may remove the property from the area at Tenant's cost.

45. Garage Space
If a garage space is included in this Lease the fee that Tenant must pay Landlord appears in the box at the top of the first page of this Lease. It is payable as added rent. The number of the garage space will also appear in the box. If a garage space number does not appear Tenant states that no garage space is leased to Tenant.

46. Voting
This Lease relates solely to the use and occupancy of the Unit and as specifically stated. This Lease does not include the transfer or exchange of any voting rights nor is it to be construed as reducing Landlord's sole right to vote without restriction, with respect to any matter related to the Unit.

47. No Affirmative Obligations of Landlord
Landlord is not obligated to provide or render any services whatsoever to the Tenant or perform any affirmative obligations under the terms of this Lease. Landlord is not liable for damages or otherwise in the event Tenant suffers them as a result of any act committed or omitted to be performed by the Association, Board of Managers, or any other party. Landlord shall not be liable to Tenant, its successors, assigns or subtenants with respect to any of the affirmative obligations to be performed by any third party including the Association or Board of Managers under the Declaration and Landlord is released from liability. Tenant must continue to pay all rent and added rent as required under the terms of this Lease in spite of any failure of performance. None of the terms of this Lease shall in any way be affected as a result of that failure. Landlord will use its reasonable efforts (provided at no expense to Landlord) in demanding the performance, by the party obligated, of its obligations under the applicable agreement including any obligation to provide services. Tenant agrees to indemnify and save Landlord harmless from and against any and all claims, liabilities or demands arising from the Declaration or other agreement related to any act, omission or negligence of Tenant.

Rider Additional terms on .... page(s) initialed at the end by the parties is attached and made a part of this Lease.

Signatures, effective date Landlord and Tenant have signed this Lease as of the above date. It is effective when Landlord delivers to Tenant a copy signed by all parties.

LANDLORD: TENANT:

....

WITNESS...............   ....

GUARANTY OF PAYMENT   Date of Guaranty ....
Guarantor and address ....
1. Reason for guaranty I know that the Landlord would not rent the Unit to the Tenant unless I guarantee Tenant's performance. I have also requested the Landlord to enter into the Lease with the Tenant. I have a substantial interest in making sure that the Landlord rents the Premises to the Tenant.
2. Guaranty I guaranty the full performance of the Lease by the Tenant. This Guaranty is absolute and without any condition. It includes, but is not limited to, the payment of rent and other money charges.
3. Changes in Lease have no effect This Guaranty will not be affected by any change in the Lease, whatsoever. This includes, but is not limited to, any extension of time or renewals. The Guaranty will bind me even if I am not a party to these changes.
4. Waive of Notice I do not have to be informed about any default by Tenant. I waive notice of nonpayment or other default.
5. Performance If the Tenant defaults, the Landlord may require me to perform without first demanding that the Tenant perform.
6. Waiver of jury trial I give up my right to trial by jury in any claim related to the Lease or this Guaranty.
7. Changes This Guaranty can be changed only by written agreement signed by all parties to the Lease and this Guaranty.

Signatures   GUARANTOR: ....
WITNESS: ....   Guarantor's address: ....

EPA and HUD Lead Paint Regulations, Effective September 6, 1996[1]

Landlords must disclose known lead-based paint and lead-based paint hazards of pre-1978 housing to tenants.[2] Use the following BLUMBERG LAW PRODUCTS (800 LAW MART) to comply:

       3140 Lead Paint Information Booklet   3141 Lead Paint Lease Disclosure Form

[1]December 6, 1996 for owners of 1 to 4 residential dwellings.
[2]Leases for less than 100 days, 0-bedroom units, elderly and handicapped housing (unless children live there) and housing found to be lead-free by a certified inspector are excluded.

Source: Blumberg*Exclesior,* Inc. Used with permission. (To order this form, call 800-529-6278 or go to http://www.blumberg .com.)

FIGURE 4.10 *Vehicle Information*

Dear Tenant:

Please complete the form below concerning your automobile. This information will allow us to update our records for the purpose of contacting you in the case of an emergency.

If you should change your home or business telephone number or purchase a different vehicle, please remember to supply us with any new information.

I thank you in advance for this pertinent information that will enable us to become more efficient in managing this complex for the overall benefit of all our tenants.

License Plate # _____ State _____

Make of Car _____ Color _____ Model _____

Owner's Name _____

Building Address _____ Apt. # _____

Home Telephone _____ Business _____

Garage Space # _____

License Plate # _____ State _____

Make of Car _____ Color _____ Model _____

Owner's Name _____

Building Address _____ Apt. # _____

Home Telephone _____ Business _____

Garage Space # _____

Lease Cancellation Rider

The Lease Cancellation Rider shown in Figure 4.12 is a useful form that can be offered to new or renewal tenants who are not able to fully complete their lease term. (For complete details on terminating or canceling a lease, see Chapter 7.) An owner may agree to this rider because the tenant has an upcoming job transfer or is in the market to purchase a home. It is not intended for use when the tenant requests to break a lease during the middle of a lease term. If tenants want to cancel their lease in midterm, a different form can be used, as shown in Figure 4.13.

Prospective tenants may ask to have a transfer clause written into the lease that would suit the same purpose of breaking a lease term early, but it is better to use the cancellation rider instead, because it clearly spells out the conditions and

FIGURE 4.11 *Lease Extension Agreement*

This agreement made this day of 20_____ by and

between (Lessor) _____

and (Lessee[s]) _____

Witnesseth _____

Whereas, Lessor and Lessee have entered into a certain lease agreement dated 20_____ for the rental of a certain property, number _____ located at _____

Whereas, Lessor and Lessee desire to extend the duration of said Lease;

Now therefore, for value received, receipt of which is hereby acknowledged by Lessor, the parties agree as follows:

1. The termination date of said Lease is hereby extended from _____ (Date) to and including _____ (Date).

2. The monthly rental amount during the aforesaid extension period will be $_____.

3. Except as modified hereby, the terms and conditions of aforesaid Lease are hereby confirmed and ratified and made a part of this agreement and said Lease shall remain in full force and effect.

In witness whereof, this agreement has been duly executed by the parties hereto on the day and year first above written.

Lessor _____ Date _____

Lessee _____ Date _____

procedures a tenant must follow to invoke it—for example, tenants must give 60 days' notice, must not be in default of the lease, must be current in their rent, and must pay a cancellation fee (the usual amount is one to two months' rent). The cancellation fee is payable in advance at the time the tenants decide to exercise their right to cancel. As with all riders, a notation should be made on the original lease that a cancellation rider exists.

Double Deposit Clause

This is not a separate rider but a clause that is typed on the face of the lease document. The intent of this provision is to allow tenants to build their credit with you.

If the salary of an otherwise desirable prospective tenant doesn't satisfy the minimum required to qualify for the property or the prospect is new to the area or has recently graduated and has not yet established a credit history, you can elect to charge an additional security deposit.

FIGURE 4.12 *Lease Cancellation Rider*

THIS RIDER is hereby made a part of and incorporated as part of a certain lease agreement dated _____ (i.e., starting date of current lease), for a property ("the Premises") located at _____ in _____, Illinois, by and between _____ ("Lessor") and _____ ("Lessee").

THE TERMS AND CONDITIONS OF THIS
RIDER SHALL GOVERN OVER THE TERMS
AND CONDITIONS OF THE ATTACHED
LEASE AGREEMENT.

The Lessee shall have the right to terminate this Lease on the last day of any calendar month during the Lease term by giving the Lessor not less than sixty (60) days prior written notice of the Lessee's intention to terminate Lease.

The Lessee's right to terminate shall only be effective under the following conditions:

1. Not less than sixty (60) days prior written notice to the intended lease expiration.
2. Lessee is not in default of the Lease terms and conditions.
3. Lessee shall remit to Lessor the sum of $300.00 (three hundred dollars) as compensation for the cancellation.
4. Fee is to be paid at the time the written notice is given.
5. Cancellation fee shall not be deducted from any security moneys on deposit.
6. All rents and late charges are paid in full up to the time of the intended Lease expiration.

LESSOR:

BY: _____   _____
                                          LESSEE

DATE: _____   _____
                                          LESSEE

Type the following clause in the special provisions section of the lease:

$_____ of security deposit may be used for (month, year) rent provided all prior rents have been paid on the first of the month.

We suggest using the seventh month of the lease in the clause. The tenant will demonstrate financial stability by paying rent on time for six months. You then apply the extra security deposit to pay the seventh month's rent.

The extra security deposit should also be listed on the top of the lease under "Other Required Deposit."

Appliance Clause

If tenants want to use their own appliances and you, as the landlord, allow it, you can type the following statement(s) on the front of the lease: "Lessee owns

FIGURE 4.13 *Agreement to Cancel Lease*

Agreement to Cancel Lease

FOR AND IN CONSIDERATION of _____, LESSOR, allowing the undersigned to cancel prior to its expiration, that certain Lease ("Lease") dated _____, 20_____ between LESSOR and _____ for an apartment located at _____ in _____ Illinois, I hereby agree to the following:

1. To pay a sum equal to two months of Lease rent prior to moving from and vacating the property;
2. To promptly return the property keys to LESSOR prior to moving from and vacating the property;
3. To provide my forwarding address to LESSOR prior to moving from and vacating the property;
4. To leave the property in a clean condition and free of any and all damages;
5. To move from and vacate the property on or before _____, 20_____ which shall be the cancellation date of the Lease.

It is further understood that my security deposit is fully refundable, provided that I have complied with the aforesaid and further provided that there are no unpaid charges of any kind on my account as of the date the Lease is cancelled.

In the event the undersigned is in default under the aforesaid Lease as determined by LESSOR, then LESSOR shall have the right to keep and apply the aforesaid cancellation fee toward any damages arising as a result of such default.

The undersigned, as additional consideration for this Agreement, does hereby forever release any claim, cause, or causes of action which it may have or which shall arise in the future against LESSOR, its officers, directors, employees, or agents arising out of the aforesaid Lease.

This agreement shall be null and void if not strictly complied with.

Dated: _____

_____   _____
Tenant Signature   LESSOR

_____
Tenant Signature

refrigerator," or "Lessee owns stove," or "Lessee owns air conditioner." Record the brand name and model number of the appliance(s) on a separate sheet of paper attached to the lease or in the tenant file. This procedure can be used for both new or existing leases.

The tenant should be required to pay for disconnecting, moving, storing, and reconnecting your appliances.

PRORATED OR FREE-RENT PROGRAMS

For a variety of reasons, tenants often do not, or cannot, move in on the first day of the month. Your property may not allow moving in on the weekends, or the first day of the month may fall on a weekday and the tenant may not be able to take the day off to move. Lease start dates almost always begin on the first, but if tenants cannot move in that day, they may request a rent adjustment because of moving in late. Alternatively, you may allow them to move in early.

For example, suppose you have a vacant property that was rented for October 1 and the tenant wants to move in on September 27, four days before the lease actually begins. You could either waive the proration and allow the tenant to live there the four days for free, or you could charge the tenant for four days' rent.

On the other hand, if the first opportunity the tenant had to move was October 4 or 5, you could rebate a couple of days' rent or elect not to make an adjustment. If your rules prevented a tenant from moving in on the first, then you would probably prorate the rent for that month. If the tenant was in possession of the keys and could have moved on October 1, you would not allow a proration.

Rent can also be prorated for middle-of-the-month leases. For example, if tenants want to move in on the fifteenth, you can charge a half-month's rent. A good idea is to require tenants to pay the half month plus the first full month before moving in. The lease date would begin on the fifteenth but end on the last day of the month one year later.

If you are in a soft rental market with a potential vacancy coming up and have decided to offer free rent as a concession, the gratuity should be taken before the year's lease goes into effect. If, for example, a tenant is going to move into a property on September 1, taking advantage of the free rent, you have two options. The first option is to give the tenant a 1-month lease at no rent for September and then a separate 12-month lease starting October 1. The second option is to start the lease on September 1 and end it on September 30 of the following year, indicating on the form that the rent begins October 1. This option has one disadvantage: the lease shows there was a rent concession. You might want to avoid revealing this in case the building is offered for sale. In both cases, the tenant occupies the property for 13 months but pays rent for only 12; and the tenant has not been allowed to move into the building without signing a lease. Security deposit moneys and the rent for October should be collected before turning over possession to the tenant.

DELIVERING THE LEASE

Tenants should not be permitted to move in until the lease is signed and all deposits are paid. Deposits should be paid with ample time to allow for checks to clear. Although some owners may elect to allow partial payments or other special deals, this is not a good policy.

Preparing the Lease

When initiating a new lease, the letter *N* can be typed on the top left-hand corner to signify that it is a new lease. For a renewal lease, type *R$* (indicating a renewal) and the previous rental amount, for example, R$550.

A replacement lease can be prepared whenever there is any change in the original lease; for example, if a tenant takes a roommate or a tenant moves from one property to another in the same building. The word *Replacement* can be typed in the top left-hand corner, and a note can be stapled to the front indicating the type of change.

For replacement leases, the starting date should be the date the change takes effect and the termination date should be the same as the termination date of the original lease. A replacement lease should not be used when an original tenant vacates and someone new moves in.

Type the name(s) of the tenant(s) under the lessee signature lines. You can then see at a glance whether you are missing signatures on move-in day. If there is a cosigner, both names should appear and the word *cosigner* should be typed after the name. Each copy of the lease and any lease riders should carry an original signature. Separate the copies for ease of signing.

If any changes or corrections are made on the lease or lease riders after typing, each change must be initialed by both the lessor and lessee(s).

Signing the Lease

Documents in the lease package should be signed *on*, or preferably *before*, the actual move-in day. When new tenants arrive, ask them to take a few moments to read the lease package documents before signing them. If the tenants seem reluctant to take the time or are in a hurry, make sure they read at least the bold print at the top of the lease, the rules and regulations on the back of the lease, and the attached riders.

Explain that these documents detail such things as the charge for late payment of rent, and the penalty for using a security deposit to pay rent. Point out that they should be aware of these rules. If you have not already done so, explain the basic policies for residency at this time, so the tenants can't claim ignorance of these policies later on.

All occupants 18 years old or older should sign all copies of the lease, the security deposit rider, and all other riders and forms. The dates the lessee and lessor signed the lease should be noted under the signatures. If one of the occupants is not present at the time of move-in (and therefore cannot sign the lease documents), the move-in can and probably should be postponed to a later date.

Keys to the property should be given out only after the lease has been signed by all lessees.

The Lease Package

After the lease and other documents have been signed by all parties, the documents are ready to be sorted and placed in the lease package to be given to the tenant(s).

Keep the originals, including all original copies of applicable riders. Staple the lease on top of all other papers. If a tenant has paid any moneys—for example, the first month's rent on a new lease or a security deposit upgrade on a renewal lease—a receipt, if issued, can be stapled to the front of the lease. The second copy of the lease and all riders are placed in the lease package for the tenant's files.

Unsigned or Undelivered Lease

If a previously agreed-to rental agreement that was signed by a tenant is not countersigned by the owner and the owner turns over possession of the property and accepts rent, the rental agreement will, in most states, still be in effect as though it had been signed by the owner and delivered to the tenant. The same conditions hold true if an owner signs and delivers a previously agreed-on lease to a tenant and the tenant doesn't countersign it. If the tenant takes possession of the property and pays rent, it will be as if the lease was actually signed.

Generally, if an unsigned or undelivered lease is provided for a term longer than one year, it is effective for only one year under the Statute of Frauds in most states and, in effect, becomes an oral lease. As an example, tenant Brown agrees to and signs a written lease covering a term of two years for a rental of $600 a month. Landlord Smith agrees to the terms of the lease but doesn't countersign nor deliver the document. Because it is oral, the lease term is effectively reduced to a period of one year.

Tenant Files

It's important to maintain an active alphabetical file containing vital information on each tenant. Keep copies of the following items in the file for each tenant: lease, application, lease riders, credit information, repair bills for the property, letters or other correspondence, rent receipts, and other receipts.

As a safeguard against possible discrimination claims, it's wise to save all rejected applications for at least two years.

5

MOVING NEW TENANTS IN

Richard Kauflin is a retired business owner and an active owner-landlord who understands what small businesses experience when dealing with commercial landlords. Because he didn't want the hassle of his business getting booted out of a rental space again, he and two partners built their own multitenant industrial building that promises a steady income for decades.

Says Richard, "I ran several small businesses, including a restaurant and a sign company, for several years. I was always at risk of being displaced by landlords who wanted to raise the rent or use my space for something else. In the early '90s, commercial rental space in Boulder, Colorado, was expensive and hard to come by, so we decided to buy land and build the right space for us.

"Besides needing a place to house my sign business and one of my partner's delivery business, we wanted a long-term investment. We were fortunate to find choice land in an industrial park that had been vacant for some time because the savings and loan company that owned it went bankrupt. By digging around, we learned that the federal government owned it. Fortunately, permits for a commercial building were already in place. The price of the land was a bargain for that area so we paid cash for it."

With two of the three investment partners self-employed, the toughest part was getting financing. Richard explained, "The Bank of Denver took a chance on us. It took nine months from the time we got the construction loan to put up a 32,000-square-foot building until the time it was ready to occupy. As we were constructing this building, we lined up another tenant and then got a well-known commercial real estate broker involved to fill the rest of the spaces. That proved to be smart because of her extensive networking contacts. Besides, we were focused on working with building contractors while still running our businesses."

Today, managing his commercial property doesn't involve much time overall. "Having that rental income means I can go fishing every day if I want to!

"My partners and I do all the tasks ourselves—accounting, signing leases, contracting for maintenance, repairs, tenant finishes, and even changing light bulbs. We do all our own customer contact, too, and our tenants really appreciate that."

As owners and managers, they might be lenient about tenants' late payments when times are tough "because we understand what small businesses go through.

"We know it's hard to keep buildings full when so many businesses are failing. But over the past decade, we haven't had vacancies except for a few months. I believe it's because we treat our customers well and deal with their problems on the spot."

Attracting commercial tenants has been easy over the years. "All we ever did was put up a sign in the beginning. We treat our customers fairly and with respect. Word gets around. That's the best marketing ever."

MAKE MOVING DAY GO SMOOTHLY

The move-in process is important in setting the stage for the business relationship between you and the tenants. Moving is an emotional and stressful experience, and if the new tenants are dissatisfied with their move-in experience, this feeling of dissatisfaction will last for months, possibly permeating their entire term of leasing.

Some factors adversely affecting a move are out of your control. There can be problems with the movers, delays in leaving the old residence, and complications in unloading in the new property. If tenants are moving out of a building with an elevator on a busy day and are unable to reserve one for their exclusive use, for example, a relatively simple two-hour move could take all day.

You can't guarantee an easy move-in, but you *can* coordinate details to make the process as trouble free and pleasurable as possible for the new tenants. Make sure the keys are in order. If an elevator is involved, schedule it for their exclusive use. Check to see that the utilities have been turned on in the new tenants' names. Give instructions on where they can store extra items. Show them the laundry room facilities. Be on hand to handle any complaints.

This is a time to keep in close communication with your tenants, being ready to assist in any way possible to ease tensions and help expedite the moving process. If at all possible, you should be on the premises during the move-in. Your physical presence can serve to reassure them that you care about them and share their desire to make this difficult day go as smoothly as possible.

PREINSPECTING THE PROPERTY

Inspecting the Unit with the Tenants

You should inspect the property with the new tenants after they sign the lease. Items that are damaged, but not to an extent to warrant replacement (e.g., minor burns in carpeting, chips in a sink, scratches on the appliances), should be indicated on preinspection forms (Figure 5.1 or 5.2). Wallpaper that is in good condition left by a previous tenant and so on should be noted. A damaged item, such as a missing closet roller or dripping faucet that is scheduled for repair, should not be listed, but it would be wise to put it on another list so it does get handled after the inspection.

By signing this form, the tenants indicate that the premises are in satisfactory physical condition at the time of move-in and promise that it will be left in the same condition at the end of the tenancy.

A check-in list should include the property manager's stated business hours as well as emergency contact numbers. Encourage tenants to call when they spot a problem, not three or four days later when a small leak in the plumbing has turned into a stream.

Last-Minute Check

A few days before the tenants arrive for move-in, inspect the property again. Fill out the Property Inspection Form (Figure 5.3). Check for cleanliness and a good paint job; see that plumbing, lights, appliances, and utilities are operating properly. Make sure doors and locks open and close easily. Ensure you have sufficient keys that work properly on all locks. This inspection should be done several days before move-in to allow time to make any necessary repairs. Then a follow-up inspection should be conducted when all deficiencies have been corrected.

When tenants check out, some property managers strongly advise taking photos of the property with a digital camera, putting the photos on a computer CD, and placing them in the tenant's file for recordkeeping. If an absentee owner wants to see photos after people move out, digitized photos can be easily e-mailed.

Videotaping is another option. Both video and digital cameras have built-in dating features so there's no dispute about when the photos were taken. The photos and/or videos can be used as documentation for insurance purposes as well.

FIGURE 5.1 *Preinspection Form*

DATE ISSUED TO RESIDENT _____ , 20 ____

RESIDENT MUST RETURN THIS FORM TO THE RENTAL OFFICE WITHIN 7 DAYS

Mid-America Management Corp.

PRE-INSPECTION

Bldg. _____ Unit _____

Resident _____ Bldg. _____ Apt. _____

Lease Date _____ No. of Occupants (Including Children) _____ Pets _____

KITCHEN	MGR.'S INITIALS	RESIDENT COMMENTS	LIVING ROOM (cont'd)	MGR.'S INITIALS	RESIDENT COMMENTS
Stove Top			Burns		
Clean			Intercom Working		
Burners			T.V. Antenna Plate In		
Light Works			Air Conditioner		
Hood			Clean		
Exhaust Fan			Working		
Light Works			Filter Inside		
Oven			**HALLWAY**		
Two Racks			Guest Closet		
Clean			Bi-fold Doors		
Broiler			Shelf & Rod In		
One Pan			Doors Clean		
One Grill			Handles On		
Clean			Linen Closet		
Refrigerator			Bi-fold Doors		
Freezer Clean			Clean		
Ice Trays			Shelves In		
Door Shelf Bars			Handles On		
Refrig. Clean			**BATHROOM**		
Shelves			Toilet		
Crisper Glass			Clean		
Crisper Drawer			Working		
Light Works			Sink		
Egg Bin			Clean		
Disposal			Faucets Okay		
Working			Medicine Cabinet/Vanity		
Removed			Clean		
Lights			Mirrors Intact		
Over Sink			Knobs on Mirrors		
Ceiling			Bathtub/Tile		
Dining Area			Clean		
Door			Faucet		
Deadbolt Lock			Shower Works		
No Deadbolt			Shower Rod In		
Chain Lock			Towel Racks		
Floor			Exhaust Fan Works		
Clean			Light Bulbs In		
Damage			**BEDROOMS**		
Cabinets Interior			Tile/Carpet Intact		
Shelves Intact			Color		
Clean			Type		
Cabinets Exterior			Doors Clean		
Clean			Closet Rod & Shelf In		
Damage			**GENERAL**		
LIVING ROOM			Bulbs In		
Sliding Door			Windows Clean		
Clean			Screens In		
Lock Bar			Screen Damage		
Lock Works			Air Conditioner		
Door			**MISCELLANEOUS**		
Deadbolt Lock					
No Deadbolt					
Chain Lock					
Carpet/Tile					
Color					
Clean					
Type					
Stains					

I have examined the said premises and am satisfied with the physical condition thereof. The said premises are in good order and repair except as otherwise specified hereon. I understand that I must leave the premises clean and undamaged, as stated in the Security Deposit Agreement.

Manager/Rental Agent _____ Lessee _____ Home Phone _____

Date _____ Lessee _____ Home Phone _____

Keys Issued _____ Deadbolt _____ Door _____ Chain _____ Mail _____ Other _____

4402 Rev. 3/01

CORPORATE OFFICE

FIGURE 5.2 *Move-In/Move-Out Report*

Source: Peachtree Business Products. Used with permission. (To order this form or a catalog, call 800-241-4623.)

FIGURE 5.3 *Property Inspection Form*

Property Name _____　Building Address _____
Inspected By _____　Date _____

Area	Condition			Maintenance Required
	Good	Fair	Poor	
Exterior				
Signs				
Grounds				
Landscaping				
Parking Areas				
Sidewalks				
Trash Area				
Light Fixtures				
Entrance/Foyer				
Door				
Windows				
Mailboxes/Nameplates				
Light Fixtures				
Floors				
Walls				
Hallways				
Doors				
Floors				
Walls				
Light Fixtures				
Stairwells				
Ashtrays				

FIGURE 5.3 *Property Inspection Form, continued*

Area	Condition			Maintenance Required
	Good	Fair	Poor	
Laundry Rooms				
Floors				
Walls				
Machines				
Light Fixtures				
Miscellaneous				
Storage Area				
Trash Chutes				
Boiler Room				
Keys to Doors				
Key to Mailbox				
Garage Door Opener(s)				

Exterior Light Timer Setting: On _____ Off _____

Comments: _____
_____
_____
_____
_____
_____
_____

Common Complaints at Move-In

Careful planning and scheduling and the physical inspections and hands-on testing of everything in the property should eliminate most potential problems. Even so, problems can arise. Here are some common complaints at move-in time, with suggested responses.

The property is dirty. Clean the property thoroughly before move-in. Hire professional cleaners if necessary. On the day before move-in, vacuum the carpet or buff the floors, dust the windowsills and countertops, and so on. This should meet the inspection standards of the most meticulous tenant.

The property is poorly painted. This complaint can be about the color of the paint or the poor quality of work. Always paint walls white or off-white, or allow the tenants to choose the colors. Hire professional painters and make sure they clean up paint spills and spatters on appliances, floors, countertops, and hardware, or do it yourself. Check the paint job as part of your preinspection and correct any problems before the tenants move in.

The dishwasher (stove, refrigerator, or other appliance) doesn't work. Appliances should be checked at preinspection; even so, problems may arise. Arrange to have them fixed as soon as possible, and tell the tenants exactly when to expect service on them.

There are bugs in the property. If your building has an insect problem, arrange early on for an adequate extermination program. If, in spite of your best efforts, new tenants see a cockroach roaming around, act immediately to reassure them that this is an isolated incident. Call your exterminator to make an emergency treatment of the property and schedule a follow-up call in a week or two.

The plumbing leaks. This should have been checked; however, like appliances, plumbing has a way of acting up on move-in day. Ascertain if it is a minor problem (dripping faucet) that can be fixed in a few days or a major disaster (overflowing toilet) that needs immediate action, and act accordingly.

Tenants have the wrong keys. If the locks and keys are checked during inspection, this problem can be avoided. Have an extra set of keys on hand in case of inadvertent mixups.

TURNING OVER POSSESSION

After all papers are signed and the rent and security deposit funds received (and any former tenants have vacated the property), the tenants are then entitled to take possession of their new leased space. From a general legal standpoint, an owner has to give possession of *habitable* premises to the tenant in compliance with the rental agreement; habitable means that the property is clean and all equipment, appliances, plumbing, and hardware are in good working condition. The definition of *habitable* can vary from city to city, county to county, and state to state. People need to find out what their local area requires, not only legally but also by custom. Local apartment and landlord associations can help you locate this information.

Turning over possession includes providing the new tenants with the keys that are necessary to enter the space, including the common area lobbies and parking facility if parking is provided in the lease.

If old tenants don't vacate a property at the end of their lease or have prohibited possession in some other manner, you will have to take legal action to rectify the situation. Either an owner or a tenant may file a lawsuit to gain possession and recover damages as provided by law. An owner may bring such action on behalf of the new tenants even though the tenants are the ones entitled to possession.

Giving Tenants Instructions (Lease Package and Move-In Kit)

Make sure you give every tenant an individual copy of the lease and move-in packet if requested; and also check the legal requirements regarding this in your state. Your move-in packet might include some or all of the documents listed below:

- Copies of the lease, security deposit agreement, applicable riders, and an "as is" letter when processing a relet
- Completed utility and telephone service hook-up forms. The electric and gas companies may require completed forms prior to move-in. If tenants pay for utilities, these services will have to be put in their names. Tenants should make arrangements as soon as they sign the lease to have their services connected on or before move-in day. Let your tenants know which utilities they're responsible for paying. As an added service, you can give them a list of utilities in the area with contact numbers and billing information. Ask the utilities to send a notice directly to you when your tenants close

the account; this gives you a heads-up that they'll be vacating and lets you know when you have to start paying utilities on the property again.

- A set of keys or access cards to the property, mailbox, and building entrance plus such common areas as laundry rooms, storage rooms, and so on. Always keep a set of spare property keys in your possession.
- Create a short form that lists everything you give tenants (e.g., keys, door openers, etc.). You both sign two copies; tenants keep one and the other goes into your file for those tenants. The form also states their costs for replacing items if they get lost.
- Change-of-address cards
- Maps of the area
- A list of often-called telephone numbers: police, fire, hospitals, schools, stores, restaurants, cab companies, chamber of commerce
- Operating instructions for appliances, laundry equipment, and so on

These materials can be placed in one folder or envelope marked with a new tenant's name, property number, address, and move-in date.

FINAL DETAILS

Moving day is made up of many details, large and small. You have to coordinate your new tenant's move-in schedule with the former tenant's move-out schedule. Other details to consider are elevator problems, mailbox and doorbell name tags, utility hookups, disposal of packing debris, and perhaps a welcome gift for the new tenant.

Consider spelling out times in your lease as well as beginning and ending dates. For example, the lease might run from 12 noon on September 1 to 12 noon on August 31 the following year. That implies that your *next* tenant is not able to move in until 12 noon the following day (September 1), giving you a 24-hour window to take care of small repair details before the new tenant moves in.

Reserving Elevators

Some buildings, including most high-rises, require tenants to schedule their move-in/move-out with the management office and reserve the elevator. Quite often, elevator buildings won't allow a move-in or move-out on weekends because most tenants are home then and the elevators are busier.

Condominium associations normally require tenants to schedule a move with the management office and sometimes ask for a deposit or charge a fee for use of the elevator. The deposit is returned after an inspection of the elevator and common areas shows no damages, but a one-time fee is not returned.

Name Tags

New tenants must usually have their names on their mailbox and doorbell. To maintain the neat and uniform appearance of doorbells and mailboxes, it is better for you to provide name tags rather than have tenants make their own. Some owners charge a fee for putting up tags. The management office usually handles this function in large buildings, but unless the property is a high-rise, a name tag fee is not a common practice.

Key Control

New tenants usually want their locks changed as a safeguard against old tenants and their friends still having keys. When locks are changed, be sure to get spare keys. If you own more than one unit, keep spare keys to all the properties and buildings in a locked key cabinet. This serves two purposes: First, you can keep the keys organized and tagged, thus making it easier to locate keys in an emergency; second, a locked key cabinet is better than a pegboard in keeping the keys safe from possible theft, thus helping maintain security at your properties.

If you manage multiple properties, have a key management system in place that's based on using a locked box in a secure area. When you get the various keys—for front door, swimming pool gate, door knob and dead bolt, storage closet, and so on—test them and then store them in the box. Establish a policy that the only way these keys will ever leave the box is to get spare ones made. That way, you'll know that one original set of keys always works. If vendors or cleaners need access to the property, set up a process of signing in and out the copied keys. Because keeping track of keys is important, your system should be failproof.

Utilities

Make sure your new tenants notify the utility companies to put the utilities in their names. If they don't, you may end up paying some of their electric or gas bills. Some owners contact these services themselves to ensure that the meters are put in tenants' names. The electric or gas service will have to be reactivated if previous tenants had them disconnected; and pilot lights must be relit. If your tenants are from out of town, you may want to make these arrangements for them.

Be aware that if the water bill doesn't get paid in single-family homes, the water company can put a lien on that property. Some utilities provide a landlord agreement or third-party notification, which means the owner and/or property manager and the tenant get a termination notice at the same time. A lien is a matter of public record and can become a cloud on the title of the property when it's time to sell it. It can also be a blemish on the credit record.

Empty Packing Cartons

New tenants usually have dozens of empty boxes and lots of waste paper to dispose of. Make sure you tell them how to dispose of this type of bulk rubbish, or your corridors or common areas may be filled with debris.

Welcome Gifts

As a gesture of good will, some owners give new tenants a welcome gift such as a plant, flowers, or a basket of fruit. These items are relatively inexpensive and can help maintain a positive feeling during this stressful time. Tenants appreciate your thoughtfulness and remember gestures of this nature throughout their lease term.

Even without gifts, the point is that when you can establish a good relationship with your tenants, everyone is happier. Make it easy for tenants to communicate with you about reasons for late rent payments, for example, but if they're running late every month, don't give them any slack before imposing your late penalties.

6

RENEWING LEASES (OR NOT)

The MBA that Clayton Niles earned in 1976 has paid off many times over because of the knowledge he's applied to developing and managing office buildings. In the past three decades, Clayton has done hands-on managing of all aspects of landlord-tenant issues for his eight office buildings. He has one staff person who handles paperwork and routine property management while he focuses on negotiating leases and dealing with new construction issues. "Having an MBA has helped because it gave me a background in bookkeeping, financial strategies, bank relations, auditing, and much more."

His mix of commercial tenants includes a mortgage company, a brokerage, a title company, and a real estate office—all in one building. In another complex, he has a legal aid office, a county office, and a wireless company. In yet other building, a flower shop is beside an orthodontist's office, with FBI and IRS agencies next door. Recalls Clayton, "Over the years, most of our tenants have been compatible with each other—though one time we had a car stereo sales and installation shop next to a hospice center. That arrangement didn't last long—we encouraged the stereo people to move out as soon as their lease expired."

Clayton's primary mode of operation has been to buy commercial lots and then have an office building designed specifically for each property. Once he has the plans in hand, he seeks people who want offices in that location. Then he gets the shell built and gradually completes the inside space while working with agents to sign up suitable tenants.

"We can't always predict the market. For example, we put up a building in Flagstaff that we thought would serve as warehouse space, so we built in 16-foot-high ceilings. But the area needed straight office space more than warehousing. We had to make the changes to suit our tenants and were left with some wasted space.

"I've learned we have to be flexible and modify plans according to the market. That's why it works best to build the shell of a building first, then make changes for specific tenants. Every circumstance is different."

In the beginning, Clayton didn't count on a federal government department showing interest to be one of his first tenants—and he didn't realize what he was in for.

"When the Social Security Administration came looking to rent space, notices were sent to all of the brokers in town. I got an RFP (request for proposal) package and completed the requirements requested by the government. After spending a lot of time and effort, we won the bid to provide the agency with office space.

"We really struggled to understand the government's purchasing process and didn't do as well financially as my pro forma said we should. But that initial effort certainly paid off. I've learned how to work with government decision makers, whereas other landlords have shied away from dealing with their requirements. The best part is that the rent check shows up like clockwork every month and the government's credit is always good."

What is Clayton's main form of marketing? Working with real estate professionals where his office buildings are located. He generally doesn't advertise, not even a listing in the Yellow Pages.

As he explains, "More than marketing, we're big on customer relations. It's expensive to change tenants because when they move out, we're faced with replacing carpets, repainting, reconfiguring walls, and doing other tenant finishes. We make a point of doing strict due diligence on new tenants and have them sign a minimum of three-year leases. Some kinds of businesses require tenants to sign longer leases than others. For example, because we had to highly customize a space for an orthodontist, we required him to sign a ten-year lease.

"If our tenants' businesses go bankrupt, it costs us a lot. Fortunately, only one tenant has moved out in the middle of the night because of a bankruptcy."

To gain advice on managing his office properties, Clayton turns to Building Owners and Managers Association (BOMA) International (http://www.boma.org) and a sub-group, Regional Owners Council. In fact, he's past president of the BOMA chapter in Tucson. "It's great for education and networking. I use BOMA's gatherings as corporate retreats to network and learn from my peers," he says.

As far as giving advice, Clayton offers these three suggestions for commercial landlords. "First, take an accounting course so you really understand where the dollars are going. They can disappear fast.

"Second, when leases are coming up for renewal, you can make a lot of concessions before it's cost effective to let tenants go. It sometimes takes six months to find new tenants and another six months to refit the space for them.

"Most important, keep tenants happy so they'll want to renew. If you suspect a problem isn't real, be sensitive and fix it anyway. For instance, landlords have been known to put non-functioning thermostats in offices so tenants believe they have more control over the heating and cooling in their space. Simple solutions like that do work.

"Remember, the longer the tenants stay, the more money you make."

FINANCIAL BENEFITS OF LEASE RENEWALS

Obtaining lease renewals can be one of your most productive activities, as tenant turnover carries many hidden costs. Turnover varies depending on local market conditions, which are affected by the economy, interest rates, and a myriad of other factors. That's why it's important to study the real estate trends in your area.

Be sure to check the common areas of your property for possible damage during a tenant's move. The unit will need cleaning and perhaps a new carpet or other redecorating. You'll have to spend time, energy, and money finding new tenants and showing the property. You may not find a suitable tenant right away, so the property could stand empty for a month or more. Even without calculating the lost income from a vacancy, it can cost hundreds of dollars each time a tenant moves out and a new tenant moves in.

Renewing a lease, on the other hand, can mean substantial savings. Advertising, maintenance, decorating, and administrative expenses are substantially reduced. The risk of damaging the halls, stairwells, doors, and elevators during the move itself is eliminated. Thus, it's important to make every effort to renew the leases of your desirable tenants.

Of course, not all tenants are good candidates for renewal. Don't renew tenants who pay the rent late, who accrue many late charges, who have unauthorized pets, or who have created noise or nuisance problems. (Procedures to follow when you don't renew a tenant are listed at the end of the chapter.)

Always consider current market conditions as they influence how strictly you adhere to the general policies and procedures discussed in this chapter. For example, if the market is soft and you have a large number of vacancies, you might decide to renew a tenant who has been slow in paying rent but has otherwise been a good tenant.

START ON DAY ONE

The process of renewing a lease begins the day a tenant moves in. The possibility of obtaining a lease renewal is tested daily by your attitude, your professionalism, and your approach to dealing with tenants. There is no substitute for dealing fairly with all tenants.

Conscientious owners work on renewals all year long through positive interactions with tenants. These landlords know their tenants well enough to identify three and four months ahead of time the individuals whose leases should and should not be renewed.

Some landlords prefer to inspect their properties quarterly to make sure they're clean and neat. Says Scott Henderson, who manages rental properties for several owners as well as for himself, "If I have problem tenants, I'll go more often than every quarter. In the lease, I state that advance notice required for an inspection is two hours. This becomes especially important near the end of a lease when I have a prospect who wants to see the property quickly. The way I have set it up in the lease, all I have to do is leave a voice mail as notice."

Reinspecting the Property

All properties should be reinspected approximately 90 days before the expiration of the current lease. Use the Renewal Inspection Notice shown in Figure 6.1 to notify a tenant in writing of the forthcoming inspection, allowing at least 48 hours' notice prior to the scheduled date. The details of the inspection are recorded on the Renewal Inspection Form shown in Figure 6.2.

A renewal inspection serves three purposes: First, it allows you to make an annual assessment of the physical condition of your properties, enabling you to observe unreported problems, such as dripping faucets, damaged bathroom wall tiles, broken windows and screens, drywall damage, and so on.

Second, it gives you the opportunity to make sure a tenant is not in violation of the lease. (Check for evidence of a pet with no pet rider, overoccupancy, poor housekeeping, and so on.)

FIGURE 6.1 *Renewal Inspection Notice*

Date:

Dear_____:

As part of our preventive maintenance program, your property will be inspected on _____ (date) at approximately _____(time). At that time we will enter your property. You need not be present at this inspection.

If this time is inconvenient, please call me at _____ to arrange a time that will be convenient for both of us.

We appreciate your cooperation.

Yours very truly,

_____

FIGURE 6.2 *Renewal Inspection Form*

Renewal Inspection

Name _____ Unit Code _____

Address _____ Lease Exp. Date _____

Phone _____

Number of Occupants _____

Pets: ❏ No ❏ Yes Type: Cat/Dog/Other _____

Carpet: ❏ No ❏ Yes Color _____ Condition _____

Appliance Colors: Stove _____ Refrigerator _____ Dishwasher _____

Comments: _____

_____

_____

I. Entry Area _____

   A. Front Door _____

      1. Locks Mastered _____ Keys _____

   B. Flooring _____ Condition _____

   C. Entry Closet Doors _____

II. Living Room _____

   A. Walls _____

   B. Floor Covering _____

   C. Windows/Screens _____

   D. Heating System _____

III. Kitchen _____

   A. Stove _____

      1. Operation _____

      2. Burners _____

      3. Oven _____

      4. Broiler _____

      5. Handles _____

   B. Refrigerator _____

      1. Operation _____

   C. Exhaust Fan _____

   D. Dishwasher _____

   E. Cabinets/Drawers _____

      1. Countertop _____

      2. Caulk _____

   F. Floor/Condition _____

   G. Sink _____

      1. Faucet _____

      2. Spout _____

IV. Bathrooms _____

   A. Vanity _____

   B. Sink _____

   C. Plumbing _____

(continued)

FIGURE 6.2 *Renewal Inspection Form, continued*

```
     D.  Toilet _____
          1. Seat _____
          2. Base_____
     E.  Shower_____
          1. Tile Grout/Caulk _____
          2. Plumbing _____
 V.  Bedrooms _____
     A.  Floor/Covering _____
     B.  Door _____
     C.  Closet _____
VI.  General _____
     A.  Door Stops _____
     B.  Air Conditioner_____
          1. Filter _____
          2. Caulk _____
          3. Tip_____
     C.  Heating Unit _____
     D.  Balcony_____
          1. Railings _____
          2. Caulk _____
          3. Doors _____
```

And third, it allows tenants to point out any defects or deficiencies they want corrected in the property.

Tenants whose properties are found in an unsanitary or damaged condition should not be renewed until a follow-up inspection indicates that the problems have been corrected and the tenants have paid in full for the work performed.

Redecorating

Lease-renewal time is a pivotal point in the landlord-tenant relationship. This is when tenants request redecorating, carpet cleaning, new appliances, and other improvements.

During the first and second years, renewals will probably not warrant any improvements, but it is a good policy to repaint the property and clean the carpet every two or three years. This is not just to please the tenants but also to prevent any serious maintenance problems through general neglect.

If a property is well maintained by the tenant and doesn't need decorating or carpet cleaning, you might give the tenant a rent rebate in an amount slightly less than what it would cost you for these expenses. This gesture on your part can also act as an incentive for the tenant to renew.

If you agree to replace or repair an item as a condition of a tenant's agreeing to renew a lease, it is a good policy to honor that commitment as soon as possible.

RAISING THE RENT

It doesn't make much sense to own and operate rental property if you can't generate a positive return on your investment. Investment properties can show a negative cash flow occasionally and for short periods, but if such a situation continues, you'll have to sell the property or see it placed in default. However, some owners and landlords strategically set up a negative cash flow because of their tax situation; losses on rental properties can be deducted against income and reduce the taxable amount owed.

Operating rental property is like any other business; to improve cash flow you must either reduce expenses or increase income. Even though Chapter 10 presents suggestions for reducing expenses, increasing income is sometimes easier to accomplish. Unless tenants are on month-to-month leases, however, the only time you can increase rents is when year-long leases terminate, assuming the market will permit an increase.

Some areas of the country allow utility and/or sales tax cost increases to be passed on to tenants if a provision is indicated in the original lease that the tenant signed.

Even professionals find it difficult to decide what percentage increase to charge renewal tenants. Rent increases in the 4 to 6 percent range are somewhat common, but it is not unusual to see hikes as low as 2 percent or as high as 10 percent. Depending on the economy and the markets, you may even have to consider dropping the rent. It's critical that you understand what's going on in the marketplace and what choices you have available to you.

The problem is complicated by several considerations. If you raise the rent too much, a tenant may not renew—leaving you with a potential vacancy as well as decorating costs. If you increase the rent too little, a tenant may stay, but you might not have enough additional income to offset inflationary increases in operating expenses.

Determining an Increase

Some professionals use the 20 percent resistance theory: After a renewal increase has been set and the tenants notified, the increase can be considered too high if more than 20 percent of the tenants resist. If fewer than 20 percent resist, then the increase was too low. This theory can be applied only to properties with multiple units and even then acts as only one factor to consider the next time an increase is due.

In the long run, renewal rent is a result of successful negotiations between you and the tenant. In order to begin the negotiation process, you need a starting point.

Know the Rental Market

The first step in determining a renewal increase is to ascertain the current market rent for vacant comparable properties in your area. This can be accomplished by looking at the classified ads in your local newspaper or by checking with other owners and managers in your community.

Find out what similar properties are instituting as an increase. How do your properties compare with others in your market? Talk to local property management companies and real estate agents. Local newspapers periodically print articles on projected rent increases for their region. Most local newsletters are available on the Internet, including the classified ads, which makes it easy to compare available properties "apples-to-apples" and determine the appropriate rental pricing. Take time to acquire this information before you determine your own increases; many property management companies show available properties on their Web sites. (Go to http://www.persmgt.com as an example.)

Calculate Tenants' Moving Expenses

Another consideration, in addition to how much it will cost you, is how much it may cost your tenants to move and redecorate a new property. Total moving expenses, including new utility service hookup charges, can be more than $1,000, depending on how much furniture the tenants own and whether they use professional movers. In addition, a move often means a new phone number, a new cable service, and new schools, so you might set a rent increase that is slightly less than the cost to the tenants if they move. Then if they object to the rent increase, you can remind them how much it would cost them to move.

Criteria for a Successful Rent Increase

Weigh all the facts you have gathered from your investigations to select a rental increase that meets the following criteria:

- The increase should offset increases in expenses, including the fixed expenses that have increased as a result of inflation and capital or decorating improvements.
- The increase, expressed on an annual basis, should not be much more than the cost of moving expenses for a tenant, unless you own properties in a high-rent district.
- The increase should not be substantially higher than those that comparable properties are charging. A comparable property would closely resemble your property in size, age, location, and amenities.
- The increased rent should be slightly higher than those that vacant comparable properties are commanding. You may be able to get an existing tenant to pay $10 to $20 more a month on a renewal than the cost of a vacant property in the same building, but you may also run the risk of creating a bad relationship with this tenant, who might resent being taken advantage of.

Having decided on an increase, your task now is to convince tenants to accept it and renew their leases. This is normally the time tenants start their negotiations, and you should be prepared to justify the rent hike with them.

Expect Some Turnover

Despite your best efforts, some tenants choose to move anyway. The national average for small investors is 45 percent retention, so if you have ten properties and five tenants renew, you are doing slightly better than average.

Tenants often leave because they have an opportunity to rent a unit in a new building. Professional managers in large urban communities that have constant new construction consider having 60 percent retention of tenants to be exceptionally good. This means that even professional managers have to cope with more than a third of their tenants moving out each year.

THE RENEWAL PROCESS

As indicated earlier, the renewal process begins on the day a tenant moves in, but the actual procedure of administratively obtaining a renewal should be initiated approximately four months before the lease expires.

As an example, one lease (Arizona Multihousing Association Property Rental Agreement) contains an automatic renewal clause stating that unless the tenant gives management a 30-day notice to vacate, the lease will be renewed on a month-to-month basis under the same terms and conditions. (A tenant is not considered renewed until all the lease documents are signed and delivered by the appropriate parties.) Management reserves the sole option not to renew.

You may use a series of *form letters* to assist in obtaining renewals, but letters and notices are not substitutes for information gathering through personal contact. When the renewal process is completed, update all tenant files and security deposit records.

90 days before the lease ends. If, in your judgment, an individual is a desirable tenant, send the 90-Day Notice (First Renewal Letter) shown in Figure 6.3. Enclose the proposed Renewal Form (see Figure 6.4) and/or lease and security deposit agreement. This packet should be sent 90 days prior to the date the current lease expires. As an added incentive for getting a prompt reply, you can offer a one-time rebate of $25 to $30 for signing the renewal lease 60 or more days before the lease ends.

If a tenant has accrued unpaid late charges or other fees and you have still decided to seek renewal, send copies of the documents with a letter requesting

FIGURE 6.3 *90-Day Notice (First Renewal Letter)*

Date:

Dear _____:

I am writing to offer to renew your lease, which is due to expire soon.

I am enclosing your proposed lease renewal agreement. You will note that there is an increase in rent. This increase is necessary because of increases in taxes, utilities, labor, overhead, and other operational expenses.

We have kept the rent increase to a minimum, and, in fact, this rental rate is available only if you sign your renewal ninety days prior to expiration of your present lease. If you sign later, the rent will be more per month to allow for further increases in costs.

I have also enclosed your security deposit agreement. Because your security deposit must equal your monthly rental, you are asked to increase your deposit by an amount equal to cover the increase in rent.

Please sign and return the lease renewal agreement and security deposit agreement, along with your payment of $_____ (to cover the additional security deposit) before _____. After that date, if you want to renew, I will issue another renewal lease at the higher rate.

Please feel free to call me if you have any questions.

Very truly yours,

_____

enc: (2): Lease Agreement
Security Deposit Agreement

FIGURE 6.4 *Renewal Form*

Form LR-202-N • P E A C H T R E E 1-800-241-4623

Your Imprint
Here

To:

The lease on your apartment will expire on:

_____

We hope that you will want to continue occupancy, so we request that you sign all copies of the lease renewal and return all copies to us on or before

_____

— Thank You.

RENEWAL OF APARTMENT LEASE

THIS RENEWAL AGREEMENT dated _____

is a rider to and forms a part of the original lease ("Lease") d_____

between _____, Lessor,

and _____, Lessee,

for the apartment located at _____
                                       APARTMENT NO.   BLD

_____
         STREET ADDRESS   STATE

known as _____
                              NAME OF APARTMENT

The Lease is hereby extended for an additional term of _____ no

commencing _____ and ending _____

and the RENTAL RATE during this period shall be _____

_____ Dollars ($ _____) per month.

ADDITIONAL DEPOSIT required is _____ Dollars ($ _____).

All other covenants and conditions of the Lease shall remain in effect, and no covenant or condition of

the Lease shall be deemed waived by any action or non-action in the past.

Lessor or Agent	Date Signed	
	Lessee/Resident	Date Signed
	Lessee/Resident	Date Signed

Source: Peachtree Business Products. Used with permission. (To order this form or a catalog, call 800-241-4623.)

that these charges be brought up-to-date. Advise tenants that their leases can't be renewed until their account balances are paid in full.

Approximately one week after sending out the renewal packet, call the tenants to make certain they received the materials and to encourage prompt responses.

60 days before the lease ends. If you have not received a reply from a tenant within 30 days of sending the packet, send a follow-up: the 60-Day Notice letter shown in Figure 6.5.

45 days before the lease ends. If the tenant has not returned the lease documents 45 days prior to the lease expiration date, send a second follow-up, the 45-Day Notice letter (see Figure 6.6). This letter informs the tenant to contact you within 24 hours if he or she chooses to renew. Otherwise, the property will be considered available for showing to prospective tenants.

30 days before the lease ends. For tenants who have not responded or have indicated in writing that they won't be renewing, send a Notice to Vacate letter (see Figure 6.8) specifying the condition in which the property is to be left when vacated. Send this letter 30 days before the lease's expiration date.

NOT RENEWING A TENANT

Occasionally you will not want to renew a tenant, a decision that might be based on any number of reasons: collection problems, poor housekeeping, over-

FIGURE 6.5 *60-Day Notice (Second Renewal Letter)*

Date:

Dear _____:

According to our records, your current lease expires on _____ and you have not yet signed and delivered the renewal lease we sent you on _____.

We need to know as soon as possible whether you intend to stay in the property so we can begin showing it for rerental.

Note also that _____ is the last date that the renewal rent of $_____ is valid. After that date, the renewal rent will be $_____.

We would appreciate your prompt attention to this matter. Please contact us if you have any questions.

Very truly yours,

_____

FIGURE 6.6 *45-Day Notice (Third Renewal Letter)*

Date:

Dear _____:

We have not yet received your signed lease document for the coming term. Since your lease expires on _____, it is extremely important that you contact us within 24 hours to let us know your plans.

If we do not hear from you by _____, we will start showing the property to prospective tenants on _____.

If you are not planning to renew your lease, please complete the bottom part of this letter, detach and return to us immediately.

Thank you for your cooperation,

Date: _____

We will vacate our property on _____ (date)

New address: _____

Signature: _____

occupancy, continual disturbance of other tenants, and so on. Give such a tenant a 30-Day Notice (see Figure 6.7) as a courtesy.

In some states you may be obligated to tell tenants why you are not renewing the lease. You currently are not required to renew a lease; however, pending legislation in at least one state proposes just that. As always, stay current on landlord-tenant legislation, and keep in touch with your attorney.

FIGURE 6.7 *30-Day Notice*

Date:

Dear _____:

This letter will serve as notification that we have decided not to renew your lease. Please turn in your keys at our office no later than _____. Also supply us with your forwarding address and new telephone number at that time.

Your security deposit is fully refundable provided your property is left in a clean, orderly, and undamaged condition as detailed in the enclosed Notice to Vacate. Also refer to the Preinspection Form, which details the condition of the property when you moved in.

If you have any questions regarding this matter, please feel free to contact me.

Very truly yours,

_____

enc: Notice to Vacate, Preinspection Form

FIGURE 6.8 *Notice to Vacate (3-Day Demand Letter)*

Mid-America Management

Reply To:

Date:_____

Dear Resident:

This letter will acknowledge receipt of your notice of intention to vacate your apartment on or before _____, 20_____. We thank you for your residency and trust your stay with us has been a pleasant one.

In order to insure the maximum return of your security deposit, please refer to the reverse side of your current lease form to be sure that all requirements regarding the move-out condition of your apartment are met. It is also suggested that you contact your site office and schedule an appointment for a final inspection walk-through of your apartment.

Should you be unable to vacate your apartment on or before the above specified date, please be advised that you will be considered a "holdover" resident and we will be strictly enforcing paragraph 31(c) of your lease which states:

> "The Lessee's continued occupancy shall be for a month to month term at a monthly rental which shall equal the monthly rental reserved herein plus a 20% increase in said amount."

As you can see, it is of utmost importance that you vacate your apartment on or before the above specified date. Failure to do so will leave you liable for an amount of _____, which represents a sum equal to 120% of your monthly rent. Please remember you are responsible for your apartment until all keys are returned to the site office.

Should you have any questions regarding your move, please contact your site office at
_____.

Sincerely,
MID-AMERICA MANAGEMENT

Site Manager

Form 4505 / 9-92

Mid-America Management Corp.
2901 Butterfield Road, Oak Brook, Illinois 60521 (708) 574-2400

7

WHEN TENANTS MOVE OUT

A young Court Gettel distinctly remembers the day he sat on the couch facing the prospect of "slaving" his way through college. He decided there had to be a better way. Then it hit him. "I've always been interested in real estate. I already had a basic idea about how rentals work for other people, so I decided to test it out for myself. I had absolutely no fears."

At age 22, Court bought his first rental property—an 11-plex apartment building. To this fearless entrepreneur, the son of a surgeon and a nurse, buying an 11-plex didn't seem like a big jump. He explained, "I didn't have a background in finance. But I did understand I needed enough dollars coming in to cover costs and put money in my pocket to live."

Fast forward to seven years later. Court, his brothers, and his father now control millions of dollars in property, most of it invested in apartment complexes. Through numerous limited liability companies (LLCs)—one for each property to isolate the risks—they own several complexes: 28 units, 38 units, 60 units, 159 units, one in escrow, and more on the horizon.

With these seven years of experience under his belt, Court feels he has "the knowledge and the guts" to go after exciting investment deals—and that's where the fun is for him. While he's sniffing out good values on properties, his brother John calmly overseas the details of their enterprise—from supervising on-site managers to dealing with maintenance and tenant issues and much more.

What are Court's criteria for selecting new rental properties? "The place has to be in a decent neighborhood, have curb appeal, and get me excited." Does he have a standard system for deciding if a property is thumbs-up or not? "I'd like to say I did, but each deal comes with so many variables to consider. I think in terms of how big the risk would be if I bought a certain property in addition to its outside potential. The numbers have to work."

Court rarely gets involved in tenant issues unless there's a problem like chronic late payments or vendors overcharging. He steps in to reinforce John's efforts if need be. Experience has taught them to be tough with their policies, such as requiring tenants to pay rents on time or pay penalties if they don't. "Every time I've given people second and third chances, it's never worked out," Court says.

The Gettel family has built a strong team of advisors who help them succeed—including their mortgage broker, accountant, banker, insurance agent, and real estate lawyers. They make time to study and network with other investors and property managers—and they're adamant about putting their profits back into their business.

What about Court's goal of getting into real estate so he could have pocket money? That's the irony. Today, his dollars don't come from rents. He earns his spending money teaching tennis—and goes about it in his characteristically fearless way.

ENDING A LEASE ON TIME

It would be nice if all good tenants stayed in their properties year after year, paying the rent on time and never creating any problems. But of course there comes a time when tenants move out.

If tenants are leaving simply because the lease has expired and they want to move on, the event should not be too stressful. But if they are being evicted, or you decided not to renew the lease, or they want to terminate the lease early, there could be a good deal of tension until the moving day is at hand and they've physically vacated the property.

When tenants inform you that they will move out at the end of the lease, there are several steps to follow.

NOTICE TO VACATE

Send the tenants a Notice to Vacate (see Figure 6.8) at least 30 days before the end of the lease. This notice reminds them that you will inspect the property before returning the security deposit and lists the particular areas of the property that will be checked for cleaning and damage.

The notice also states the date the property must be vacated, asks for a forwarding address, and tells the tenants where to return the keys.

Move-Out Inspection

The move-out inspection can be conducted on the day a tenant vacates the property or a few days before. The purpose of this inspection is to document the condition of the property and ascertain what needs fixing or replacing. Based on this inspection, you then calculate the amount of the security deposit to return to the tenant.

To conduct the inspection, use a copy of the Preinspection Form shown in Figure 5.1 that was completed when the tenant moved in. Review this form along with any completed property work orders to verify deficiencies accepted by the tenant and defects corrected through work orders.

Refer also to the Notice to Vacate, which requires the tenant to leave the property clean and free of debris.

If possible, conduct a move-out inspection together with the tenant to avoid disputes about the condition of the property and appropriate charges for repairs and cleaning. If time permits, you might allow the tenant to correct such minor deficiencies as touching up the paint, cleaning the oven, and so on.

Regain possession. Once you ascertain the exact day tenants will be leaving, be on hand to receive the keys and regain possession of the property.

ENDING A LEASE EARLY

When tenants want to move out before their lease is over, you have several options. If you want to enforce the lease, you have a legal right to hold your tenants to the signed agreement to pay for a complete year. A lease is a contract; both parties mutually agreed to uphold their obligations in compliance with the stated terms and conditions. However, it may not always be wise to take such a hard line.

There are ways, on the other hand, in which each party can mutually agree to terminate a lease early. You can elect to cancel the lease completely. Or you might allow tenants to sublet the property or assign (relet) the lease to substitute tenants.

If you let your tenants know that you are willing to negotiate an early termination of the lease, they will be less likely to move out without giving notice. In the latter case, the landlord can initiate a legal suit, but it is a good idea to avoid costly and stressful legal battles.

Subletting

Subletting occurs when a tenant enters into a separate agreement with a third party (subtenant) to use the property on a temporary or permanent basis. The two parties are responsible to each other for performing whatever obligations they have agreed on. Be sure you get involved with the transaction and don't let the tenants make arrangements on their own.

As an example of a temporary sublet, tenant Smith gets a business assignment out of town for three months and decides to sublet his property to a friend for the period he will be gone. The friend, subtenant Jones, agrees to pay Smith an amount of rent for use of the premises. Smith, in turn, continues to pay rent to you and when the three months have expired, Smith returns and Jones moves out. If everything went well, you might not even know about the transaction.

Smith could also decide to permanently move out of his property before the lease expired and sublet the property for the balance of the lease. He could collect rent from the subtenant and pay rent to you, the landlord, and would remain obligated to you until the old lease expired. The sublet tenant usually accepts the property in an "as is" condition and doesn't benefit from any redecorating until the lease expires.

In this case you are more likely to be a party to the sublet because the new tenant would probably want to enter into a new lease with you when the sublet expires, where permitted by law. It is a common practice to charge a small fee to cover administrative expenses when allowing a sublet.

Subleasing can be an accounting and tracking nightmare. If your tenant wants to sublease, you can charge money (e.g., $300) for that privilege and for the extra paperwork it requires. The renter is responsible to find the sublessee and is responsible for paying for any advertising or promotions and making sure that the sublessee is acceptable to the landlord. It's advisable to do your own credit and background checks, then start a fresh lease with the new person.

Assignment (Reletting)

When tenants must terminate their lease early, you may choose to assign the lease (or relet) to new tenants who will finish the remainder of the term. If it takes several months to locate a suitable replacement, the original tenants are still liable and must pay rent, even though they may not be occupying the unit.

"Assignment" differs from subletting in that once new tenants have signed the lease, the original tenants are fully released from any additional obligation. In some cases, landlords ask the replacement tenants to sign a brand new one-year lease instead of completing the obligation under the old lease. Landlords usually charge a higher fee to accommodate an assignment.

Assignment is, in effect, a termination of one lease and creation of a new one. Thus, when the old tenants move out, be sure to inspect the property for damages and deduct the cost of repairs and redecorating from the security deposit. Refund the original tenant's security deposit and collect a new one from the replacement tenants.

Why assignment is preferable to subletting. The reasons are clear when you think how involved and complicated the situation would be if subtenants had to first contact the original tenants to get repairs and service for the property. And if landlords had to enforce the rules and regulations of occupancy with a sublet, they would have to contact the original tenants, who may have moved to another state.

With an assignment, you have what amounts to a new lease with new tenants, and your dealings with the former tenants end.

Sublet/Assignment Clauses in Standard Leases

Many lease and rental agreement forms address the issue of subleasing and assignments in a similar fashion. State laws generally allow rental agreements to require tenants to obtain the owner's prior consent in order to sublet or assign a property. Written permission may be necessary if the lease is in writing.

Owners should not withhold permission unreasonably, and sublease/assignment clauses in form leases normally don't contain any language that would constitute an unreasonable withholding of permission.

The following common provisions are considered generally acceptable by both landlords and tenants:

- Tenants may be prohibited from transferring their lease interest to a trustee in bankruptcy or for the benefit of the tenants' creditors or any other act of bankruptcy or insolvency.
- Owners may reserve the right to rent other vacancies in the premises before consenting to reletting the dwelling unit. [This clause could be considered antagonistic and you can waive the right if the tenants are responsible for finding their own sublessee.]
- Prospective tenants may be required to meet the criteria customarily used to evaluate the acceptability of tenants for similar units in the premises.
- Sublet/assignment may be restricted during the last 90 days of the lease term. During this period, a landlord could require prospective sublessees to sign new, full-term leases.

Obligations and Liabilities

Current tenants usually remain liable for responsibilities under the lease until a new lease is signed. You may require financial assurance from the old tenants or the prospective lessees, including advance payment for rent and expenses of reletting. Such expenses might include decorating, repairs, replacements, advertising, commissions, and reasonable administrative fees for performing the details involved in this type of transaction.

Unless agreed, you generally don't have a responsibility to advertise or incur expenses on behalf of the tenants or yourself in conjunction with reletting a property. A tenant who subleases is normally liable to his or her sublessee for the performance of the owner's obligations under the rental agreement.

A landlord is not directly liable to a sublessee in regard to obligations under the rental agreement, and the sublessee is not directly liable to the owner with respect to the tenant's obligations unless otherwise agreed.

Obeying State and Local Laws

Even though some states have given tenants a right to sublet or relet, most states honor a rental agreement if subletting or reletting is specifically prohibited. If you're in doubt about your rights in this regard, it is best to check with your local municipality or Realtor association on the issue of subletting and assigning leases. Unless your city has a landlord-tenant law, the lease document and specific subletting policies that have been agreed to by the tenant prevail.

The Relet Agreement

If you agree to relet, execute a Relet Agreement that spells out the terms and conditions of a relet.

A Relet Agreement gives the tenants the responsibility for finding suitable new tenants for the property. Suitable tenants are ones who meet your usual financial and other requirements, and who are willing to assume the balance of the lease term. You have the right to reject the prospective sublessees on the basis of a credit check.

The agreement spells out exactly when the old tenants' responsibilities end. Only on the new tenants' paying a full security deposit, signing a lease, paying the first month's rent, and accepting the keys are the old tenants given their security deposits back and released from the lease.

The agreement lists the amount of the reletting fee (if any) and states the exact day the property will be vacated. It also provides new tenants with two options.

The first option is to accept the property in "as is" condition at the same rent and without redecorating or cleaning. In this case, you should have the new tenant sign an "As Is" Letter (see Figure 7.1), which indicates in writing that the new tenant accepts the unit in its existing condition.

The second option is to sign a new one-year lease at a higher rent. This option provides for redecorating and cleaning the property as with any new lease. In this case, the old tenant agrees to leave the property a few days before the reletting tenant's move-in date to allow the landlord to prepare for the new tenant.

In either case, you should send the old tenant a Notice to Vacate and inspect the property for damage. This inspection should be done in the presence of both the old and the new tenant, if possible.

The relet agreement also deals with details about the return of security deposits, payment of outstanding bookkeeping charges, providing forwarding addresses, and the return of keys. Both you and the old tenant should sign the relet agreement, and you should keep a copy of the form in your permanent files.

Note that the laws in Arizona, for example, state that the landlord has an obligation to keep up with repairs on a property but isn't expected to do inside cleanup during the duration of the tenancy and has no obligation to upgrade or redecorate the property during that time.

FIGURE 7.1 *"As Is" Letter*

Date:

Dear _____:

We are glad to welcome you as a new tenant in _____.

This letter is to verify that you are accepting the property "as is" and will not request further cleaning or redecorating for the duration of the lease.

Also, you agree that upon termination of your lease, you will leave the property in the same condition to comply with the provisions of your security deposit agreement.

Very truly yours,

_____

Accepted by: _____
         (tenant)   (date)

Cancellation

When tenants must terminate a lease early, they may choose to cancel the obligation rather than take the time to find a suitable subtenant. In such a case, you may agree to cancel the lease.

In a lease cancellation, tenants buy out their lease by agreeing to a set of conditions. In return for a fee, you take on the responsibility of finding a new tenant and fully release the old tenant from any further obligation as of the effective date. To cancel a lease, execute an Agreement to Cancel Lease (see Figure 4.13). If tenants requested a cancellation rider when they signed their lease, this form can be used in conjunction with that rider.

Terms and conditions of this agreement to cancel require tenants to pay a fee equal to two months' rent. This fee can vary, but it is intended to cover your costs of reletting a property, including cleaning and redecorating. It also covers the risk of losing a month's rent if you can't find suitable tenants right away.

The form specifies the day the property will be vacated, which is also the cancellation date of the lease, and deals with details of returning keys and providing forwarding addresses.

Be sure to send a Notice to Vacate and inspect the place for damages before returning a security deposit. As in any move-out, tenants must leave a property in good condition.

RETURN OF POSSESSION

However a lease is ended, your goal is always the same: to regain possession of the property in good condition and on time.

Tenants' Rights to Possession

When tenants rent a property, they are given, and retain, possession of the unit throughout the term of the lease term. If tenants are in compliance with the terms of the lease during the lease term, you may not take any action to regain possession except in the case of an abandonment or as otherwise permitted by law.

Even if the tenants aren't in total compliance with the lease, you can't take possession of the property by locking the tenants out, removing part of the dwelling unit (for example, the front door), or withholding services (utilities, water, garbage removal).

Turning Over Possession

When a lease is terminated, tenants must relinquish possession immediately. They do this by removing all personal belongings from the property and delivering all keys to the owner.

Turning over possession is usually a routine, businesslike procedure. You and the tenants agree to terminate the lease or to sublet the property; the old tenants move out on the agreed-on day; and the new tenants move in without a hitch.

However, sometimes things don't go smoothly, as explained in the following.

Forcible detainer. Tenants may fail to return possession by not vacating the unit or not returning the keys. This normally constitutes a forcible detainer, meaning that you, the owner (or new tenants, if there are any), may initiate eviction proceedings (see Chapter 8) and request actual and punitive damages.

Abandonment. Occasionally, tenants abandon a property without notice. This sometimes happens when you are in the process of filing an Owner's Five-Day Notice for nonpayment of rent (see Figure 8.3) or a Termination Notice for breach of contract. If you check the property and find it is, or appears to be, vacant and not occupied for a period of at least seven days, an Abandonment Notice (see Figure 7.2) should be prepared. (Comply with state and local laws governing the posting of notices.) A copy of the form must be posted on the property door for ten days. The original is kept in your files.

When the ten-day period has elapsed, you regain full dominion and control over the premises and property, and can begin preparing the property for rerental.

Abandoned Personal Property

Tenants occasionally move out and return the keys but leave behind some personal property, which must be disposed of properly.

Generally, personal property left in a property is considered abandoned if the tenants appear to have moved out (except in the case of eviction) and the property no longer contains food or clothing. *Abandonment* is a term that has a technical meaning in the law, and some states have specific statutes defining it.

Your lease form may contain language governing abandoned property and your rights to dispose of it. The general procedure to follow for disposing of the property is as follows:

FIGURE 7.2 *Abandonment Notice*

Notice and Declaration of Abandonment

Date:

To:

Please be advised that as of this date your rent has been outstanding and unpaid for ten (10) days and you have been absent from the premises without notice to the Management/Owner for seven (7) days and there is no reasonable evidence that you are occupying the premises; or your rent has been outstanding and unpaid for five (5) days and you have been absent from the premises for five (5) days and none of your personal property remains in the premises.

Consequently, you are advised that the premises have been deemed abandoned in accordance with A.R.S. § 33–1370 and unless you contact the Manager/Owner within five (5) days of the listing and mailing of this Notice, the Manager/Owner will take the following action:

1. Enter the premises and take possession of the premises;
2. Make reasonable efforts to rent your property at the fair rental value;
3. Your refundable security deposit will be forfeited and applied to damages, if any, accrued and unpaid rent, and any other costs incurred by the Manager/Owner as a result of your abandonment of the property;
4. Your personal property in the premises (if applicable) will be removed and you will be notified of its location; and
5. Your personal property will be stored for a period of ten (10) days after the completion of the abandonment and if you fail to claim and remove your personal property, it will be subject to being sold with the proceeds of the sale being applied to any outstanding rent, taxes, late charges, damages and any other reasonable costs incurred by the Manager/Owner.

Should you prefer to avoid these actions, please contact the Manager/Owner and make arrangements for the payment of all outstanding rent and other charges immediately.

Sincerely,

By _____ Manager

Time and date personally delivered/mailed
by certified mail:

_____

- Try to contact the tenants by telephone through their new number or through the emergency or employment telephone numbers provided on the lease application. If you reach the tenants, request that their personal property be removed from the property during the next seven days.
- If tenants fail to claim personal property at the end of the period, then take an inventory of the property, noting any damaged items.

- If you reasonably believe that the abandoned items are valueless or of such little value that the cost of storage would exceed the amount that would be realized from their sale or if the items are subject to spoilage, dispose of them immediately.

- If the items are of value greater than the cost of storage, then store them for a reasonable time, not exceeding 60 days, taking reasonable care against loss or damage. You should not feel responsible to the tenants for any loss not caused by your negligence. The tenants may claim the items during the term of storage by paying for transfer and storage costs. Items not claimed during the term of storage may be disposed of in any reasonable manner without liability to you.

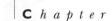

8

RENT COLLECTION

Some parents buy condos for their college kids, but Alexis Papahadjopoulos's dad took that idea further. He bought Alexis and his brother an eight-bedroom Edwardian house near the campus in Berkeley, California. That's where they got their start as landlords.

After graduating, they stayed in the house and continued to rent to students. That big Edwardian house opened up the world of investment income to Alexis, who went on to buy a partial interest in two other properties with members of his family. Then, for a while he owned 5 of 7 units in a tenancy in common arrangement (it's a California thing!) and sold them as condos. With seed money from these ventures, he took a leap and bought a 14-unit apartment building on his own in 2002.

Says Alexis, "As a career choice, landlording crept up on me. I had spent several years traveling and never really started a career. I realize it's natural for me to work independently; it suits my history and temperament." Purchasing a 14-unit apartment building that needed a lot of tender loving care, however, "pushed me over the top toward being serious in this career." He says, "As a result of having more properties, I can't be too undisciplined taking of care them or I'll get into trouble. People get really upset when something in their home doesn't get fixed right away.

"It's become critical to find a good, steady crew of workers and stay on top of things. In the long run, that approach requires less effort than dealing with each issue on an ad hoc basis."

The best rewards from this career come for Alexis when he sees his efforts to improve properties add value to the neighborhood—something he's proud to be part of. About one of the biggest projects he's ever done, he says, "We added a second story to a small house that had been neglected for nine years. It now has a beautiful upstairs view of the San Francisco Bay." Although this project involved the difficulties of getting permits and working with building inspectors, he realizes they all have the same purpose in mind: to retain and improve the building standards in the neighborhood.

The more serious Alexis becomes in his landlording career, the more interested he is to learn from others. That's why he's part of a loosely formed group called Property Opportunity Players and goes to owner-landlord gatherings. When the group gets together, they discuss finding good suppliers, seeing new trends, and diversifying their holdings beyond the Bay Area. Alexis also turns for advice to his real estate agent who's "been around a long time" and is actually partnering with Alexis in one venture.

In a sense, Alexis regards his tenants as business partners too, for without them he wouldn't have a business or a career. He strives for the best combination of being laid-back and being strict with his tenants. "I like to be helpful and give extra service whenever I can. I've found that when they're happy, they rarely complain. But when they're annoyed, they find lots to complain about."

THE MOST IMPORTANT MANAGEMENT TASK

Many of your property management activities occur once a year (renewal of leases, inspection of apartments, and so on), and others, such as maintaining positive resident relations, are a continuing responsibility. Collecting the rent, however, is a regular, once-a-month task, and in many ways this function is the owner's most important management activity. The rent is your income from the property. Without it you won't be able to operate and maintain your property.

That's why you need to set a policy of when and how the rent should be paid each month and then consistently enforce this policy. Try to anticipate problems that might arise—for example, tenants who habitually pay rent late or the need to evict a tenant—and decide ahead of time how to deal with these eventualities. You can avoid a lot of stress if you plan ahead and deal with these matters in a businesslike way.

Payment Policies

The strictest policy would be to demand that rent be paid in full on or before the first of the month. A more lenient policy is to have a five-day grace period, which allows tenants to pay the rent any time between the first and the fifth of the month, inclusive, without penalty. Either of these policies might include a provision for a late fee. Whatever policy you establish, the key is to enforce it consistently and not waver from one month to the next or from one tenant to the next.

Where to collect. You can go about collecting the rent in several ways. One is to ask the tenants to bring it to you in person, but they may object to this unless you live on the property or have an office there. Another way is to go to tenants' apartments on the first day of each month; some owners prefer this method, but it may not always be convenient. The most common procedure is to have tenants mail the rent; and to make it easy, you may provide tenants with 12 preaddressed envelopes.

When to collect. Rent is due at the beginning of any term of one month or less; otherwise, rent is payable in equal monthly installments at the beginning of each month. Unless otherwise agreed, rent is normally uniformly apportioned from day to day using a 30-day month.

Most leases clearly state that rent is due and payable in full on or before the first day of each month. It's important to note that if your rental agreement does *not* address this issue or if you don't have a written lease agreement providing that rent is payable in advance on the first of the month, then the rent is generally payable at the end of the rental period—that is, at the end of the month.

Methods of payment. The rent is considered paid if it is made by any means or in any manner customarily used in the ordinary course of business. This includes cash, money orders, certified and cashier's checks, and the like. It does not include farm animals, produce, food stamps, products or goods, or other personal property.

Payment by check is conditional. If a tenant gives you a check on the first of the month that is subsequently returned for insufficient funds, it is tantamount to that tenant never having paid. An owner may require a bad check replaced by cash along with a penalty for non-sufficient funds and all future payments made in cash. Money orders or certified checks can also be requested if you don't feel comfortable carrying large amounts of cash.

Second-party checks, including payroll checks and/or government checks, should not be accepted. Be sure you tell tenants to whom they should make out the rent payment checks.

Give a receipt. A receipt book, which can be purchased in most stationery stores, can be used to show receipt of all money, including application fees, initial security deposits, rents, credit check fees, partial payments, relet fees, lockout fees, and cancellation fees. You may want to keep copies of receipts and place them in the tenants' files.

Delinquencies and late charges. The lease indicates when rent is to be paid and at what point it becomes delinquent. If the rent is due on the first of the month, it is considered delinquent on the second (or the fifth, if you allow a grace period). At this point you could choose to immediately file An Owner's

Five-Day Notice (see Figure 8.3) and proceed with an eviction. However, unless you want to get rid of a tenant because of other lease violations, you may want to consider taking less extreme action.

Reminder letter. If the rent is late, you may want to send a tenant a Rent Reminder Letter (see Figure 8.1). If it is your policy to charge a late fee as soon as rent becomes delinquent, indicate this on the letter. Otherwise, send a Late Charge Notice (see Figure 8.2) on the day the late charge goes into effect.

Late charges. Some form leases have a built-in late charge, and most leases at least have a provision allowing it. Depending on the specific lease, the late charge is usually assessed between the sixth and tenth day of the month, but it can be assessed as early as the second day. Certain leases specify the exact amount to be charged; for instance, a charge of $5 on rent paid after the fifth and $10 after the tenth. Without a written provision stated somewhere in the lease, a late charge cannot be demanded.

FIGURE 8.1 *Rent Reminder Letter*

Date:

Dear _____:

Our records indicate that your rent is not yet paid. To avoid late fees, please remit your past due rent immediately.

Sincerely,

_____

FIGURE 8.2 *Late Charge Notice*

Date:

Dear _____:

Our records indicate that your rent is still not paid. A $10.00-per-day late charge is now in effect. I am sure you will want to take care of this matter immediately.

If I can be of any help to you in this matter, please feel free to contact me at _____.

(Phone Number)

Sincerely,

_____

The charge should be high enough to discourage habitual lateness but not so high as to be unreasonable. An exorbitant late charge, say over $75, could be challenged as unreasonable.

A valid argument can be made against charging late fees. Although they are intended to encourage tenants to pay rent on time, late fees indirectly give tenants permission to pay the rent late. Tenants may think that it is acceptable to pay late so long as they agree to pay the late charge. You must decide what is more important to you: getting the rent on time or getting additional income from the late fee. If you have enough funds in reserve to make the mortgage payment before receiving the rent, a late charge, if rigidly enforced, can provide additional income.

You can choose to waive the late fee, but by doing so you are excusing the lateness and encouraging it to happen again. If you habitually allow late payments, you can't suddenly change your attitude and begin eviction proceedings when tenants are again late. If you want to return to the strict terms of the lease, you must first notify the tenants of your intention—yet another area to consider under fair housing laws. If you waive late fees for some residents but act inconsistently and not waive them for others, you may be making yourself vulnerable to a discrimination suit. Whatever policy you establish, you must make every effort to enforce it uniformly with every resident.

Whether or not you charge a late fee, do attempt to make personal contact with tenants whose rent is outstanding and find out why it's late. Get them to set a firm date when the rent will be paid, and remind them to include fees for late payment. Start eviction procedures if they don't pay on the promised date.

COLLECTING LATE RENT

Most tenants pay their rent on time or within a reasonable grace period. But some won't. If sending reminder letters or making personal contacts is not effective, you'll have to take further action. Typically, you'll serve a five-day notice, send a follow-up letter, and then begin eviction proceedings.

The Five-Day Notice

In most states, an Owner's Five-Day Notice (see Figure 8.3) is the first step in processing rent-delinquent tenants through the court system. It is usually served on the sixth day of the month, but you can issue it as early as the second. Don't put off sending a five-day notice just because they've promised to pay. Issue the notice anyway; if and when the tenants pay, you can tear up the notice.

FIGURE 8.3 *Owner's Five-Day Notice*

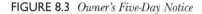

OWNER'S FIVE DAY NOTICE
FORM 16R COPYRIGHT 1990
CHICAGO BOARD OF REALTORS®

RECOMMENDED BY THE CHICAGO BOARD OF REALTORS® FOR USE WITH CBOR® APARTMENT LEASES 15, 15C, 15C-TH

You are hereby notified that there is now due the owner the sum of $_____

(1) Rent per month $_____, (2) Rent Due from_____to_____

being rent for the premises situated in_____, County of_____

and State of Illinois, and known and described as follows, to wit: _____

_____together with all

buildings, storage areas, recreational facilities, parking spaces and garages used in connection with said premises.

And you are further notified that payment of said sum so due has been and is hereby demanded of you, and that unless payment thereof is made on or before the expiration of five days after service of this notice, your right of possession under the lease of said premises will be terminated.

ONLY FULL PAYMENT of the rent demanded in this notice will waive the landlord's right to terminate the lease under this notice, unless the landlord agrees in writing to continue the lease in exchange for receiving partial payment.

To_____

_____ is authorized to receive said rent, so due.

_____

OWNER

_____

By _____

Dated this_____day of_____ 20 _____

AGENT OR ATTORNEY

FORM 16-R UNIVERSITY PRINTING CO., CHICAGO 60613

— FOLD —

STATE OF ILLINOIS

COUNTY OF_____ } SS.

AFFIDAVIT OF SERVICE

_____, being duly sworn, on oath deposes and says

(Served by)

that on the_____day of_____, 20 _____he served the above notice on the tenant named above, as follows:*

☐ (1) by delivering a copy thereof to the above named tenant, _____.

☐ (2) by delivering a copy thereof to _____, a person above the age of twelve years, residing on or in charge of the above described premises.

☐ (3) by sending a copy thereof to said tenant by certified or registered mail, return receipt requested, postage prepaid, at the address for tenant at the beginning of tenant's lease or such other address as tenant may previously have designated by written notice.

☐ (4) (in the event of apparent abandonment only) by posting a copy thereof on the main door of the above described premises, no one being in actual possession thereof.

Subscribed and sworn to before me this_____day of

_____, 20 _____.

_____ Notary Public

X _____

*Identify the method of service used by placing a check in the proper box. Sign on line marked X.

Source: Chicago Association of Realtors®. Used with permission.

Be aware that, in effect, this is a six-day notice. If you serve the notice on the sixth of the month, you cannot file any further papers in court until the twelfth of the month.

At the same time that you issue the five-day notice, you can include an explanatory cover letter (see Figure 8.4).

Filling out the notice. Office supply stores that sell legal forms can supply you with a five-day notice form. (Use Figure 8.3.) The top part of the notice must be filled out before being delivered to a tenant. States vary in their requirements of posting and delivering notices, so check with your attorney to make sure the method described below is the correct one in your area.

FIGURE 8.4 *Five-Day Notice Cover Letter*

Mid-America Management

Dear Resident:

Enclosed, please find a copy of a five-day notice for your unpaid rent. This five-day notice is a legal notice that you have five days in which to pay your rent. This is a demand for payment! Do not construe this as a release from your responsibilities for the apartment which you now occupy. Should you not pay your rent in the prescribed time, legal action in the form of forcible eviction will be entered against you. Should you move out and not pay your rent, a five day notice is not a release. As stated earlier, this is a demand for payment.

Under the law, you will be responsible for the apartment for the reminding term of the lease, whether you are occupying the apartment or not, until the apartment is re-rented. Therefore, it is important that you understand that merely vacating the apartment does not release you from the responsibility of the lease. To avoid any further charges, such as late charges and legal fees, which the lease states you are required to pay, please pay your rent within the prescribed five-day period. Please be advised that, to assist you with your debt, we do accept VISA and MASTERCARD for rent payments. Should you vacate without paying, a judgement will be entered against you which will appear on your credit record. You would also be liable for wage garnishments against your earnings or any savings or checking accounts you may have in effect.

Should you have any further questions concerning this matter, please contact your site manager.

Regards,

4704 3/00

Mid-America Management Corp.
2901 Butterfield Road, Oak Brook, Illinois 60523 (630) 574-2400

The amount indicated as due must be rent only; it should not include late charges, security deposit, repair charges, and so on. Write in the amount of one normal month's rent as shown on the lease or extension. If a partial payment has been made, fill in the actual amount of rent still owed.

The rent is considered due for the full month, even if the resident has already paid a partial amount. A month's rent is not considered paid until the full amount is received. Be sure to record the beginning and ending dates of that month on the notice.

Other information to record on the top part of the form is the complete name and address of the tenant, and a complete description of the property, including location (city and county), street address, and apartment number, if applicable.

The bottom part of the five-day notice ("Affidavit of Service") is completed after the tenant has been served with the notice. On delivery, the original copy is filled out according to the sample. The first line of the bottom section ("Served by") is for the name of the person who actually serves the notice. This individual should be the owner or the owner's agent.

The person who served the notice signs the form at the bottom in the presence of a notary public any time prior to the time of filing for court eviction.

Delivering the notice. The form offers four possible modes of delivery. The preferred mode is for the owner to personally serve the notice to the principal adult tenant. The notice may also be served to an occupant above 13 years of age or to an individual in charge, such as a babysitter.

Delivery by certified mail is not recommended because the eviction cannot be filed until the proof of receipt has been returned. It used to be permissible to post the notice on the apartment door, but this practice is no longer acceptable in most states.

Partial payments. Tenants may attempt to pay part of the overdue rent during the period covered by the five-day notice, but you don't have to accept a partial payment. You are only obligated to accept the full amount indicated on the five-day notice.

If you want to keep the tenants, it might be a good idea to accept a partial payment, but if you want to evict them, insist on full payment. Accepting partial payments may only delay the inevitable.

If you accept a partial payment, you can still pursue the tenant for the balance due. Whatever you do, be consistent in the treatment of all residents. Don't make exceptions for some and not for others.

Follow-up action. In most cases a five-day notice motivates tenants to pay; if not, you'll have to take further action. If a tenant has not given you rent on the sixth day following service of the five-day notice, you can issue a Legal Action Notice Letter (see Figure 8.5). This form lets the tenant know that you are serious about an eviction, and it may motivate him or her to pay. Otherwise, proceed directly to filing eviction papers if you seriously want to evict the tenant.

Eviction

It's a good idea to retain a lawyer to represent you for your first eviction; after that you can probably carry out evictions yourself. The following four steps describe the usual process:

1. On the seventh day after filing the five-day notice, file eviction papers in county circuit court and obtain a court date, usually in two or three weeks. The court (or possibly you or your lawyer) will serve the eviction papers on the tenant.
2. Show up for court on the court date. If the tenant doesn't show up, the judge will order in your favor but will give the tenant at least a seven-day stay. If the tenant does show up, a lenient judge may grant an automatic

FIGURE 8.5 *Legal Action Notice Letter*

Date:

Dear _____:

We have referred your delinquent rental account to our attorneys. They will file an eviction suit against you _____ (date) in the County Circuit Court. They will ask for possession of your apartment and for a judgment against you for all rent due, plus late charges, attorneys' fees, and all costs and expenses involved with this matter. You will be served with a copy of the complaint and a summons to appear in court.

However, if you pay the rent due plus late fees and other costs (total costs to date: $_____), we will stop the legal proceedings that have been initiated against you. We will not accept partial payment.

To avoid a forcible eviction by the County Sheriff's Department, possible damage to your credit standing, a judgment and garnishment of wages, and future credit bureau and collection agency action, please phone me immediately at _____ and arrange to make payment.

Sincerely,

_____

two-week stay to allow the tenant more time to come up with the rent. If the tenant claims hardship (illness, unemployment, small children involved, difficulty finding other housing), the delay could be a month or more.

3. If the tenant doesn't pay within the court-decreed stay, another stay is possible for hardship. You take the eviction order to the sheriff's department to set up an eviction date, usually in two or three weeks. Again, these papers are served on the tenant.

4. The tenant will usually move out before an actual physical eviction; if not, a moving company hired by the sheriff (and paid for by you) will come and move the tenant out. At this time you regain possession of the property.

This is clearly a long, time-consuming process. And even if you don't retain an attorney, a number of filing fees must be paid. If the tenant has decided not to pay, you will lose a month or more of rent during the eviction process. Attorney fees to process an eviction vary and may be awarded to you by the court.

COLLECTING A JUDGMENT

Partial Payments

If the tenant attempts to pay part of the overdue rent during the period covered by the five-day notice, you don't have to accept it. You are obligated to accept only the full amount indicated on the five-day notice. In general, accept partial payments from tenants you want to keep; but don't accept partial payments from tenants you want to evict. After a resident makes a partial payment, you can—but do not have to—serve another five-day notice indicating the balance due.

After a delinquent tenant moves out, you can begin activities to recover the amount due. Winning in court doesn't mean you will automatically be paid. The court may award you a judgment, but you must enforce it, so you'll probably have to take additional action to collect the funds.

Using a Collection Agency or Attorney

When tenants have moved out without notice, have been evicted, have damaged the property in excess of the security deposit, or have moved owing you back rent, the debt can be turned over to a collection agency or attorney.

Depending on the circumstances, it might be better to use a collection agency rather than an attorney. Collection agencies are usually licensed by the state, and licenses can be revoked in the event a collection law is violated. Collection attorneys operate on their own and are controlled only by their peers in the bar association. In either case, it is vital to select a reputable and talented attorney or agency. Collecting bad debts requires special skills and experience, and is usually best handled by professionals. Collection agencies normally work on a contingency basis, generally charging a percentage of the amount collected as their fee.

Even with the help of a professional collection specialist, you may not suceed in collecting bad debts from tenants. Thus, you should initiate legal proceedings promptly to minimize potential loss.

A collection agency needs as much information as possible to track down a former tenant. You can use the Transmittal Form (see Figure 8.6) to forward

FIGURE 8.6 *Transmittal Form*

Date: _____

_____

_____

_____

Gentlemen:

Enclosed are the necessary documents relating to the EVICTION, POSSESSION, FORCIBLE DETAINER and/or COLLECTION of Accounts Receivable for apartment: _____ at

_____

Names of Residents: _____/_____

Monthly Rent:	$ _____ times _____ months		=	$ _____
Months Included:				
Other Charges:	$ _____ for _____		=	$ _____
SUBTOTAL:			=	$ _____
Attorney Fees:			=	$ _____
Court Costs:			=	$ _____
TOTAL DUE:			=	$ _____

Please send COLLECTION letter before beginning suit. _____

Please begin suit immediately. _____

Please send a letter demanding tenant take remedial action to cure default as listed.

Comments: _____

_____

Please notify us of any actions taken by tenant as a result of your efforts. We will notify you immediately of any action or receipt of any funds on behalf of the tenant.

information to the collections manager. If possible, obtain the tenants' forwarding address before he or she leaves the property for the purpose of forwarding mail or returning the security deposit. It's important to obtain the current place of employment in case it becomes necessary to garnishee wages, if permissible by law. Other approaches that might prove successful in obtaining a forwarding address include the following:

- Recording the license plate number on the tenant's car and contacting the secretary of state
- Contacting the moving company
- Calling the old telephone number to see if calls are being referred to a new number
- Contacting the referred person listed on the application for notification in case of emergency
- Sending a notice to the previous address and stamping the envelope "Do Not Forward"

INSURANCE

Dan Nixon has been involved in some aspect of real estate—both independently and with others—since he joined his father's firm, Nixon and Nixon, at age 21.

"Our history has been to diversify our portfolio over time." That's one reason why Dan is focusing on the self-storage side of the Utah-based investment-landlord business. Another reason is that it's performing well compared with other real estate sectors, which are experiencing high vacancy rates. Indeed, several investors have been eager to get involved in financing the storage facilities that Dan's company has built in four Utah locations.

"Studies tell us that 17 to 18 percent of the American population never use self-storage. But that's because self-storage facilities tend to be tucked away out of sight in undesirable industrial parks. Now they're being built in residential areas—right beside high-profile commercial centers with grocery stores, banks, and other retailers—and people are seeing them." In addition, many existing buildings are being converted to self-storage facilities in urban neighborhoods that are going through a renaissance.

In recent years, more facilities offer climate-controlled storage, which attracts, for example, pharmaceutical reps who store samples there rather than in warehouses or their homes. Although it can be difficult to get storage units zoned in residential neighborhoods and in high-traffic locations, an owner-operator like Dan takes up the challenge to "sell" municipalities on their benefits: self-storage complexes are safe and secure, they generate little traffic, they don't impact schools, and new ones are designed to fit in with upscale neighborhoods.

Self-storage developer Eric Bush in Denver, Colorado, agrees that getting approval for zoning in desirable locations can be tough. "Self-storage properties are among the most difficult pieces of real estate to get entitled because they don't generate sales tax. Still, I consider self-storage among the best real estate investments out there." Typically, it takes a 60 to 70 percent occupancy rate to break even, depending on how the property is financed. Operating expenses tend to run 35 to 40 percent of gross income.

Whether it's self-storage property or other kinds of property, Dan believes investing and landlording go hand in hand. When he first got into the self-storage business, he performed a lot of due diligence and was eager to learn new things. "I'd hire consultants and attend conferences, aggressively seeking the good advice of experts in the business."

About property management in general, he says, "So many people try this business for a short time and quit because it's difficult. I tell aspiring landlords not to expect it to be fun. After all, they still have to deal with those calls in the middle of the night when something goes wrong.

"Give this time," he advises. "You can have fun when you get rich. Make a solid, committed effort for 20 years to build your asset base in real estate. Move slowly and methodically but rarely sell. When you need to generate cash to buy other properties, it's almost always better to carefully leverage against your current ones than to sell them. Be conservative with your finances and don't live off the income from them, at least not for a long time."

A fellow member of the Self-Storage Association (SSA), Charlie Broomfield used to be in politics and government in his home state of Missouri before he got into lobbying. As a lobbyist, he was asked by a group of self-storage owners to assist in getting a specific law passed. "I had to learn about the industry to do a good job for them. I agreed to help them if they'd show me the ropes. That's when I bought my own storage business—20 years ago."

Self-storage attracted him because, compared to other kinds of properties, headaches are minimal, plus laws exist to protect owners when the headaches show up. For example, if a payment doesn't come in within 45 days of its due date and the manager has given the delinquent renter sufficient notice, the business can confiscate all the items left in storage and sell them.

"We have about ten no-pays a year, and we hold a sale to get rid of their possessions two or three times a year. The last thing we want to do is sell someone's property so we often wait longer than 45 days. But once a renter's payment is six months late, we toss in the towel."

Charlie, Eric, and Dan would agree that having excellent drive-by visibility is the secret to success. Charlie's 500-unit self-storage is adjacent to a busy highway. In addition to this visibility, his marketing centers on four tactics: Yellow Pages ads, good signage, referrals, and repeat customers.

Convenience proves to be more important than price in this industry, and the average amount of time someone rents a unit for is 6 months (although Charlie has one customer who has kept his unit for 15 years). "For many years, we thought this industry wasn't strongly affected by changes in the economy, but over time we're finding that's not true. Storage rental rates are tied to real estate sales and unemployment, which can affect our business as much as 15 percent."

Both Dan and Charlie highly recommend getting involved in the Self-Storage Association (http://www.ssa.org). In fact, Charlie is founder, executive director, and president of the Missouri Self-Storage Association and treasurer of the national association. He points out that the SSA holds a convention and trade show every year as does Virgo Publishing (http://www.insideselfstorage .com/expo)—both places where education and networking go hand in hand.

THE LANGUAGE OF INSURANCE

The following definitions, explanations, and examples are provided so you may better understand this chapter.

All-risk. Insurance policies that provide coverage for all perils except those excluded. Be sure to read the exclusions portion of your policy.

Bailee. Whenever property is delivered into the custody of a person other than the rightful owner, the person in control of the property becomes the bailee and assumes certain responsibilities for the safety of property in his or her care.

Care, custody, and control. Damage to the personal property of others that is in the care, custody, or control of the insured is excluded under all standard liability forms. You should purchase a bailee endorsement or policy to cover this exposure.

As a bailee, you may store an article for another, accept packages for your tenants to pick up from you, and/or borrow a piece of equipment. Discuss with your agent your possible bailee exposure.

Certificates of insurance. You should require contractors who do work for you to supply a certificate of insurance in order to limit your liability in case of mishaps. Certificates should show liability coverage for bodily injury and property damage and for workers' compensation and employers' liability. Figure 9.1 shows how a certificate of insurance looks when completed.

If a suit arises and you can't provide proof that the contractor had insurance, your policy may pay on your behalf when you are sued. However, your insurance company may then require you to pay a premium for this additional exposure or may cancel your coverage as a result of this discovery.

Coinsurance. Coinsurance indicates a sharing of the insurance by the insurance company and the insured, but the word *coinsurance* has a more limited and restricted meaning within the insurance business.

The mandatory and minimum amount of coinsurance is usually 80 percent. Illustrating the coinsurance clause by example best explains its meaning and application. For example, a property with an actual cash value of $100,000 must be insured for at least 80 percent of the value of the property, or $80,000.

In this case, $80,000 would be the minimum coverage required to avoid a penalty in the event of a loss. If the same building is insured for $60,000 in lieu of the required $80,000, it would be insured for only three-fourths of the minimum coverage demanded by coinsurance requirements. In this instance, a penalty would be imposed should a loss occur.

In the event of a $1,000 loss, exclusive of all deductibles, the insured would receive, not $1,000, but three-fourths of the loss, or $750. In the event of a total loss, however, the insured would collect the full face value of the policy, or $60,000. Because the property was valued at $100,000 before the loss, the insured is still penalized for not having insured sufficiently—a $40,000 penalty.

The coinsurance clause is taken very seriously in the insurance business; an insured who doesn't adhere to its requirements can expect to receive less than full value when faced with a loss.

Deductibles. The use of a deductible means the insured pays the first dollar amount for a loss, as specified in the policy. Unless changed by endorsement, a standard $100 deductible may apply separately to each building (and its contents), subject to a $1,000 aggregate per occurrence.

Premium dollars can be saved by increasing the deductible. A larger deductible will mean a larger financial outlay in the event of a loss and may mean total responsibility for smaller losses, but it will also result in an immediate savings on the premium.

Deductibles are applied in three different ways:

1. Occurrence: One fire or other insured loss equals one occurrence and one deductible applies.
2. Per claim: This applies to every claim filed regardless of the number of occurrences. One fire may produce six or more claims, and six or more deductibles will apply.
3. Aggregate (either occurrence or annual): With a $25,000 annual aggregate deductible, the insured retains a maximum of $25,000 of losses in a given year and the insurer is responsible for any additional loss payments in that year.

Physical hazard. This is a characteristic that increases the chance of loss. Some hazards arise from a repairable defect in the property (for example, a broken step); others are inherent characteristics of the property (for example, a building is of frame construction).

Premium. This is money that the insured pays the insurer for coverage of a defined nature, an exchange that must take place prior to or at the inception date of coverage. You may be surprised to find you are not insured if a loss occurs prior to premium payment. A large premium can be financed with monthly or quarterly payments by a premium finance company at interest rates close to bank prime rates.

Property values. Insured values reflect not market value but the construction cost; that is, the cost to rebuild at the time of loss. Unless specifically endorsed or stated in the coverage form, all property is valued at actual cash value (ACV) at the time of loss. ACV is defined as the cost to repair or replace the damaged property less an amount for physical depreciation. This basis of adjustment may be modified, however, by the attachment of a replacement cost endorsement.

Punitive or exemplary damage awards. Most companies exclude responsibility for payment of any award for punitive or exemplary damage. Responding to and complying with insurance company recommendations adds to your noticeable effort to provide a safe environment for your tenants and is beneficial in the defense of suits that may arise.

Self-insured retention (SIR). That portion of a loss that you pay (similar to a deductible). Excess insurance is usually purchased over a large retention reserve.

Vacancy. This means there are no furnishings or other personal property in the building. Some insurers consider a property to be vacant when there are no full-time occupants. Most policies contain a clause that suspends coverage when a building is vacant beyond a stated period, normally 30 days. Vacancy policies are available but are very expensive.

PROPERTY INSURANCE

As the owner of an income property, carrying insurance to protect your investment and its income against catastrophe is a good practice. The following summary is provided for general information purposes only and is subject to the terms and conditions of your individual policies, which may vary.

Because no two properties are alike, there is no all-purpose insurance policy that will cover all buildings. Instead, an insurance agent issues a multiperil package (sometimes called a business owner's package), which consists of property and liability insurance along with a number of endorsements and/or riders. The purpose of this coverage is to protect you from loss from damage to your property.

Two types of property are to be considered: (1) real property and (2) business personal property. Virtually all real property, except foundations and underground improvements, is included in the definition of a building under a policy.

Most policies define a building as buildings, structures, additions, fixtures, appliances, permanent equipment, and machinery used for the maintenance and service of a building. Some companies include fences and TV antennas, but most do not. Piers, wharves, docks, pools, and valuable landscaping must be separately insured. Be sure to check what is included in the definition of real property on your policy.

Business personal property includes rental office contents on premises, lobby and recreational room contents, model apartment contents, and furnished unit contents.

Limitations or Exclusions

Types of property that might have limited coverage or be excluded from this package of coverage include tenant improvements and betterments, boiler and machinery, leased equipment, money and securities, valuable papers, private collections, landscaping, and mobile equipment, such as trucks, automobiles, watercraft, and aircraft.

ENDORSEMENT OPTIONS

Endorsements are separate documents attached to policies that modify a policy's original terms. These are the ten common endorsements:

1. Agreed-amount endorsement
2. Inflation-guard endorsement
3. Replacement-cost endorsement
4. Demolition-and-increased-cost-of-construction endorsement
5. Difference-in-conditions (DIC) endorsement
6. Earthquake endorsement
7. Fine arts schedule
8. Glass endorsement
9. Loss-of-rents endorsement
10. Flood
11. Terrorism
12. Mold

Agreed-Amount Endorsement

It is practical to establish a fixed value on your real insurable property to which the insurance underwriter will agree in advance. This agreement serves to eliminate coinsurance. For superior property, an agreed-amount clause is a means of protecting against the consequence of inadvertent underinsurance in an inflationary environment.

Through this endorsement, a coinsurance clause is superseded and a specified amount of insurance takes the place of a specified percentage of actual cash value (ACV) or replacement cost. Partial losses are paid in full after the deductible has been applied. Total losses are paid to the policy limit after the deductible.

Inflation-Guard Endorsement

Under this type of endorsement, the property coverage is automatically increased by a specific percentage each month (or quarter) to help meet rising construction and replacement costs.

Ask your agent to include this feature in your policy to prevent future coinsurance penalties or underinsurance.

Replacement-Cost Endorsement

This endorsement eliminates the deduction for depreciation in property valuation at the time of a loss. It is used in lieu of actual cash value (ACV) or depreciated value.

Coverage is limited to either the cost of restoring the property to its original (non-depreciated) condition or the actual cost of repairing or replacing the property, whichever is less.

Policies will pay on a replacement cost basis only if the damaged property is repaired or replaced at the same premises within a reasonable time after the loss.

Where replacement may take a significant amount of time, you may elect to settle on an ACV basis initially and, after the property has been restored, settle the balance due on a replacement-cost basis.

Demolition-and-Increased-Cost-of-Construction and Contingent-Liability Endorsement

The ordinance or law exclusion in most property policies excludes loss from operation resulting from the enforcement of building codes that require demolition of partially damaged structures and mandate superior construction in new or replacement buildings. Demolition coverage, which may be included by endorsement to the standard fire or all-risk policies, provides coverage for the cost of demolition and the loss from that remaining undamaged portion of the building that must be demolished when required by local ordinance.

The demolition endorsement is often combined with an increased-cost-of-construction endorsement that affords coverage for the difference in costs between the original damaged construction and the new, upgraded construction required by current building codes. Ordinances mandating superior construction are common in many cities where fire or earthquake codes have been changed over the years. Check your local ordinance.

Difference-in-Conditions (DIC) Endorsement

This endorsement can add back coverage for some of the normal exclusions found in most policies. Backup of sewers and drains, wind-driven rain, off-premises power failure, and off-premises water damage (example: a break in a city water main resulting in damage to premises) are normal exclusions under the basic fire policy.

Earthquake Endorsement

Coverage for damage from earthquakes and resulting aftershocks within 72 hours may be provided by endorsements to the standard fire or all-risk policy or by special all-risk forms and DIC policies. Coverage includes damage to excavations, foundations, and pilings, which are excluded under the standard fire policy.

Deductibles are generally quite high and rates are determined primarily by location and type of building construction.

Fine Arts Schedule

Any sculptures, antiques, and other artwork must be scheduled by endorsements on the policy. Be sure to advise your agent of the existence of these objects if you wish to insure them.

Glass Endorsement

Most apartment package policies limit glass coverage. If there is a large percentage of glass in the makeup of the building structure, additional coverage should be purchased. This may be accomplished by endorsing the apartment package policy or by purchasing a separate policy.

Discuss with the insurance agent any unique types of glass such as stained glass, neon and fluorescent signs, and structural glass and lettering or ornamentation on these items. Coverage includes the repair or replacement of frames when necessary.

Loss-of-Rents Endorsement

This clause provides for reimbursement of rents lost, less any discontinued expense, when the loss is caused by an insured peril under the policy. It's best to purchase this coverage on the basis of actual loss sustained within a 12-month period or 100 percent of annual value.

Flood

The Federal Flood Program will provide coverage up to $250,000 per building for flood damage when the building is located in a designated flood zone. Your local zoning or building code office will be able to tell you if your property is located in such a zone. This is a separate policy, not an endorsement. Apply for coverage through your insurance agent. The coverage is not effective until 30 days after a completed application and payment of premium is received by the Federal Flood Program Agency. An exception to this: If the property is a new purchase and a mortgagee is involved, the 30-day wait is waived.

Additional coverage may be purchased through a DIC (difference in conditions) policy. You may use the Federal Flood Program as coverage for the large deductible required under the DIC policy.

Terrorism

Since the events of 9/11, all coverage exclusions for terrorism are prohibited by the Terrorism Risk Insurance Act of 2002. All insurers of direct commercial property and casualty insurance are required to participate in the program. The insurance company must notify you of the cost of the terrorism coverage. You will have a 30-day window to reject or accept the coverage. If you do not reply and/or pay the additional premium, the coverage will be rendered void.

Mold

Insurance companies are beginning to exclude mold-related claims, so be sure to check with your agent. If the exclusion is in your policy, you may consider a buy-back.

LIABILITY INSURANCE

The purpose of liability insurance is to protect you against a lawsuit arising from some accidental or unintended occurrence. General liability protects against claims arising from premises, products, incidental contracts, libel, false arrest, and so on.

The liability portion of a policy is generally written on a comprehensive basis for any occurrence arising out of the ownership, maintenance, or use of the premises and for operations that are necessary or incidental to the property, such as lawsuits arising out of slips and falls, and certain liabilities assumed under contracts or agreements. The limits are usually combined single limits for bodily injury and property damage liability and range from $300,000 to $1,000,000. Coverage of employee injuries is not included and must be purchased under a workers' compensation and employers' liability policy.

An annual aggregate limit restricts the total amount that will be paid for liability coverage in any one policy year. Most policies include a limit for all occurrences within a policy year as well as the per occurrence limit. Be sure to check which limit you have purchased because of this annual aggregate limitation. An umbrella, or excess, policy purchase will be important to your protection.

Liability Policies

Liability policies are of two types: (1) claims-made and (2) occurrence-based. A claims-made policy differs from an occurrence policy primarily in the manner in which coverage is triggered.

Occurrence-based policies cover events that occur during the policy period, and the insurance company is obligated to defend and pay for claims that arise from such covered occurrences at any time in the future, even years later. On the other hand, claims-made policies obligate the insurance company to defend and pay for only those claims reported while the policy is in force and for incidents that occurred on or after the retroactive date (usually the policy effective date). In other words, in a claims-made policy the company will pay claims for any occurrences on or after the retroactive date and only up until the policy expires.

If your coverage is the claims-made type, yet you want coverage to last for a certain period after the policy expiration or cancellation, one option is to purchase an extended reporting period (sometimes called tail coverage) for your policy. This extends coverage to protect against claims that may be made after a policy is no longer in force.

Umbrella, or Excess Liability Policy

It is prudent to protect your assets with an umbrella, or excess limits liability, policy. The policy adds at least $1,000,000 of protection to primary liability policy limits of commercial, auto, and employers' liability, and insures many uncovered liability exposures for $1,000,000 or more over a self-insured retention, normally $10,000 or $25,000.

Pollution Liability Exclusion

The commercial liability policy excludes all pollution coverage. The exclusion is built into the policy itself and cannot be removed by endorsement. You should research your property to determine whether you have an exposure to pollution liability. If an exposure exists and coverage is desired, a special application and survey must be completed.

As the result of a growing need for property owners to protect themselves against financial liability associated with environmental damage, environmental impairment insurance is available.

Broad Form Commercial General Liability (CGL)

Broad form commercial includes contractual, personal injury that includes libel, slander, and false arrest (discrimination or humiliation coverage is included but limited), advertising, premises medical, host liquor, fire legal, incidental medical malpractice, non-owned watercraft, limited worldwide coverage, employees as additional insured, automatic coverage for newly acquired entities, and broad form property damage that adds back coverage for property in your care, custody, and control. Some of these are discussed below; others were defined earlier in this chapter. Your agent can explain how these options apply to your property.

Contractual (Independent Contractors)

You may have occasion to enter into contracts employing others, such as painters, roofers, and so on. When the contractor enters your premises or does work on your behalf, she or he may incur or cause injury claims for which you may be held liable. Some of the claims asserted against you by people injured by the contractor are covered by your own policy under the commercial general liability section if your agent has included independent contractors on an "if any" basis.

In some states, if a contractor cannot respond to a workers' compensation claim, the person for whom the injured employee is working (you) may have to respond. Therefore, you should request evidence that the contractor carries liability and workers' compensation insurance before he or she begins the job. This evidence is normally provided in the form of a certificate of insurance, which is obtained from the contractor's insurance broker (see Figure 9.1).

Medical Payments

Coverage is automatically provided in the amounts of $1,000 or more per person and $10,000 or $25,000 for all persons requiring medical attention as a result of a single accident arising from owned or rented premises. Some policies exclude payments on behalf of tenants or residents; and liability need not be proven.

Personal Injury

You face risks for claims other than bodily injury or property damage. If you libel or slander someone, invade a person's privacy, commit a trespass, or mistakenly accuse someone of a crime, you can be sued by the person so injured. Indemnity for certain personal injuries is in the insuring agreement of the commercial liability section of the policy.

Host Liquor

If a host serves liquor (without charge) to guests who subsequently, while intoxicated, cause bodily injury or property damage to others, the host may be held liable.

FIGURE 9.1 *Certificate of Insurance Form*

ACORD™ CERTIFICATE OF LIABILITY INSURANCE		DATE (MM/DD/YYYY)

PRODUCER	THIS CERTIFICATE IS ISSUED AS A MATTER OF INFORMATION ONLY AND CONFERS NO RIGHTS UPON THE CERTIFICATE HOLDER. THIS CERTIFICATE DOES NOT AMEND, EXTEND OR ALTER THE COVERAGE AFFORDED BY THE POLICIES BELOW.	
	INSURERS AFFORDING COVERAGE	**NAIC #**
INSURED	INSURER A:	
	INSURER B:	
	INSURER C:	
	INSURER D:	
	INSURER E:	

COVERAGES

THE POLICIES OF INSURANCE LISTED BELOW HAVE BEEN ISSUED TO THE INSURED NAMED ABOVE FOR THE POLICY PERIOD INDICATED. NOTWITHSTANDING ANY REQUIREMENT, TERM OR CONDITION OF ANY CONTRACT OR OTHER DOCUMENT WITH RESPECT TO WHICH THIS CERTIFICATE MAY BE ISSUED OR MAY PERTAIN, THE INSURANCE AFFORDED BY THE POLICIES DESCRIBED HEREIN IS SUBJECT TO ALL THE TERMS, EXCLUSIONS AND CONDITIONS OF SUCH POLICIES. AGGREGATE LIMITS SHOWN MAY HAVE BEEN REDUCED BY PAID CLAIMS.

INSR LTR	ADD'L INSRD	TYPE OF INSURANCE	POLICY NUMBER	POLICY EFFECTIVE DATE (MM/DD/YY)	POLICY EXPIRATION DATE (MM/DD/YY)	LIMITS	
		GENERAL LIABILITY				EACH OCCURRENCE	$
		☐ COMMERCIAL GENERAL LIABILITY				DAMAGE TO RENTED PREMISES (Ea occurence)	$
		☐ CLAIMS MADE ☐ OCCUR				MED EXP (Any one person)	$
						PERSONAL & ADV INJURY	$
						GENERAL AGGREGATE	$
		GEN'L AGGREGATE LIMIT APPLIES PER: ☐ POLICY ☐ PRO-JECT ☐ LOC				PRODUCTS - COMP/OP AGG	$
		AUTOMOBILE LIABILITY				COMBINED SINGLE LIMIT (Ea accident)	$
		☐ ANY AUTO					
		☐ ALL OWNED AUTOS ☐ SCHEDULED AUTOS				BODILY INJURY (Per person)	$
		☐ HIRED AUTOS ☐ NON-OWNED AUTOS				BODILY INJURY (Per accident)	$
						PROPERTY DAMAGE (Per accident)	$
		GARAGE LIABILITY				AUTO ONLY - EA ACCIDENT	$
		☐ ANY AUTO				OTHER THAN AUTO ONLY: EA ACC	$
						AGG	$
		EXCESS/UMBRELLA LIABILITY				EACH OCCURRENCE	$
		☐ OCCUR ☐ CLAIMS MADE				AGGREGATE	$
							$
		☐ DEDUCTIBLE					$
		☐ RETENTION $					$
		WORKERS COMPENSATION AND EMPLOYERS' LIABILITY ANY PROPRIETOR/PARTNER/EXECUTIVE OFFICER/MEMBER EXCLUDED? If yes, describe under SPECIAL PROVISIONS below				☐ WC STATU-TORY LIMITS ☐ OTH-ER	
						E.L. EACH ACCIDENT	$
						E.L. DISEASE - EA EMPLOYEE	$
						E.L. DISEASE - POLICY LIMIT	$
		OTHER					

DESCRIPTION OF OPERATIONS / LOCATIONS / VEHICLES / EXCLUSIONS ADDED BY ENDORSEMENT / SPECIAL PROVISIONS

CERTIFICATE HOLDER	**CANCELLATION**
	SHOULD ANY OF THE ABOVE DESCRIBED POLICIES BE CANCELLED BEFORE THE EXPIRATION DATE THEREOF, THE ISSUING INSURER WILL ENDEAVOR TO MAIL _____ DAYS WRITTEN NOTICE TO THE CERTIFICATE HOLDER NAMED TO THE LEFT, BUT FAILURE TO DO SO SHALL IMPOSE NO OBLIGATION OR LIABILITY OF ANY KIND UPON THE INSURER, ITS AGENTS OR REPRESENTATIVES.
	AUTHORIZED REPRESENTATIVE

ACORD 25 (2001/08)   © ACORD CORPORATION 1988

Source: ACORD. Used with permission.

MAKING CLAIMS

One of the conditions of an insurance policy is that you promptly give notice to the insurer of any accident or occurrence and of any claim or suit brought against you. An occurrence is an incident such as someone falling on your premises, an error that causes loss or injury to a person, or any unplanned event that could give cause to a lawsuit.

If you fail to give reasonable notice, you may be shocked to find that the insurance company's obligations to defend you and pay any claims have been waived. Therefore, report any notice of a lawsuit the same day it is received, if possible.

Notice is normally given by contacting the agent or broker who sold you the policy. To protect yourself, it is wise to give notice in writing and to get written confirmation from the agent acknowledging that your notice has been received and forwarded to the insurer.

Don't attempt to judge whether insurance applies before reporting. You should make a report regardless of coverage. If there is a serious question in your mind whether the policy covers the claim, consult your attorney for assistance in giving notice to the insurer. A poorly drafted notice may prompt the insurer to deny coverage rather than investigate and pay the claim.

Property Claims

Property damage claims should be made promptly. To report property claims, use the property loss form provided by your insurance carrier. A sample Property Loss Report is included as Figure 9.2.

Photos should be taken when damage to your property occurs and you have to make immediate repairs to prevent further loss. It isn't necessary to wait for the claims adjuster before you do whatever emergency repairs are necessary to prevent further loss. Be sure to retain any damaged, replaced materials or objects for the adjuster to view on arrival. Most property policies cover your insured property if you move it to a safer place to avoid loss or further damage.

Liability Claims

To report liability claims use the Liability Loss Report form (see Figure 9.4) and the Incident Report form (see Figure 9.3) provided by your carrier to assist you in providing necessary information to the insurance company's claim adjuster.

FIGURE 9.2 *Property Loss Report*

Property Loss Report

Reported By: _____ Date: _____

Complex: _____

Date of Loss: _____

Contact Person: _____ Phone Number: _____

Location of Loss: _____

Kind of Loss (Fire, Wind, Explosion, etc.): _____

Description of Loss and Damage: _____

_____

_____

_____

_____

Estimated Amount of Loss: _____

Police or Fire Department Reported to: _____

Claimant's Name, Address, and Phone Number: _____

_____

_____

_____

Additional Comments: _____

_____

_____

_____

_____

_____

FIGURE 9.3 *Incident Report*

PRIVILEGED & CONFIDENTIAL

INCIDENT
LOSS REPORT

** FOR CORPORATE USE ONLY **	
DATE REPORTED:	_____
AGENT REPORTED TO:	_____
INSURANCE CARRIER:	_____
POLICY NO.:	_____
POLICY PERIOD:	_____
LOCATION CODE:	_____
REPORTED BY:	_____

Property Name: _____

Address:_____

Date of Report: _____ Date Reported to You: _____

Date of Incident: _____ Time of Incident _____ am/pm

Person Claim Reported To: _____ Title: _____

Contact Person: _____ Title: _____ Telephone No.: _____

PERSON INVOLVED IN INCIDENT (Please print or type)

Name: _____ Spouse: _____

Address:_____

Telephone No.: Home _____ Work _____ Age: _____ Sex: _____

Is person involved a tenant, employee, other?_____

Did person involved report the incident?   Y   N

Alleged injury/personal property damage: _____

Exact location/address where incident occurred i.e., parking lot/sidewalk/stairs (interior/exterior):

_____

How incident allegedly occurred/cause (describe in detail): _____

_____

Weather conditions: _____

Type of shoes worn (if slip & fall): _____

Any indication of the involvement of alcohol in this incident?   Y   N   Unknown

    Specify:_____

Were pictures taken of incident area?   Y   N   Contact: _____

Reported to Police/Fire/Paramedics?   Y   N   Specify: _____

Treating Hospital (if known): _____

Renter's Insurance Company: _____ Policy No.: _____

Name of Agent: _____ Telephone No.: _____

ANY KNOWN WITNESSES

Name: _____ Telephone No.: _____

Address: _____

Additional Comments: _____

_____

_____

Signature: _____ Title: _____

Incident Report.pub Rev. 5/13/02

FIGURE 9.4 *Liability Loss Report*

Liability Loss Report

Reported by: _____ Date: _____

Complex: _____

Date of Loss: _____

Contact Person: _____ Phone Number: _____

Injured Party or Damage to Personal Property of Tenants, etc.

Name: _____

Address: _____

Phone Number: _____ Work Number: _____

Age: _____ Sex: _____ Date of Injury: _____

Where Injury Sustained (Address): _____

How Injury Sustained: _____

_____

_____

_____

_____

(If additional space is required, please use reverse side.)

Type of Injury: _____

_____

_____

Treating Hospital: _____

Was Police Department Called? If So, Please Indicate: _____

Additional Comments: _____

_____

_____

_____

_____

The incident report is beneficial in tenant-landlord communications. Using this form to extract information from the tenant or visitor at the time of complaint assures the complainant that proper attention is being given to the incident. The report is then forwarded to the insurance carrier, who responds to the complaint. These are important notes to remember regarding liability incidents:

- Make no statement admitting liability or authorizing medical treatment.
- Take photos of the area when an accident occurs before proceeding with any necessary immediate repairs. If any machine or object may have been responsible for the accident, preserve it, as is, in a safe place until it can be examined by experts.
- Advise any employees not to discuss the case with anyone until instructed by your claims adjuster or attorney.

OTHER TYPES OF INSURANCE

FAIR Plan

In the past, if you were unable to buy insurance for property because it was in a riot-prone or environmentally hazardous urban area, coverage was made available through the Federal Riot Reinsurance Program under the FAIR (Fair Access to Insurance Requirements) Plan. Although this program is no longer federally active, in many states it has become a statewide program, and it is still active in Illinois, for example.

Under this plan, a building must be otherwise insurable except for its location in a blighted or deteriorated but eligible urban area. You must submit an application for eligibility and may be accepted, conditionally accepted, or unconditionally declined. You cannot be declined by reason of environmental hazards in urban areas.

Coverage is generally limited to fire, extended coverage, vandalism, and malicious mischief. Maximum limits are $500,000 at any one location.

Tenants Insurance

As a landlord, encourage your tenants to carry adequate personal property and liability insurance. Landlords have limited liability for injury or damage occurring within the rental portion of the premises. Both landlords and tenants have a duty to take reasonable care in the portion of the premises under their control. For example, if tenant Jones on an upper floor allows his bathtub to overflow and the water drips through the ceiling and ruins rugs in tenant Smith's apartment below, the landlord is not liable because Smith is in exclusive possession of his apartment. The landlord, however, on being advised, must attempt where possible to aid the tenant suffering the loss by turning off the water.

If a tenant causes a fire, damages are paid by the owner's insurance company, which could then seek recovery from the tenant's liability policy, thus protecting the good claims record of the building owner. A high and frequent claims record usually means higher premiums for the building owner as well as the risk of having the policy cancelled or not renewed.

Boiler and Machinery Insurance

Boiler and machinery insurance can be endorsed into many packages or written on a separate policy. Protection includes property damage and legal liability for damage to the property of others in your care, custody, and control, and associated defense costs. A large component of the boiler and machinery premium is for engineering and inspection services.

Boiler coverage. Almost all apartment building policies exclude damage to the insured property resulting from internally caused explosions of boilers or other pressure vessels. Consequently, boiler coverage is needed if the property contains any heating or process boiler or steam generator that operates under pressure. Boilers include hot water boilers, steam boilers, and steam piping.

Boiler explosions are rare, but even one such explosion can be a catastrophic event in terms of destruction and injury. A far more common occurrence is the less destructive, but still costly, cracking, burning, bulging, or collapse of boilers and pressure vessels.

One of the most common failures of boilers is that of the low-water cutoff, the control that shuts off the burner when the water level is low. Such failure generally results in damage from overheating and, in the case of cast-iron boilers, cracked sections. Some building insurance policies don't include coverage for damage caused to the building as a result of a boiler problem (consequential damage). In this case, an insurance policy that includes a boiler inspection service can be as valuable as the coverage itself.

Machinery coverage. Machinery coverage provides insurance against damage and loss resulting from the breakdown of machinery on the premises. Machinery includes such objects as air compressors, fans, air conditioners, blowers, pump units, engines, turbines, and miscellaneous electrical equipment like switchboards and other apparatus used for power distribution. This coverage also extends to surrounding property that is excluded under a building package policy.

It is wise to insure only those machines that are extraordinarily expensive and time consuming to repair or whose function is critical to the entire operation. Again, the insurance company's machinery inspection service can be a valuable component of the insurance policy.

Coverage options in boiler and machinery insurance. Following are some options to consider when choosing how to allocate insurance dollars:

- Repairs and replacement: essentially an elimination of depreciation
- Extra expenses for the period of restoration
- Joint loss agreement (loss-adjustment endorsement) should be obtained when you have different insurers for building and boiler and machinery. This means the boiler carrier will settle the loss and subrogate against the property insurer if necessary.
- Business interruption (loss of rents): on a valued daily or weekly indemnity basis. There are two coverage options:
  1. *Actual loss sustained:* The loss of net profit plus specified fixed charges and expenses that continue despite the accident. This loss must be proven. If coverage is on a coinsurance basis, you should obtain a waiver of coinsurance, if possible. Care must be taken in establishing the valuations.
  2. *Valued form:* A daily indemnity is specified and is the amount of recovery for each day during which rents are totally suspended. In the case of a partial suspension, a portion is paid based on reduction of current business.

Workers' Compensation

Each state has its own workers' compensation law, whereby all workers suffering injury or illness related to the job are reimbursed for medical costs, lost earnings, and rehabilitation costs. When death occurs, an employee's heirs are entitled to death benefits provided by statute.

If you hire employees such as rental agents, cleaners, or maintenance personnel, you must purchase workers' compensation and employers' liability insurance.

Even if you have no direct employees, you should still have voluntary workers' compensation and employers' liability insurance for those situations in which a subcontractor is uninsured or an independent contractor can show employee status. State workers' compensation courts don't always recognize independent contractor arrangements.

The objective of workers' compensation is to indemnify the employee for loss of earnings and expenses. The employer is obligated to pay for the reasonable cost of medical, surgical, hospital, and nursing services as required. An injured employee is also entitled to weekly compensation payment for the length of the disability and rehabilitation services. Workers' compensation statutes in all states now include disease.

Every worker injury involving medical treatment or lost time must be reported on the form used in your state. Each state has its own form; copies are available from your local adjuster or agent. For samples of the Illinois, Indiana, Arizona, and Wisconsin forms, see Figures 9.5 through 9.8.

EMPLOYERS' LIABILITY

A further exposure facing an employer is an action instituted by a third party. This could arise when an injured employee sues and recovers from a legally responsible third party, such as the manufacturer of machinery. This third-party manufacturer may in turn seek recovery from the employer, contending, for example, that the employer is liable for having negligently maintained the machine or having inadequately trained the employee.

A few work-related injuries do not fall under workers' compensation law. If that is the case, the claim is one of employers' liability, which is part of the workers' compensation policy.

Employers' liability coverage, in contrast to workers' compensation coverage, is subject to a specified limit of liability, customarily written at a limit of $100,000 but allowed to be increased to $500,000. It is advisable to have this coverage scheduled on the umbrella, or excess liability, policy to assure that the higher umbrella limits apply. Some umbrella insurers have refused to insure employers' liability incurred by employee disease; therefore, you should request a higher employers' liability on the workers' compensation and employers' liability policy.

DEALING WITH INSURANCE COMPANIES

Begin shopping for insurance coverage at least 90 days before your current coverage expires to allow time to find the best coverage for the lowest premium.

FIGURE 9.5 *Workers' Compensation Claim Form—Illinois*

ILLINOIS FORM 45: EMPLOYER'S FIRST REPORT OF INJURY

Please type or print.

Employer's FEIN	Date of report	Case or File #	Is this a lost workday case? Yes / No

Employer's name	Doing business as

Employer's mailing address

Nature of business or service	SIC code

Name of workers' compensation carrier/admin.	Policy/Contract #	Self-insured? Yes / No

Employee's full name	Social Security #	Birthdate

Employee's mailing address	Employee's e-mail address

Male / Female	Married / Single	# Dependents	Employee's average weekly wage

Job title or occupation	Date hired

Time employee began work AM PM	Date and time of accident	Last day employee worked

If the employee died as a result of the accident, give the date of death.	Did the accident occur on the employer's premises? Yes / No

Address of accident

What was the employee doing when the accident occurred?

How did the accident occur?

What was the injury or illness? List the part of body affected and explain how it was affected.

What object or substance, if any, directly harmed the employee?

Name and address of physician/health care professional

If treatment was given away from the worksite, list the name and address of the place it was given.

Was the employee treated in an emergency room? Yes / No	Was the employee hospitalized overnight as an inpatient? Yes / No

Report prepared by	Signature	Title and telephone #

Please send this form to the ILLINOIS INDUSTRIAL COMMISSION 701 S. SECOND STREET   SPRINGFIELD, IL 62704. IC45 9/03

By law, employers must keep accurate records of all work-related injuries and illness (except for certain minor injuries). Employers shall report to the Commission all injuries resulting in the loss of more than three scheduled workdays. Filing this form does not affect liability under the Workers' Compensation Act and is not incriminatory in any sense. This information is confidential.

FIGURE 9.6 *Workers' Compensation Claim Form—Indiana*

INDIANA WORKER'S COMPENSATION
FIRST REPORT OF EMPLOYEE INJURY, ILLNESS

State Form 34401 (R9 / 3-01)

Please return completed form electronically by an approved EDI process.

FOR WORKER'S COMPENSATION BOARD USE ONLY		
Jurisdiction	Jurisdiction claim number	Process date

PLEASE TYPE or PRINT IN INK

NOTE: Your Social Security number is being requested by this state agency in order to pursue its statutory responsibilities. Disclosure is voluntary and you will not be penalized for refusal.

EMPLOYEE INFORMATION

Social Security number	Date of birth	Sex ☐ Male ☐ Female ☐ Unknown	Occupation / Job title		NCCI class code

Name (*last, first, middle*)	Marital status ☐ Unmarried ☐ Married ☐ Separated ☐ Unknown	Date hired	State of hire	Employee status

Address (*number and street, city, state, ZIP code*)

Hrs / Day	Days / Wk	Avg Wg / Wk	☐ Paid Day of Injury ☐ Salary Continued

Telephone number (include area code)	Number of dependents	Wage Per $ ☐ Hour ☐ Day ☐ Week ☐ Month ☐ Year ☐ Other

EMPLOYER INFORMATION

Name of employer	Employer ID#	SIC code	Insured report number

Address of employer (*number and street, city, state, ZIP code*)	Location number	Employer's location address (*if different*)
	Telephone number	
	Carrier / Administrator claim number	Report purpose code

Actual location of accident / exposure (*if not on employer's premises*)

CARRIER / CLAIMS ADMINISTRATOR INFORMATION

Name of claims administrator	Carrier federal ID number	Check if appropriate ☐ Self Insurance

Address of claims administrator (*number and street, city, state, ZIP code*)	☐ Insurance Carrier ☐ Third Party Admin.	Policy / Self-insured number
Telephone number		Policy period From To

Name of agent	Code number

OCCURRENCE / TREATMENT INFORMATION

Date of Inj./ Exp.	Time of occurrence ☐ AM ☐ PM	Date employer notified	Type of injury / exposure	Type code
Last work date	Time workday began	Date disability began	Part of body	Part code

RTW date	Date of death	Injury / Exposure occurred on employer's premises? ☐ Yes ☐ No	Name of contact	Telephone number

Department or location where accident / exposure occurred	All equipment, materials, or chemicals involved in accident
Specific activity engaged in during accident / exposure	Work process employee engaged in during accident / exposure

How injury / exposure occurred. Describe the sequence of events and include any relevant objects or substances.

Cause of injury code

Name of physician / health care provider	**INITIAL TREATMENT**
	☐ No Medical Treatment
	☐ Minor: By Employer
Name of witness	Telephone number	Date administrator notified	☐ Minor: Clinic / Hospital ☐ Emergency Care
			☐ Hospitalized > 24 Hours
Date prepared	Name of preparer	Title	Telephone number	☐ Future Major Medical / Lost Time Anticipated

An employer's failure to report an occupational injury or illness may result in a $50 fine (IC 22-3-4-13).

FIGURE 9.7 *Workers' Compensation Claim Form—Arizona*

EMPLOYERS REPORT OF INDUSTRIAL INJURY	INDUSTRIAL COMMISSION OF ARIZONA P.O. BOX 19070 PHOENIX, ARIZONA 85005070	FOR CARRIER USE ONLY
COMPLETE AND MAIL THIS REPORT WITHIN 10 DAYS FROM NOTICE OF ACCIDENT. FATALITIES MUST BE REPORTED WITHIN 24 HOURS. Employer must, on this form, notify his insurance carrier of every injury or disease suffered by an employee, fatal or otherwise, which is claimed to arise our of or in the course of employment. ARIZONA REVISED STATUTES 23-908 & 23-1061	MAIL TO: (CARRIER NAME & ADDRESS)	FOR OSHA PURPOSES ONLY OSHA Case #: _____ RECORDABLE INJURY _____ NON-RECORDABLE INJURY _____

EMPLOYEE

1. LAST NAME / FIRST / M.I. 2. SOCIAL SECURITY NUMBER✱ 3. BIRTH DATE

4. HOME ADDRESS (NUMBER & STREET) / CITY / STATE / ZIP CODE 5. TELEPHONE

6. SEX ☐ MALE ☐ FEMALE 7. MARITAL STATUS: ☐ SINGLE ☐ MARRIED ☐ DIVORCED ☐ WIDOWED

EMPLOYER

8. EMPLOYERS NAME 9. POLICY NUMBER 10. NATURE OF BUSINESS (MANUFACTURING, ETC.)

11. OFFICE ADDRESS (NUMBER & STREET) / CITY / STATE / ZIP CODE 12. TELEPHONE

ACCIDENT

13. DATE OF INJURY OR ILLNESS 14. TIME OF EVENT ☐ A.M. ☐ P.M. 15. TIME EMPLOYEE BEGAN WORK ☐ A.M. ☐ P.M. 16. DATE EMPLOYER NOTIFIED OF INJURY

17. LAST DAY OF WORK AFTER INJURY 18. DATE OF RETURN TO WORK 19. EMPLOYEES OCCUPATION (JOB TITLE) WHEN INJURED

20. CLASS CODE ON PAYROLL REPORT 21. EMPLOYEES ASSIGNED DEPARTMENT 22. DEPARTMENT NUMBER 23. DID INJURY OCCUR ON EMPLOYER PREMISES? ☐ YES ☐ NO

24. ADDRESS OR LOCATION OF ACCIDENT / CITY / COUNTY / STATE / ZIP CODE

25. WHAT WAS THE INJURY OR ILLNESS? Tell us the part of the body that was affected and how it was affected; be more specific than "hurt," "pain," or sore." *Examples:* "strained back", "chemical burn, hand", "carpal tunnel syndrome."

26. PART OF BODY INJURED 27. FATAL ☐ YES ☐ NO 28. IF THE EMPLOYEE DIED, WHEN DID THE DEATH OCCUR? DATE OF DEATH

29. WAS EMPLOYEE TREATED IN AN EMERGENCY ROOM? ☐ YES ☐ NO NAME OF PHYSICIAN OR OTHER HEALTH CARE PROFESSIONAL ADDRESS (STREET, CITY, STATE & ZIP CODE)

30. WAS EMPLOYEE HOSPITALIZED OVERNIGHT AS AN IN-PATIENT? ☐ YES ☐ NO IF HOSPITALIZED, HOSPITAL NAME ADDRESS (STREET, CITY, STATE & ZIP CODE)

31. IF VALIDITY OF CLAIM IS DOUBTED, STATE REASON

CAUSE OF ACCIDENT

32. **WHAT HAPPENED?** Tell us how the injury occurred. *Examples:* "When ladder slipped on wet floor, worker fell 20 feet", "Worker was sprayed with chlorine when gasket broke during replacement", "Worker developed soreness in wrist over time."

33. **WHAT OBJECT OR SUBSTANCE DIRECTLY HARMED THE EMPLOYEE?** Examples: "concrete floor", "chlorine", "radial arm saw." *If this question does not apply to the incident, leave it blank.*

34. **WHAT WAS EMPLOYEE DOING JUST BEFORE THE INCIDENT OCCURRED?** Describe the activity, as well as the tools, equipment, or material the employee was using. Be specific. *Examples:* "climbing a ladder while carrying roofing materials", "spraying chlorine from hand sprayer", "daily computer key-entry."

35. IF ANOTHER PERSON NOT IN COMPANY EMPLOY CAUSED ACCIDENT, GIVE NAME AND ADDRESS

EMPLOYEES WAGE DATA

36. WAS WORKER IN YOUR EMPLOY WHEN INJURED? ☐ YES ☐ NO 37. HOURS PER DAY EMPLOYEE WORKED FROM A.M. P.M. THRU A.M. P.M. 38. WAS EMPLOYEE ON OVERTIME WHEN INJURED? ☐ YES ☐ NO 39. NUMBER OF DAYS PER WEEK USUALLY WORKED EMPLOYEE COMPANY

IMPORTANT IF WORK LOSS IS EXPECTED TO EXCEED SEVEN CALENDAR DAYS, COMPLETE ITEMS 40 THRU 47 40. DATE OF LAST HIRE 41. WAS WORKER PAID FOR DAY OF INJURY? ☐ YES ☐ NO IF YES, $ 42. WAS EMPLOYEE HIRED FOR PERMANENT EMPLOYMENT? ☐ YES ☐ NO

43. NUMBER OF MONTHS EMPLOYMENT AVAILABLE DURING THE YEAR 44. GIVE EMPLOYEES WAGE STATUS AS APPLICABLE HOUR ☐ DAY ☐ WEEK ☐ MONTH ☐ $ _____ PER 45. IS EMPLOYEE FURNISHED ☐ LODGING ☐ BOARD ☐ BOTH VALUE $

46. ACTUAL GROSS EARNINGS OF EMPLOYEE FOR THE 30 CALENDAR DAYS PRECEEDING INJURY (EXAMPLE: IF INJURED APRIL 8, GIVE EARNINGS FROM MARCH 9 THRU APRIL 7) 47. DOES EMPLOYEE CLAIM DEPENDENTS? ☐ YES ☐ NO

IMPORTANT IF EMPLOYEE IS PAID OTHER THAN FIXED WEEKLY OR MONTHLY SALARY, COMPLETE ITEMS 48 THRU 55 48. IF EMPLOYEE EARNS EXTRA PAY FOR OVERTIME, WHAT IS BASIS OF PAYMENT? PER HOUR 49. NUMBER OF HOURS OVERTIME CONSIDERED NORMAL PER WEEK

50. GROSS WAGES OF EMPLOYEE DURING 12 MONTHS PRECEEDING INJURY FROM _____ THRU _____ $ 51. IF EMPLOYEE WORKED LESS THAN 12 MONTHS, SHOW GROSS WAGES FROM DATE OF HIRE THROUGH DAY PRIOR TO INJURY FROM _____ THRU _____ $

52. DATE OF LAST WAGE INCREASE IF WITHIN 12 MONTHS PRIOR TO INJURY $ 53. WAGE BEFORE INCREASE $ 54. WAGE AFTER INCREASE $ 55. GROSS EARNINGS FROM DATE OF INCREASE THRU DAY PRIOR TO INJURY

AUTHORIZED SIGNATURE DATE AUTHORIZED SIGNATURE TITLE

NOTE TO EMPLOYER:
1. Mail one copy to the Industrial Commission within 10 days.
2. Mail one copy to your insurance carrier within 10 days.
3. Keep one copy, for not less than five (5) years, as your supplementary record of injuries required by the Federal Occupational Safety and Health Act of 1970.

✱ The mandatory requirement that the social security number be included in forms filed with the Claims Division or Special Fund Division of the Industrial Commission of Arizona is permitted by Section 7(a)(2)(B) of the Federal Privacy Act of 1974, because the Commission forms, prescribed under the Commission's Rules in existence prior to January 1, 1975, required disclosure of the social security number. The number is used as a means of identifying all the various records in the Claims Division or Special Fund pertaining to an individual. The use of social security numbers is made necessary because of the large number of persons who have similar names and birth dates, and whose identities can only be distinguished by the social security number.

Form ICA 04-0101 (Rev. 7/01)   THIS FORM APPROVED BY THE INDUSTRIAL COMMISSION OF ARIZONA FOR CARRIER USE

FIGURE 9.8 *Workers' Compensation Claim Form—Wisconsin*

EMPLOYER'S FIRST REPORT OF INJURY OR DISEASE

Department of Workforce Development
Worker's Compensation Division
201 E. Washington Ave., Rm. C100
P.O. Box 7901
Madison, WI 53707-7901
Imaging Server Fax: (608) 260-2503
Telephone: (608) 266-1340
Fax: (608) 267-0394
http://www.dwd.state.wi.us/wc/
e-mail: DWDDWC@dwd.state.wi.us

An employer subject to the provisions of ch. 102, Wis. Stats., shall, within one day after the death of an employee due to a compensable injury, report the death to the Department of Workforce Development (DWD) and to the employer's insurance carrier, if insured. In cases of permanent disability or where temporary disability results beyond the 3-day waiting period, an insured employer shall also notify its insurance carrier of a compensable injury or illness within 7 days after the injury or beginning of a disability from occupational disease related to the employee's compensable injury.

Insurance carriers and self-insured employers must report all compensable claims to DWD on this form, the EDI system, or the internet format within 14 days of the date of injury.

The provision of your social security number is voluntary. Failure to provide it may result in an information processing delay. Personal information you provide may be used for secondary purposes [Privacy Law, s. 15.04(1)(m)]. **(Please read the instructions on page 2 for completing this form)**

EMPLOYEE

Employee Name (First, Middle, Last)		Social Security Number - -	Sex ☐ M ☐ F	Employee Home Telephone No. ( ) -
Employee Street Address	City	State	Zip Code -	Occupation
Birthdate	Date of Hire	County and State where accident or exposure occurred		

EMPLOYER

Employer Name		WI Unemployment Insurance Account No.	Self-Insured? ☐ Yes ☐ No	Nature of Business (specific product)
Employer Mailing Address	City	State	Zip Code -	Employer FEIN -
Name of Worker's Compensation Insurance Co. or Self-Insured Employer				Insurer FEIN -
Name and Address of Third Party Administrator (TPA) used by the Insurance Company or Self-Insured Employer				TPA FEIN -

WAGE INFORMATION

Wage at Time of Injury $	Specify per hr., wk., mo., yr., etc. Per:	In Addition to Wages, ☐ Meals No. of Meals/wk. Check Box(es) if ☐ Room No. of Days/wk Employee Received: ☐ Tips Avg. Weekly Amt. $

Is worker paid for overtime? ☐ Yes ☐ No   If yes, after how many hours of work per week?

For the 52 week period prior to the week the injury occurred, report below the number of weeks worked in the same kind of work, and the total wages, salary, commission and bonus or premium earned for such weeks.

No. of Weeks:	Gross Amount Excluding Tips: $	If Piece-Work, No. of Hrs. Excluding Overtime:

	Start Time	Hours Per Day	Hours Per Week	Days Per Week
Employee's Usual Work Schedule When Injured:	☐ AM ☐ PM			
Employer's Usual Full-Time Schedule For This Type of Work At Time of Employee's Injury:				

Part-Time Employment Information:	Are there other part-time workers doing the same work with the same schedule? ☐ Yes ☐ No If yes, how many?	Number of **full-time** employees doing the same type of work:

INJURY INFORMATION

Injury Date	Time of Injury AM PM	Last Day Worked	Date Employer Notified	☐ Date Returned to Work ☐ Estimated Date of Return
Did injury cause death? ☐ Yes ☐ No	Date of Death	Was this a lost time or other compensable injury? ☐ Yes ☐ No	Did injury occur because of: ☐ Substance Abuse ☐ Failure to Use Safety Devices ☐ Failure to Obey Rules	

Was employee treated in an emergency room? ☐ Yes ☐ No   Was employee hospitalized overnight as an in-patient? ☐ Yes ☐ No
Name and Address of Treating Practitioner and Hospital:

Case Number from the OSHA Log:

Injury Description - Describe activities of employee when injury or illness occurred and what tools, machinery, objects, chemicals, etc. were involved.

What happened to cause this injury or illness? (Describe how the injury occurred)

What was the injury or illness? (State the part of body affected and how it was affected)

Report Prepared By	Work Phone Number ( ) -	Position	Date Signed

WKC-12 (R. 03/2002)   SEND REPORT IMMEDIATELY - DO NOT WAIT FOR MEDICAL REPORT

New agents typically request three years of past claims history. This information should be requested annually from your insurance company and retained with your records.

Be sure to provide accurate information about construction and square footage of your building because the premium you pay is partially based on this information. Tell your agent about any improvements or updates, such as new roofing, heating, plumbing, and electrical wiring that have been done within the past ten years. This information can reduce your premium as much as 50 percent in some cases.

Coverages are essentially the same throughout the United States, but local variations apply. Your insurance agent can assist you in choosing your insurance format and assembling an appropriate insurance program.

Rating Insurance Companies

Insurance companies are rated on their financial condition and operating performance; these are called Best ratings (named after the company that does them). Your mortgage may require that you obtain coverage from a company with a Best rating of A 9 or better (superior) or A+ 9 or better (excellent). This is a good idea, as companies may experience financial or service difficulties from time to time. A good Best rating gives you some assurance that you are obtaining your insurance from a financially strong company. Your insurance agent can provide this information.

Insurance Agents

There are two types of insurance agents: independent and direct writers. An independent agent may represent many different insurance companies, such as Hanover, St. Paul, Hartford, Cigna, Chubb, Fireman's Fund, Travelers, Continental, USF&G, and Reliance to name a few. A direct writer normally represents one company, such as Allstate, State Farm, Farmers, Nationwide, and Liberty Mutual. You may wish to obtain quotes from both direct writers and independent agents, which allows you to obtain the most competitive coverage.

Your agent should be insured for errors and omissions, and you should require proof of this coverage, which can be produced in the form of a certificate of insurance. You may have recourse under this coverage if your agent mistakenly fails to provide coverage for which you paid.

Inspections

Your insurance company may inspect your property before or after the inception of your policy. If it finds conditions and/or physical hazards that would encourage or contribute to a loss on your premises, it issues a notice of recommendations for eliminating or reducing these exposures.

Inspectors from fire, liability, boiler and machinery, and workers' compensation insurance companies should be given every cooperation. Boiler and machinery inspectors (but no others) have the authority to shut down any object that they feel poses an imminent danger.

Respond to an inspector's notice of recommendations by informing your insurer in writing of your intentions to comply with the recommendations and supply an estimate of the time needed to comply.

Recommendations with which you agree should be carried out. For those on which there is any question, your objections should be put in writing to the insurance agent. It is a good idea to comply, whenever reasonable, because eliminating or minimizing losses results in direct savings in the long run.

If you don't respond and a reinspection reveals the same hazardous conditions, the insurer may cancel your coverage within the first 60 days of inspection. Coverage will then be more difficult to obtain elsewhere.

The insurer may cancel for reasons of increased hazard by giving the named insured and the mortgagee at least 30 days' notice in writing. If possible, negotiate a 60-day or 90-day notice to allow ample time to shop for a different insurance company.

10

MAINTENANCE

It can be common for a couple just getting together to find themselves in the landlord business. He owns a house; she owns a town house; they live in one and rent out the other.

That's exactly what Brenda and Tom Smith did when they said their vows in 1999. That's also when they caught the property-owning bug, and it just kept biting. By 2003, they had sold his house, bought a new home in a Minneapolis suburb, rented her town house, and later bought a foreclosure in the same complex. Then they refinanced both the town houses to purchase 17 rental units in Morris, Minnesota, and later sold one town house to buy a vacation home on Lake Minnewaska that rents by the week!

Add to that raising four boys—two boys on board before the wedding and two born afterward—plus Tom and Brenda both hold down jobs. Yet it's their family's future they're working for today. Says Brenda, "We believe in diversifying now so we can have some retirement income later and won't have to depend on Social Security." They're also looking ahead to provide for their sons' formal schooling (though the older boys are quickly getting an education taking care of properties through all their parents' activities).

Still in their first five years as landlords, the Smiths are already reaping the rewards of their hard work because of tax deductions and appreciation. And they're occasionally reminded of the downside—especially on holiday weekends.

"One New Year's Day, our family had gone skiing when the call came through on our cell phone. The pipes in one of our rental buildings had frozen. So we had to drive two hours to get there, and Tom rigged up a quick fix. On a July 4th weekend, we had to deal with the damage caused by galelike winds that ripped shingles off the roof. Any day but a holiday, we would have phoned a repair company. That happens in this business!"

What has worked well for the Smiths is buying fixer-uppers. That includes a fourplex built in 1890 and a 13-unit apartment complex in the town of Morris, where the University of Minnesota has a satellite campus specializing in agricultural, engineering, and education programs.

"In the beginning, it was exhausting taking care of repairs and remodeling the units. My husband started redoing one bathroom himself, but we soon learned what made sense to do ourselves and what to hire others to do," Brenda explains. They treat their fourplex as a long-term rental and carefully screen prospective tenants, but they set up their 13-unit building as month-to-month efficiencies for temporary housing. A caretaker lives on the premises of the 13-unit building and deals with collecting rents and other management duties. Explains Brenda, "These efficiency units fill an important marketing niche in the community. We provide short-term housing for migrant workers, students, and others just getting on their feet. Being in a small town has helped us get good tenants because our caretaker seems to know everyone."

When they're not doing hands-on work, the Smiths can be found attending meetings of the Minnesota Multi Housing Association. "We've attended lots of seminars for small landlords to network and learn from professionals. For example, one expert talked about protecting properties. Another told us about services for screening tenants. That alone has saved us from getting burned by prospective tenants," says Brenda.

The association also shares its paperwork, forms, Minnesota-approved leases, and much more with its members. "It's been a great resource for us." So has the Web site mrlandlord.com (http://www.mrlandlord.com). Says Brenda, "I can chat with other landlords online, get handy tips, and avoid a lot of trial and error in running our business." Being online has been a bonus, both in communicating with tenants and marketing their weekly vacation rental. As the Smiths seek more investment properties, their online connections become a necessity. "In rural areas especially, real estate agents don't want to put in the time traveling to show properties, so we view as much as possible on the Internet."

The real estate bug continues to bite Brenda, who is working toward getting her own real estate license so she can be a real insider when it comes to finding good properties. As she says, "We're just getting our feet wet."

PRESERVING THE ASSET

One of the primary responsibilities of owning rental property is the preservation of tangible assets: you must safeguard your property from physical damage and loss of income. Beyond keeping the property in excellent physical condition, a good maintenance program that includes regular upgrades or cosmetic improvements can actually increase the value of your investment.

Owning and operating rental property requires ongoing physical maintenance. Vacant homes, properties, and offices must be cleaned and decorated to make them more appealing and rentable; and broken or worn-out items need to be repaired or replaced. You can either hire a contractor to maintain your property or do it yourself.

For residential properties, routine maintenance expenses should run about 5 percent of gross income. As an example, if the gross annual income from your property is $10,000, maintenance expenses may total around $500. By setting aside $45 a month, you'll have enough in reserve for normal anticipated repairs. Having the money handy when you need to get a job done is less stressful than having to delay a repair until the funds are available.

Good preparation and planning helps keep maintenance problems under control. Preparation includes keeping spare parts, tools, and service telephone numbers on the property or in some other convenient location. Preparation also means developing the skills and acquiring the equipment necessary to do the work yourself or developing relationships with good electricians, plumbers, cleaning and decorating contractors, and so on.

Residential Repair and Deduct Laws

A comprehensive cleaning and maintenance program will help you fulfill your responsibility to provide habitable living accommodations to your tenants.

In many states, maintaining habitable premises is mandated by law, and the rules are getting tougher all the time. New state and local ordinances being introduced contain a provision called *repair and deduct,* a provision already existing in the landlord-tenant acts of many states and municipalities. Its intent is to force landlords to keep their properties in good condition.

The old general rule was that tenants and landlords could negotiate the landlord's basic obligation to make repairs through mutual agreement. For example, a landlord could require a tenant to maintain everything *inside* a property and the landlord would maintain the *outer* shell of the building and common areas. If a landlord agreed to make repairs and failed to do so, a tenant had little recourse.

Under a repair and deduct ordinance, tenants are allowed to have repairs made and can deduct the expenses from the rent, regardless of any preexisting agreement with the landlord. If a landlord doesn't maintain the property in habitable condition, a tenant can take action by calling professional contractors to perform the work and deducting the amount of the invoice from the rent. The only requirement generally is that the tenant give the landlord sufficient notice, usually 10 to 14 days.

Even if a municipality has a repair and deduct ordinance, an owner and tenant may still agree in writing that the tenant is to perform specific repairs, maintenance tasks, or minor remodeling. The four conditions for such an agreement to be enforceable are the following:

1. The agreement is entered into in good faith and is not for the purpose of evading the obligations of the owner.
2. The agreement does not diminish the obligations of the owner to other tenants.
3. The terms and conditions of the agreement are clearly and prominently disclosed.
4. The consideration for such agreement is specifically stated.

Renting "As Is"

Some landlords rent properties "as is," requiring tenants to decorate and upgrade. In this way, the landlords save money, and tenants can decorate to their specific tastes. But most tenants don't want to invest their own money and time improving someone else's property; also, you may get a tenant who wants purple walls with a dragon mural. If you do allow tenants to do their own decorating, limit the colors of paint and the wallpaper patterns.

Another drawback to renting a property "as is" is the reality that few prospective renters can visualize how a shabby-looking place can be transformed with new carpeting, freshly painted walls, and a thorough cleaning job. Thus, good tenants are reluctant to rent a residence "as is," so you may have to allow a big deduction on the rent.

UPGRADING

From time to time, you'll have to spend money to upgrade a property, including replacing aging appliances, worn-out carpets, and outdated lighting fixtures. You may also have to remodel a kitchen or bathroom. Upgrading should be planned for and done on a regular schedule. It's always better to replace a refrigerator before it breaks down on a hot Sunday in July.

Sometimes you may upgrade a property for an existing tenant at or before lease renewal time, whereas other times you will make these improvements to ensure the property is attractive for a prospective tenant.

The decision of whether to repair or replace is based on economics, and some upgrading can be put off. However, a malfunction in an essential appliance, such as a furnace, air conditioner, stove, or refrigerator, requires immediate action.

How do you make the decision to upgrade?

- Consider the market for rental units in your location. If the demand is strong, you may not have to do any upgrades; if the market is weak, however, you may need to invest in some improvements to remain competitive and attract renters.
- Look realistically at the overall condition and physical appearance of the unit. Check for worn-out shades, draperies, or blinds; torn or stained carpeting and flooring; broken, deteriorated, or severely outdated appliances, light fixtures, or plumbing fixtures. Perhaps the property needs a total rehab. Good tenants expect and demand a unit be in like-new condition before they move in. And existing tenants also deserve an attractive, well-maintained unit.

Decide how much money can be invested in upgrades compared with how much the rent can be increased to amortize these expenses. Suppose you put $2,000 worth of improvements into a property that is currently renting for $400 a month. If rents are increased 6 percent a year for the next three years, the additional income would be only $915. To amortize a $2,000 expense over three years, rent would have to be increased 13 percent per year. At a 6 percent rent increase, it would take almost seven years to pay off the cost of improvements.

The easiest practical way to determine how much can be spent on improvements is to work backwards from the projected rent increases. If the $400 property has a 10 percent rent increase per year for the next five years, the additional income would amount to $2,928. If you deduct a conservative figure for inflationary operating expenses of 2 percent per year, approximately $2,432 would be available for necessary improvements for the five-year period.

Doing Your Own Maintenance

If you want to perform your own routine maintenance tasks, you need tools and equipment. Following is a list of what the pros say is necessary:

Cleaning supplies

- Canvas trash bag with shoulder strap
- Steel wool
- Furniture polish
- Straw broom
- Scouring powder
- Whisk broom
- All-purpose cleaner (powder and/or liquid)
- Dustpan
- Plastic trash bags
- Spray deodorizer
- Mop and mop wringer
- Spray wall-tile cleaner
- Sponge mop
- Sponges
- Wooden pick-up stick with pointed end
- Five-gallon paint bucket
- Scrub brush
- Wide floor broom
- Spray bottles
- Shovel
- Razor blade scraper
- Rags
- Spray window cleaner
- Buckets
- Liquid floor wax and applicator
- 6″ and 12″ squeegees
- Wax stripper
- Handy box carrier
- Metal polish
- Three-foot stepladder
- Toilet-bowl cleaner (liquid or crystal)
- Toilet brush
- Floor cleaner and wax for hardwood floors
- Spray oven cleaner
- Drop cloths

Basic tools

- Claw hammer
- Needle-nose pliers
- Phillips screwdriver
- Wire strippers
- Metal files or rasps
- Putty knives
- Channel-lock pliers
- Razor knife
- Black electrical tape
- Paint roller
- Electric continuity tester
- Razor blade scraper
- Flathead screwdriver
- Flashlight (plastic cover to avoid electrical contact)
- Awl or punch (ice pick)
- Regular pliers
- Pipe wrenches
- Vise-Grip pliers
- Wood saw and hacksaw
- Wire cutters
- Spirit level
- 20-foot tape measure
- Crescent wrenches
- Paint brushes
- Electric or battery-operated drills and saws

PREPARING A VACANT PROPERTY FOR RENTAL

Vacant properties must be in good rentable condition when they are shown to prospective residents. The preparation process consists of possible upgrading, surface cleaning, painting, and thorough cleaning and repair. Use the Make-Ready Checklist in Figure 10.1 as a guide to prevent overlooking or forgetting an important item.

Surface Cleaning

Vacant properties should be cleaned as soon as possible after tenants move out. This initial cleaning includes removing all trash, wiping down appliances and countertops, sweeping and vacuuming floors, and cleaning windows. Once a property is clean, you can show it to prospective tenants, even if it still needs painting and repairs.

Minor Repairs

Inspect vacant properties, using the preinspection checklist in Figure 5.1. You will usually see a number of things that need repair or replacement, such as some of the following common maintenance items:

- Broken or loose doorknobs on cabinets and closet doors
- Loose closet shelving or rods
- Loose shower rods, towel bars, and hooks
- Leaky faucets or toilets
- Clogged faucet aerators
- Clogged drains
- Burned-out light bulbs
- Broken electrical switches or outlets
- Blown electrical fuses
- Torn window screens, shades, and blinds
- Broken windowpanes
- Torn or missing wall or floor tiles in kitchens and baths
- Doors that stick (entrance, bedroom, or bathroom)
- Dirty heating and air-conditioning filters

FIGURE 10.1 *Make-Ready Checklist*

Property _____	Unit _____
Unit Size _____	Date to be Occupied _____
Inspected by _____	Date _____

Checklist	Instructions (C) clean (P) paint (R) repair (RPL) replace
Check all plumbing (toilets, faucets, pipes). Check for leaks, pressure, etc.	
Check all appliances for proper operation, bulbs, etc.	
Check all hardware (doorknobs, hooks, rods, locks, catches, etc.)	
Check all windows and screens (tracks, locks, operation, cracks, tears, etc.)	
Check all walls, ceilings, baseboard (holes, cuts, nail pops, seams, woodwork trim).	
Check all floors (cleaned and waxed, carpet rips, shampoo, vacuum).	
Check bathrooms (cleaned tubs, toilets, walls, vanities, mirrors, medicine cabinets, sinks, towel bars, toilet paper holders, soap dishes polished).	
Check all closets (shelves, lights, floor, doors).	
Check all thresholds for cracks, dirt, loose screws.	
Check all other doors (warping, rubbing, cracks, squeaks, etc.).	
Check all vents, registers (dirt, operation).	
Check heating and air-conditioning for proper operation (filters, thermostats, etc.).	
Check all kitchen cabinets (doors work, cleaning, peeling, etc.).	
Check all lighting (new bulbs, switches, cleanliness, hanging properly).	
Check for chips or cracks in sinks, countertops, appliances.	
Check mailbox and key	
Check intercom and locking door operation	
Check unit for proper address/unit number	
Replace These Missing Items	
Cleaning Date	
Painting Date	
Maintenance Date	
Follow-Up Inspection Date	
New Carpeting Date	

Most items listed above can be repaired with the tools suggested earlier; and replacement parts can be purchased in most hardware stores. Inspect the property personally to determine if you can restore the broken items yourself before calling in professionals.

PAINTING

The next step in getting a vacant property ready is painting. Although you may decide to hire a professional painter, you should know the basic process of painting a vacant property. The task is divided into three steps: preparation, painting, and cleanup.

Preparation

Remove all nails, screws, anchors, and so on, and fill all holes with matching plaster. Patch holes five inches in diameter and smaller following directions on the package. Holes larger than five inches need a section of drywall or plaster lath inserted before patching.

Remove electric switch plates and outlet plates. If walls are very dirty, scrub them; don't try to paint over dirt. Seal water marks, grease marks, crayon marks, and so on with a product designed for this purpose. Scrape loose paint.

Painting

Paint the entire property with one coat of flat white latex paint, including ceilings, walls, closets, doors, frames, windows, and trim, if applicable. Use semigloss paint in kitchens and bathrooms (some people prefer to use semigloss paint for trim as well). Use brushes for trim and rollers for walls and ceilings; using extension poles make ceiling painting easier. Use drop cloths to facilitate cleaning up.

Cleanup

Reinstall switch plates and outlet plates. Remove all paint splatters on countertops, cabinets, appliances, floors, and woodwork. Scrape paint smears off windows. Clean paint out of bathtubs and sinks; and sweep up paint chips on the floors.

Final Cleanup

When the property is painted and all repairs have been completed, the unit can now undergo a final cleaning. Follow these procedures for a comprehensive cleaning program.

Kitchen. To clean the oven, take out any removable parts and put them in the sink to soak. Spray the oven with oven cleaner (if it's not self-cleaning). Follow directions on the package, as oven cleaners are corrosive; some cleaners take a few minutes to work, whereas others must be left on overnight.

Using an all-purpose cleaner, wash the outside of the range: top, front, sides, and doors. Clean the countertops and interiors and exteriors of cabinets and drawers. Clean the interior and exterior of the refrigerator, defrosting it if necessary. Clean the dishwasher inside and out. Vacuum and scrub the range hoods and vents.

By this time the oven cleaner will have had time to act, so clean the oven, following directions on the package. Clean and replace the oven parts.

Using scouring powder, clean the sink and faucets. And, finally, pull appliances away from the walls, and sweep up where appliances were. Scrub the floor and wash all walls. Replace the appliances. Resweep and mop the floors.

Bathroom(s). Put toilet bowl cleaner in the toilet, following instructions on the package.

- Spray and clean the shower tile walls with a product designed for this purpose.
- Using an all-purpose cleaner, clean the medicine cabinet, vanity, light fixtures, walls, and toilet bowl.
- Using scouring powder and a spray cleaner, scrub the sink, tub, and chrome fixtures.
- Vacuum and scrub the exhaust vent.
- Finally, sweep and scrub the floor.

Closets. Vacuum the shelves, doors, and tracks, scrubbing if necessary. Be sure door handles or knobs and door tracks and hinges are tightened.

Lighting. Clean the light globes. Replace bulbs as needed.

Heating and air-conditioning. Clean or replace filters in heating and air-conditioning units. Vacuum, wipe, or scrub the units if necessary.

Windows. Clean trim and tracks; make sure windows open and close freely. Use a razor scraper to remove dried paint on glass surfaces. With a spray window cleaner, clean interior window panes (also exterior, if possible).

Floors. Sweep and/or vacuum all hard-surface floors and carpeting. For tile floors, mop with an all-purpose cleaner and apply liquid wax. For hardwood floors, clean and wax with products designed for hardwood floors, and use a wax finish that minimizes slippery surfaces.

Carpets. Carpet cleaning is the last step in property preparation, a job often performed by outside contractors. The best results are obtained with a process that employs water extraction equipment.

If you decide to do the job yourself, follow the instructions that accompany the carpet-cleaning equipment. Prespotting heavily stained areas will improve the final result. Don't use too much shampoo, a common mistake that makes the job of rinsing the carpet next to impossible.

When you have finished, cover the wet carpet with an absorbing paper that is available at most hardware stores. If no one will be in the property for a few days, you can omit the paper and let the carpet dry in the open air.

After the carpet dries, vacuum it to pick up any residue. At this point the property should be ready for new tenants.

USING OUTSIDE CONTRACTORS

Certain maintenance functions are best handled by outside contractors. You may have to hire a contractor for snow removal; landscaping; garbage removal; roofing; painting (interior and exterior); tuckpointing; pest control; carpet cleaning; and electrical, plumbing, heating, and air-conditioning repairs.

Compile a list of recommended service companies for various types of mechanical problems, including plumbers, electricians, heating and air-conditioning contractors, and appliance repairers. If you can't get a recommendation for a particular job, look in the Yellow Pages and take a chance with a company that can give you a reference list of satisfied customers. You may want to check out various companies with the Better Business Bureau.

Some owners of small property buildings hire a local janitor, possibly someone who lives nearby, to perform daily or weekly housekeeping tasks. Inquiries of neighbors and property owners in the area may result in a few good recommendations.

When using an outside contractor, refer to the Contractor Guidelines in Figure 10.2 to avoid problems.

FIGURE 10.2 *Contractor Guidelines*

Contractor Guidelines

The following was prepared to inform you of our procedures and expectations regarding your business relationship with us.

Insurance

All contractors that perform work on our property are required to carry appropriate insurance coverage. A certificate of insurance must be provided before work begins. See the attached page for the specific coverage required.

Proposals

Proposals, when required, should be submitted to the appropriate individual. The proposal must be as specific as possible containing the job address, description of work, types of materials to be used, any warranty/guarantee information, and the dollar amount. If specific payment terms are required, they should be specified (see also payment terms).

Purchase Orders

Before starting any work, you must get a purchase order or purchase order number. The purchase order should contain all pertinent information regarding the job. You will receive the white copy for your records. All correspondence regarding a job must contain the purchase order number.

Invoices

All invoices should be sent directly to _____.
Invoices must contain the following information:

  1. Job address
  2. Purchase order number
  3. Description of work per the purchase order
  4. Dollar amount

Payment Terms

Send your invoice immediately after completing the work. It will be processed and paid within 30–45 days upon completion and acceptance of work and upon receipt of invoice.

If you do not receive payment in 45 days, provided there are no discrepancies, you should contact us at _____.

Quality of Work

All work is expected to be completed according to specifications in a professional and workmanlike manner in accordance with accepted practices.

Work Area

Upon completion of work or at the end of each workday, the work area must be left clean or in the same condition it was before start of the work.

Damage to Property

In the event that your company causes any damage to any property, personal or otherwise, your company will be held liable and expected to resolve the matter immediately.

FIGURE 10.2 *Contractor Guidelines, continued*

Extras

Any extra work not included in the original price must be approved in advance, in writing, prior to the commencement of such extra work.

Keys

If you must use a key to gain access to a work area, you will be required to sign for the key. All keys must be returned at the end of each workday.

Discrepancies

If there are any discrepancies regarding the terms and conditions of the services rendered, you are expected to resolve them immediately.

Business Conduct Policy

The intent of the policy is to preclude the development of any situation or relationship that might compromise good business judgment or create, or appear to create, the image of unethical practices. Accordingly, this policy prohibits our company's employees, or their family members, from accepting gifts, loans, or use of accommodations from anyone with whom we do business. Gifts of inconsequential value may be accepted in circumstances when such minor gifts are customary.

Insurance Requirements for Contractors

All contractors that do work for us must have a certificate of insurance on file.

The requirements are as follows:

General Liability	$100,000 minimum
Property Damage	50,000 minimum
Workers' Compensation*	100,000 minimum
Auto Liability and Property Damage	100,000 minimum

*The only people exempt from workers' compensation are sole proprietors and partners and corporate officers. All policies must contain the following clause:

Cancellation: Should your policy be canceled before the expiration date, the issuing company will endeavor to mail ten (10) days' written notice to the certificate holder, but failure to mail such notice shall impose no obligation or liability of any kind upon the company.

The certificate must be mailed to _____

_____

_____

_____

_____

Any questions regarding this should be directed to _____

at_____.

Thank you.

CONDOMINIUMS

The governing association of a condominium may have a maintenance staff that can perform routine maintenance tasks, charging the owner for time and materials. Association rates are usually less expensive than those of outside contractors; a property's maintenance personnel are generally better prepared to deal with problems particular to that building.

PEST AND INSECT CONTROL

Almost every building will have problems with pests and/or insects from time to time. The most common nuisance is the cockroach, but others are mice, rats, ants, and termites.

Pest control is best left to professional exterminators. At the first sign of trouble, have the building treated and set up a regular schedule of follow-up treatments. If tenants know that you have a regular extermination program, they won't panic if they see an occasional cockroach.

You and your tenants can do several things to help control pest problems, although these practices are not a substitute for a good, ongoing, professional pest extermination program. For example, you can caulk cracks and openings around windows, foundations, drains, and pipes to prevent pests from entering the building.

Enforce good housekeeping and sanitation practices: Garbage and trash must be covered and removed promptly; kitchens should be scrubbed regularly to minimize grease buildup; debris and junk should be thrown out—even accumulated newspapers can harbor pests.

When screening prospective tenants, find out if the building where they formerly lived had roaches. If so, the roaches will probably move in with the tenants.

CUTTING COSTS

Often the difference between a positive and negative cash flow is simply a matter of prudently monitoring controllable expenses. Your biggest costs are usually fixed: mortgage payments, real estate taxes, and insurance. There isn't much you can do about these costs except to file a tax protest or refinance the mortgage.

Other expenses, such as utilities and maintenance costs, however, can be substantially reduced. For example, if you are paying for common area lighting, you can install timers to turn off the lights during the day. If you pay for heat, air-conditioning, and hot water, installing programmed thermostats and timers can control the output and keep costs down. Make sure all mechanical equipment is in peak operating condition. Boilers and air conditioners will run more efficiently if you have them inspected and adjusted annually.

Always be on the lookout for more ways to cut costs. Are you paying for certain routine services that you or one of your tenants can perform? Can you make some of the minor repairs or do your own painting?

Use the Cost-Cutting Checklist (see Figure 10.3) for suggested ways to save money on maintenance.

FIGURE 10.3 *Cost-Cutting Checklist*

Cost-Cutting Checklist

General

Bring in utility companies to explain present rate structure and revise to the most favorable rate.

Heating/Air-Conditioning

Check boiler efficiency.

Maintain the boiler regularly to ensure the highest efficiency.

Lower daytime and nighttime thermostat settings for heat. (Follow local ordinances.)

Clean radiators and air registers.

Repair all leaks.

Reduce water temperature in hot water systems.

Check operation of automatic controls.

Balance heating system.

Check operation of all electric heating units.

Install indoor/outdoor controls.

Tune up heating plants.

Install flue restrictors.

Reduce air-conditioning and/or heat in unoccupied units.

Keep doors closed as much as possible when heating and air-conditioning are in operation (specifically service and fire doors).

Leave thermostat on a desired temperature rather than adjusting it all the time.

Maintain thermostat controls for heating public areas at not more than 68° from October to April.

Increase moisture in air to increase tenant comfort and at the same time reduce use of heating fuel.

Check out motors and pumps on heating systems for cleanliness; investigate the possibility of using a lower wattage motor.

Keep air filters clean; change them often.

Do not block registers or ducts.

If the building has window air-conditioning units and a central heating furnace, cover or close the floor or side-wall registers and low return-air grills while air-conditioning is on.

With a forced-air system, keep the return-air grills and warm air ducts clean.

If laundry facilities are available in the building, keep dryer lint filter clean.

Eliminate humidity controls for all but certain circumstances.

Insulation

Install heat-absorbing and heat-reflecting glass to reduce heat from direct sunlight by 40 to 70 percent.

Repair broken glass.

Repair window putty.

Replace caulking.

FIGURE 10.3 *Cost-Cutting Checklist, continued*

Adjust door closers.

If feasible, redo roofing and sidewalls to provide insulation.

Use storm windows and doors or double-pane glass to reduce the loss of heat.

Waterproof foundations to minimize heat loss.

Install weather stripping and caulking to seal cracks around windows and doors.

Electricity

Reduce lighting levels.

Clean bulbs and fixtures.

Investigate the most efficient light sources that can provide the illumination required:

- High-pressure sodium vapor (most efficient)
- Metal halide
- Fluorescent
- Mercury
- Incandescent (least efficient)

Put reflective covers or backers on fluorescent lights to maximize light refraction.

Reduce hall lighting to minimum safe levels.

Reduce exterior lighting (around building and parking areas) by removing every other bulb.

Repaint dark-colored areas (lobbies, halls) white to increase reflected light.

Install photocells in place of electric timers.

Install fluorescent light in place of incandescent.

Locate refrigerators away from heating equipment and direct sunlight.

Keep refrigerator coil surfaces clean to provide maximum cooling.

Notify tenants to defrost their refrigerators when frost in the freezer compartment is about one-quarter-inch thick.

Water

Reduce water heater temperature.

Repair leaks.

Check boiler water level.

Check combustion efficiency of boiler.

Ask utility company to check the efficiency of the hot water tanks being used.

Instruct tenants to use cold water when operating a garbage disposal. This solidifies the grease, reduces hot water usage, and cuts down on maintenance.

Insulate pipes so that less energy will be wasted in running until it "warms up."

Repair dripping faucets.

Investigate use of smaller water-saving nozzles and spray heads on water fixtures to increase pressure but reduce total gallons of water used.

11

PROPERTY TAXES

Sharon Niccum knows profits can be made as a landlord of mobile home communities when two things happen consistently: rents get collected and both properties and tenants are well taken care of—exactly what she has strived to do for 25 years.

Sharon owns and operates eight mobile home communities in Indiana. Her days are filled with taking care of roads, signage, landscaping, wells, or sewage treatment centers. At the same time, she focuses on attracting working-class families to her "bread and butter" communities— and keeping them happy.

"Luckily, the biggest complaint we get is about drivers speeding through the communities. If that's the nature of most of our complaints, we must be doing something right," she says.

Sharon has earned respect as a landlord over the years by establishing guidelines and rules as well as meeting requirements of fair housing regulations. "Requirements keep changing, and we keep up with them ourselves rather than turning to a lawyer for everything. The state Manufactured Housing Association has been an excellent source of information in helping us do this."

As an independent owner, she works long hours but prefers that to having partners in her business. Sharon has a full-time assistant, and her husband helps with the maintenance and management of the communities; she also has on-site resident managers at each property. Duties of the managers vary; some are responsible for new resident interviewing, rent collecting, maintenance, and enforcement of rules. A few have minimal duties, such as picking up trash, watching for violations of rules, and communicating with the property manager. Sharon also counts on help from part-time maintenance people. "They religiously perform thankless duties and are important to our overall operation. My people are what makes all this happen—I couldn't possibly do it all myself."

Rents for monthly lots in Sharon's communities start as low as $175 plus water and sewage costs. But pricing the lots is tricky. As Sharon says, "If lot rents get too high, a tenant's total housing costs per month would go above $500 including the mortgage. People know they can buy their own tract house and pay a total of $600 to $650 for their housing. So that's our competition."

Even so, this entrepreneurial property owner has been able to keep the vacancy rate on her properties low at 5 percent through strict management. Her working philosophy: "I know from experience that I can't lower my standards for the bad tenants and still keep the good ones."

This story Sharon loves to tell demonstrates how she approaches her business. "The farmer's crop was failing, so he sought advice from a wise man. This wise man told the farmer to take a magic box to every corner of his field every day. If he does that, his crops will grow. Before long, the farmer's fields grew lush with healthy crops, and the farmer was very happy. He told the wise man the box was indeed magic. To that, the wise man replied, 'Your crops are growing because you paid attention to them every single day.'

"Pay attention—that's what we have to do with our property management businesses, too," Sharon concludes.

HOW TO READ A TAX BILL

The following discussion is intended to help you understand how your tax bills are calculated. Laws vary from community to community so consult your local tax authority.

Market Value

The public assessor or appraiser has the responsibility of determining a market value for each property in a jurisdiction (county, township, borough, or parish). The market value of a property is the price the property would probably sell for in a competitive market. If there has not been a recent sale of a property comparable to yours, the assessor uses other methods to determine a market value.

One method that could be used—especially on newer or special-use buildings—is the *cost approach,* which determines the current cost of replacing the building less depreciation from all causes plus the value of the land. Another method, used for income-producing property, is the *income approach.* It establishes market value by determining the income the property either produces or is expected to produce.

Assessors usually don't inspect each building. They determine a market value for a representative building, determine the value per square foot for that building, then multiply that value by the square footage of other buildings.

Public assessors are required by law to reassess property at mandated intervals. A reassessment period may be every year, every three years, every four years, or even longer. Our 12-unit apartment building example has been determined to have a market value of $240,000 (see Figure 11.1).

FIGURE 11.1 *How to Read and Calculate a Tax Bill*

Example 12-Unit Apartment Building	**Your Tax Bill** Your Building
Market Value $240,000	Market Value . . . . $_____
Assessment Rate . . . . × 33.33%	Assessment Rate . . . . × ? %
Assessed Valuation $79,992	Assessed Valuation. . . . . $_____
Equalization Factor (multiplier) . . . . × 1.4153	Equalization Factor . . . . × (multiplier)
Equalized Assessed Valuation $113,212.68	Equalized Assessed Valuation . . . . . . $_____
Tax Rate . . . . × 8.785*	Tax Rate. . . . . × (tax rate)*
Tax Bill $9,945.73	Tax Bill . . . . $_____
*For each $100 of Equalized Assessed Valuation	*For each $100 of Equalized Assessed Valuation

Assessed Value

Once the market value is determined, the assessed value can be calculated. The *assessed value* is a legal term denoting on what value a property will be taxed (not necessarily the sale value of a property). Assessed value is a percentage of the market value and varies between states, within a state, and/or by type (or classification) of property. The assessed value is set by the same body that determined market value; it can be 100 percent of the market value or some fraction of the market value. This percentage of market value is known as the assessment rate. In our example, the *assessment rate* is 33.33 percent of the market value; this property therefore has an assessed value of $79,992.

Multipliers

Between reassessment years, some assessed values may need to be adjusted. As an example, there may be times when sales in a given area indicate a property value change, either upward or downward. Or inflation may bring about substantial increases in property values. Sometimes values between taxing jurisdictions get too far out of line, and it may be necessary to make them more uniform so taxpayers are paying proportionately. In any case, making a reassessment adjustment saves the assessor a lot of time and work—saving the taxpayers money in the cost of running the assessor's office.

The assessor may perform a reassessment on a property-by-property basis, or the state, county, and/or other supervisory body may step in and adjust all the values in a given jurisdiction. Instead of reassessing each property in a given area, adjustments are made by applying a multiplier to each property. When an intervention like this takes place, the adjustment to the assessed values is accomplished by applying a multiplier, or equalization factor, to the assessed value. When the multiplier is applied to the assessed value, it either increases or decreases the assessed value by the percentage of the multiplier. The process thus produces the adjusted, or equalized, assessed value of the property.

In our example, because the multiplier is more than 1, the assessed value will increase. Our assessed value of $79,992 times the 1.4153 multiplier results in an equalized valuation of $113,212.68.

Tax Rate

Once the adjusted assessed value is determined, the tax rate (in many states called the millage rate) is calculated. Local taxing bodies (schools, municipality, county, etc.) add up assessed values on all properties in their jurisdictions. The total operations amount budgeted for those bodies is divided by the total adjusted assessed value base to determine the tax or millage rate. Multiplying the equalized assessed value by the tax or millage rate gives you your total taxes due (tax bill). The tax rate for our building has been set at 8.785 per $100 of equalized assessed valuation. To see how much we owe, we would divide the valuation of $113,212.68 by 100, getting $1,132.12, which is then multiplied by the tax rate of 8.785 to calculate a tax bill of $9,945.73. (You can save a step by turning the tax rate into a percentage [.08785] and multiplying the equalized assessed valuation by that number.)

ARE YOU OVERASSESSED?

Your property may be either over- or underassessed, even though the assessors have done their jobs properly. Assessors have many properties to assess at any given time, and they tackle this problem by using a mass appraisal approach. An assessor places comparable market values on comparable properties in comparable areas and therefore places comparable assessed values on the properties. Because the assessors are not inspecting properties for their unique features, the values they place are almost always inexact. An individual appraisal is much more accurate for determining market value because it focuses on the unique characteristics of a particular property.

Purchase prices are not always good indicators of true market value. When purchasing property in a state that doesn't tax personal property, it is generally a good idea to allocate a reasonable portion of the purchase price specifically to personal property (ask your accountant for details). The amount should be specified on the closing statement and also, if possible, in the contract. Another factor skewing the value of a property is below-market financing. If below-market financing is involved, the selling price may be inflated and, if so, should be adjusted downward to reflect the effects of the financing. The assessed value shouldn't indicate a market value higher than the amount of money paid for the property after the adjustments for personal property tax and financing.

You may discover comparable properties near your property that are assessed lower than your building. Bringing in photographs of these properties may be helpful when filing a complaint with the assessor. In some cases, the assessor may either lower your assessed value or raise the assessed value on the comparable properties.

When using an income approach (rental property), keep in mind that assessors usually employ guideline percentages in determining normal operations of a property. They follow these guidelines when looking at vacancies, expenses, and taxes as percentages of taxes of gross possible rents and taxes per unit or per square foot.

If your percentages are higher than the guidelines used by the assessor, it is up to you to prove that these problems should be considered in assessing the property and are not the result of poor management. Assessors don't have to lower the value on a property simply because the owner or manager isn't doing an adequate job. Be ready to justify and support variances from the guidelines, especially major, unexpected, and necessary expenses. Also be ready to give reasons why you are experiencing higher-than-normal vacancies.

Any natural disaster, such as a flood, fire, or tornado, that causes major damage to the property should be brought to the attention of the assessor immediately; documentation supporting the cost of the damages should be submitted to the assessor. Any problem with the property that would have a negative effect on value should be documented for the assessor.

VALUATION COMPLAINTS

As noted above, all property by law must be reassessed at certain intervals, although the assessor may reassess your property each and every year. Also, you may file a complaint every year, even if your property has not been reassessed the year you file a complaint.

A call to the local assessor will inform you of the proper forms that are required to be filed, the date by which the complaint must be filed, the documents that must be filed with the complaint, and the number of copies of each document that are required. If you have trouble finding the proper office, which may happen in some rural areas, a call to the town hall may provide the answer. Some jurisdictions are not so formal and may just require that you mail the pertinent documents by a certain date. Assessors in these jurisdictions will work with you to determine the value of your property before formally issuing a notice. By working in this manner with the assessor, you may be able to avoid the appeal process altogether.

Some assessors won't accept a complaint if it isn't on their specific forms, so it's important that taxpayers work with the assessor and know the filing deadline. Filing deadlines may vary from year to year, and it may be very difficult to file a complaint for a given year if it is missed.

Legal representation is not required to work with an assessor concerning an assessed value; you may file the required information on your own behalf. If you and the assessor don't reach a mutually satisfactory decision, however, the next step is an appeal to a supervisory board. The name of the supervisory board may vary between states and even within states—Board of Appeals, Board of Review, Board of Equalization, Board of Assessors, or any number of other titles. In some jurisdictions, you may represent yourself before the board, whereas in others, you may require a lawyer. Complaint forms are required and filing deadlines must be met. A hearing or meeting is arranged at which the taxpayer may present the pertinent information about the property to the board, and questions and answers may pass back and forth. A decision is rendered by the board within a specified period.

In most cases, if you aren't satisfied by the decision of the board, a court remedy is available but requires hiring an attorney to represent you.

TAX RATE PROTESTS

Some states allow tax rate protests, or they at least have some type of procedure for protesting the tax rate. The basis for a tax rate protest is that the tax rate being levied, or some portion of it, is excessive and/or illegal. Normally, you would hire a local law firm to determine what portion of the tax rate is illegal and/or excessive and to file the lawsuit for you. There may be forms that have to be filed at the time the taxes are paid as well as other procedures that must be followed. The local treasurer should be able to guide you through the necessary procedures and perhaps provide you with the names of law firms to assist you in the process. Be advised, though, that tax rate protests are allowed only in some areas of the country.

SPECIAL ASSESSMENTS AND INCENTIVE PROGRAMS

Before contracting to purchase a property, check if there are any special assessments on the property. Special assessments for sidewalk or street light installation or the construction of a new sewage treatment plant are examples that would be passed on to a property owner and could lead to significantly higher taxes for a number of years. Taxes attributable to special assessments or special service areas cannot be reduced through an appeal process, so you would want to negotiate payment of these taxes with the seller at the time of purchase.

On the other hand, if the property needs major rehab work, you may want to find out if any incentive programs, tax credit programs, or exemptions are offered. Check with the local assessor's office or with the state to discover if any of these programs are available and how you qualify your property for them. Programs vary from state to state, between types of properties, and between local jurisdictions.

Before you start upgrading, ask about anything that might reduce the assessed value of the property during the work period and even for several years after the work is completed. If a landfill is going to open near you or the city is planning to rebuild the streets (eliminating parking spaces for a period), you may want to reconsider upgrading it.

CHOOSING A RELIABLE ATTORNEY OR TAX CONSULTANT

Many property tax consulting firms as well as law firms are available to represent taxpayers before the various assessors, boards, and courts. Their degree of success can vary significantly based on their level of expertise, their diligence, and their reputation with the various assessing bodies, so it's a good idea to speak to several different consultants or attorneys. Look for one who is established in the field and preferably works exclusively in the field of property taxes with a reputation for honesty, reliability, and imagination. Request examples of the types of cases they have handled, with a list of references, and then call several references. Request that they explain the steps in a typical appeal process, your role in the process, and the information you need to provide as well as anything you don't understand about the process. Don't hesitate to contact the assessor to determine if the information provided by the consultant or attorney is accurate.

Ask about fees. Call as many different firms as possible to determine the normal fees in a given area. Some firms work on a contingency basis, whereas others work on flat fees. A contingency fee is a percentage of the tax savings, usually payable over two or more years; a flat fee is exactly what it implies and is a specified amount per year for the term of the agreement. Flat fees are normally employed in situations in which it's difficult to determine actual savings or a contingency fee would be outrageously high because of the size of the property. Fees are usually negotiable.

It's usually preferable to hire a consultant or attorney in the geographic area where the property is located. However, if you own property in many different locations, such as in several different states, a national firm may be the answer. Question how long the firm has worked in these different locations; the type of relationship it has with different assessors; what, if any, professional designations its lawyers possess; and to what local, national, and international professional organizations it belongs. Preferably, the firm belongs to organizations that work with assessors in these areas, which usually signals that the consultant or attorney has a good rapport with the local assessor.

FOR MORE INFORMATION

If you have questions but are not quite ready to hire a consultant or attorney, there are several organizations you can contact. All states have their own organizations formed for assessor education and interaction that almost always allow nongovernment members to make inquiries. Ask the local assessor for the name and location of the organization for your jurisdiction.

You can also contact the International Association of Assessing Officers (IAAO), 130 East Randolph Street, Suite 850, Chicago, IL 60601-6217, 312-819-6100. This is the foremost authority on assessment practices worldwide. It accepts nongovernment members and offers several professional designations. It may be able to provide a list of associate members in a taxpayer's areas. This organization is also an excellent source for reference materials covering assessment practices and procedures, and it offers classes.

The Institute of Property Taxation, 3350 Peachtree Road, NE, Suite 280, Atlanta, GA 30326, 404-240-2300, is an organization of nongovernment members only. It has its own education programs and professional designations; its members are willing to exchange ideas, give referrals, and explain the property tax system in areas where they own property.

ACCOUNTING

Ellen Martig and her husband, Roger, became owners of a 14-unit, 20,000-square-foot strip mall in Mesa, Arizona, after doing an extensive 1031 tax-free exchange for ten rental properties they owned. Their company, Rogellen Properties, managed the mall for 13 years during a highly cyclical time before selling it in 2002 for their retirement nest egg. Through these years, they enjoyed an average of 95 percent occupancy.

"I did the leasing, bookkeeping, marketing, and overall customer communication on our mall as well as setting up maintenance contacts from my list of vendors. It helped tremendously that I took a course in how to be a commercial landlord from a real estate school. In addition to that, I'd ask advice from Richard, the agent who put together the 1031 tax-free exchange sale for us in 1989," Ellen says.

Many factors affected the management of this mall during that 13-year time frame. Demographic factors around it changed and more low-income people moved into the neighborhood. Ellen found that more women went into business during this time, but instead of renting commercial space, they opted to set up home offices. In addition, new megamalls were being built in the metro Phoenix area, drawing some businesses away from small neighborhood strip malls.

Telemarketing to tenants of other strip malls around the area and enticing them to move to her mall proved to be a good learning experience. "I realized that people want to do their own legwork. They prefer to case out a location and check traffic patterns and demographics for themselves." Still, through good management that took her an average of four hours a week, she was able to sustain low vacancy rates.

"We did well because we sought and attracted tenants who'd bring in their own customers, such as doctors, chiropractors, and dance teachers. Franchised hairdressing businesses, for example, tend to have a hard time making it in a strip mall because they really need the walk-in traffic of a megamall."

As she looks back on her landlording years, Ellen says the key to success is having good relationships with her tenants. With some, she even developed a business coaching relationship. "They liked me and they knew I really wanted them to succeed. It encouraged me to start a coaching business now that I'm no longer a landlord. Working with people—that's the rewarding part."

BOOKKEEPING

The bookkeeping for your rental property can be as simple or sophisticated as you like. However, the type of accounting system you use will depend to a large extent on the size of your income portfolio. Using a personal computer or hiring a computer service company may be helpful if you operate more than 24 units. On the other hand, a simple receipts-disbursements bookkeeping system is adequate for managing a few units.

The Internal Revenue Service (IRS) requires that taxpayers be able to substantiate rental income and expenses reported on their tax returns. By using a bookkeeping system such as the one illustrated in this chapter, you will not only satisfy IRS requirements but will also determine your cash flow or deficit on a month-by-month basis.

Operating income property is a business. Just as in any other business, you want to make intelligent decisions based on sound economic reasoning and facts. Maintaining adequate records enables you to monitor the expenses of your property, allowing you to determine if any of the expenses can be reduced and thereby increasing your cash flow.

Your accountant will be able to prepare your tax return more easily if the history of the past year is readily available. Funds received and cash disbursed as part of a business need to be treated with more sophistication than your personal checkbook transactions. Even if your accountant or computer service bureau keeps your records, you need some knowledge of bookkeeping.

USING A LEDGER TO PRODUCE A MONTHLY FINANCIAL STATEMENT

Checking Accounts

The IRS does not require that you maintain a separate checking account for each building you own (unless the property is not owned by you personally; for example, it's owned by a partnership), but keeping separate accounts facilitates recordkeeping. By keeping the cash receipts and cash disbursements separate from your personal transactions, it is much easier to prepare the monthly operating statement because all of your transactions are in one checking account.

If you use a separate checkbook for each property, and the account doesn't have sufficient cash to pay a certain bill, you will have to put your personal funds into the checkbook. If you have to do this, be certain to indicate in your building checkbook where the money came from; for example: "transfer from personal checkbook." Later, when the building checkbook has sufficient cash, you can write a check reimbursing yourself from the building account.

Rent Schedules

As you receive the monthly rental checks, deposit them into the appropriate building account checkbook. Next, record the rental receipt on a Rent Schedule (see Figure 12.1) for the appropriate building. By recording the receipts when you receive the rent, you can determine at a glance which tenants still owe you money. As your number of units increases, this rent schedule becomes very important; without it you might overlook a nonpaying tenant as a result of the high number of units you own. Your rent schedules function as a cash receipts journal.

Record cash disbursements in the building checkbook when they occur. At the end of each month, complete the Cash Disbursements Journal (see Figure 12.2). Make the recordings each month on a new sheet, and keep all sheets for your accountant to review at year-end.

To prepare the monthly Cash Disbursements Journal, go through the building checkbook, recording each disbursement by check number, payee, and description. In the sample journal, six columns are used for types of disbursements

FIGURE 12.1 *Rent Schedule*

Building Location or Name																20___
Security Deposit	Tenant Name	Apt. No.	Jan.	Feb.	Mar.	Apr.	May	June	July	Aug.	Sept.	Oct.	Nov.	Dec.	Total	
$550	Smith	1	$550													
$600	Jones	2	$600													
$575	Adams	3	$575													
$575	Johnson	4	$600													
	Total rents		$2,325													
Plus laundry income			$50													
	Total income		$2375													

FIGURE 12.2 *Cash Disbursements Journal*

Check Number	Payee	Mortgage Payment	Supplies	Utilities Gas	Utilities Water	Office Supplies	Other
101	Citizens Mortgage	$1,250.00					
102	Ace Supply Store		$13.31				
103	Utility Co.—Gas			$192.72			
104	Water Company				$39.41		
Cash	Smith Hardware		$10.00				
105	Ace Supply Store		$15.00				
106	All-Office Supply Store					$22.00	
		$1,250.00	$38.31	$192.72	$39.41	$22.00	

Building Location or Name _____ For the Month of _____, 20___

(mortgage, supplies, utilities, and so on). The building and the number of checks written each month determines the number of columns you will need to record the transactions. Use 13-column accountant's worksheets, which can be purchased at most office supply stores, or a computer-based program.

Monthly Cash Disbursements Journal

If you pay cash for a supply or service instead of writing a check, get a receipt and indicate on the receipt what type of service was performed or supply purchased from whom, on what date, and for which building. You can then reimburse yourself from the building checkbook for the cash you spent, or on the Monthly Cash Disbursements Journal write "cash" in the check number column. Attach all receipts to each month's Cash Disbursements Journal. By doing this, you leave an "audit trail," so should you ever have to substantiate the building operation numbers, all of the paid receipts are attached to the appropriate month's disbursements journal.

Operating Statement

At the end of each month, tally the income and expenses from your journals and enter the figures on the Cash Flow Statement (see Figure 12.3). The operating statement shows a summary of activity during the month and is broken down by line items.

FIGURE 12.3 *Cash Flow Statement*

| Building Location or Name _____ | | | | | | | | | | | | | 20_____ |

Cash Receipts (table 1)	Jan.	Feb.	Mar.	Apr.	May	June	July	Aug.	Sept.	Oct.	Nov.	Dec.	Total
Rent	$ 2,325.00												
Laundry	$50.00												
Other													
Total Receipts (a)	$ 2,375.00												
Cash Disbursements (table 2)													
Mortgage payment	$1,250.00												
Accounting													
Advertising													
Cleaning and maintenance													
Insurance													
Legal													
Repairs													
Supplies	$38.31												
Real estate taxes													
Utilities													
Electric	$192.72												
Gas													
Water	$39.41												
Scavenger													
Landscaping													
Snow removal													
Wages and taxes													
Carpeting													
Appliances													
Office supplies	$22.00												
Other (describe)													
Total disbursements (b)	$1,542.44												
Net Cash Flow (Deficit) (a – b)	$ 32.56												

LINE ITEM DEFINITIONS
FOR THE CASH FLOW STATEMENT

Cash Receipts

- Rents: all moneys received as rent, not including security deposits or other deposits. Security deposits received from tenants are not considered income for tax-reporting purposes. It is a good idea to maintain these in a separate checkbook (or an interest-bearing account) until the tenants vacate the units. If you use some or all of the security deposit to pay for past due rent or damages to the property, it becomes taxable.
- Laundry: income received from laundry equipment
- Other: such items as application fees, late fees, and credit-check fees
- Total receipts: equals total of above items
- Fees: application fees, credit check fees, cleaning fees, etc.

Cash Disbursements

- Mortgage payment: principal, interest, tax escrow, and insurance escrow. Get an amortization schedule from your lender for your mortgage payments. Using the amortization schedule, you will be able to record each month's principal and interest payments. If your real estate taxes and insurance are included in your monthly mortgage payments, the lender can also provide you with the specific amounts.
- Accounting: fees paid to accounting companies or individual accountants for services rendered
- Advertising: signs, print ads, promotions, printing of fliers, and so on
- Cleaning and maintenance: labor only (does not include supplies)
- Legal: fees paid for legal services
- Repairs: parts and labor for appliances, electrical, plumbing, air-conditioning and heating, and do-it-yourself maintenance or contractor work
- Supplies: cleaning, janitorial, maintenance, and so on
- Landscaping: service contract or new purchases
- Snow removal: service contract
- Wages and taxes: administrative and janitorial
- Carpeting: new purchases
- Appliances: new purchases
- Other: miscellaneous
- Total disbursements: total of above expenditures

- Net cash flow (or deficit) from property: total cash receipts less total cash disbursements

ANALYZING AND USING OPERATING STATEMENT DATA

To further refine your operating statement, determine the rental income and other items on the operating statement on a per unit basis. Do this by dividing each income and expense category by the total number of units you own. You can use this information to determine relationships that may help you increase your cash flow.

Operating statements provide historical data for preparing your annual budget and detail important information that is useful when you purchase more investment property. For example, suppose you own a 4-flat property building with utility costs of $14 per unit and are considering purchasing a 12-flat. By using information from your other properties, you can project a per unit utility cost for the building you are considering buying. Don't arbitrarily use the data, however, without giving thought to the details of the potential building. For example, if your 4-flat building is gas heated and the 12-flat building for sale has electric heat, the heating costs are not comparable.

In addition to per unit totals, income and expenses can be expressed as a percentage of gross rents and other values, such as vacancy loss comparisons of the properties. Maintaining good records makes preparing your tax return easier and helps you analyze your building operations on a monthly and annual basis.

When you are ready to sell your real estate investment, you'll have information readily available to show a potential buyer.

COMPUTER SOFTWARE

If you own and operate at least six units, you may want to consider using a personal computer to keep track of your tenants and to perform all your accounting and bookkeeping functions. Many of the electronic spreadsheet programs (for instance, Microsoft Excel, or Quicken, or QuickBooks) can be used to create your basic functions, along with several canned programs that come preloaded on some new computers. Beyond these basic spreadsheets, you can also purchase a software package designed specifically for property management.

Using a computer allows you to generate graphs and tables that make analyzing the details of your investment easier.

As of this writing, at least three software packages were reasonably priced for the individual owner and/or operator of rental properties. These, or any other good software systems, should have the following minimum characteristics:

- Improve management of daily and monthly routines
- Easy to install or to use
- Cost effective
- Have free technical support
- Handle all the accounting, recordkeeping, and file maintenance
- Customizable
- Handle multiple properties
- Include a good set of manuals or instructions
- Allow for future updates
- Backed by a reputable company

Three software options developed specifically for landlords are: *Tenant Pro 100*, Property Automation Software Corp. (800-964-2792, http://www.propertyautomation.com and http://www.tenantpro.com); *Tenant File*, WG Software, Inc. (800-398-3904, http://www.tenantfile.com); *EZ-Units*™ Z-Law Software, Inc., (800-526-5588, http://www.z-law.com). See the Resources section in this book for more information.

INCOME TAXES

Tax reform has significantly changed real estate as an investment, and real estate experts believe it will be good for real estate in the long run. The following information only touches the surface of the changes affecting real estate investing. Contact your own tax advisor for a more in-depth analysis of how tax laws affect your situation.

Active Owners

Tax reform eliminated many tax shelters associated with real estate investments. However, the revisions did leave a substantial portion available to active owners who make less than $150,000 per year in earned income and are actively involved in the management of their real estate.

An owner-operator of income property who has less than $100,000 per year (or $50,000 if married and filing separately) in earned income can still deduct up to $25,000 for depreciation and operating losses to reduce taxable income from all sources. The $25,000 tax loss is phased out in stages for incomes between $100,000 and $150,000. If your adjusted gross income stays below $100,000, you could purchase several properties before reaching the $25,000 limit. The elimination of tax incentives for builders has led to a reduction in the construction of new property units and should result in increased rents.

Passive Owners

The following advantages exist for passive real estate investors (those who are not involved in the management of their real estate):

- Limited liability: The mortgages are nonrecourse (only the specific property is at stake), and you have no personal responsibility for any bills or operating expenses of the building.
- Professional management: A professional management company handles all of the day-to-day concerns. A passive investor enjoys worry-free ownership.

Depreciation

Depreciation is defined as the allocation of the cost of an asset to the periods benefited in a rational and systematic manner. This means a noncash deduction on your tax return.

For example, suppose you purchased a four-unit property building for $150,000, of which $30,000 is allocated to the land. Land is a nondepreciable asset, so the higher the land allocation, the lower the amount remaining that you can depreciate. Allocating a portion of the original purchase price to Section 1245 personal property, which is depreciated over five years, can provide a larger depreciation expense than allocating it over 27.5 years. The building value is then $120,000, and, for simplicity's sake, let's assume you depreciate this using the straight-line method for a period of 27.5 years. You can then deduct $4,363 annually from your rental income as an expense, but you did not pay $4,363 as a current year *cash* expense. On your tax return, you would claim a deduction of $4,363 for *depreciation* expense. This is what is meant by a noncash expense.

Tax reform increased the life over which you depreciate the residential building from 19 years to 27.5 years (39.5 years for commercial property). In addition, you are now required to use the straight-line method of depreciation as opposed to using the accelerated method that was used in the past.

Active versus Passive Income

There are three different types of income, and each is reported differently on your tax return. Wages are earned income; dividends and interest are considered portfolio income; most real estate investment is classified as passive income. Check with your tax consultant about the exact rules.

In general, if you own property personally (as opposed to a limited partnership investment), you are able to deduct any losses you may incur against your other income. For example, you earn $50,000 from your job and your property investment has a $10,000 loss (remember depreciation is a noncash expense, so it is not unusual to report a loss on your tax return). You would be able to deduct the $10,000 rental loss on your tax return, in effect decreasing your earned income from $50,000 to $40,000. Depending on your individual tax bracket, this could save you up to $3,850 in taxes.

Congress has limited the deduction you can claim from real estate losses to a maximum of $25,000. So if you have more than $25,000 in passive losses, you cannot deduct any amount over the $25,000 limit. Also, if your earned income is more than $100,000, you start to lose 50 percent of the loss. At $150,000 of earned income, you cannot deduct any losses from your property. These nondeductible losses become "suspended" losses to be used when the property is sold or in future years if your income decreases. You don't lose these rental losses; it merely becomes a difference in timing—changing from a current deduction to a deduction that will decrease your gain on the sale of the property in the future.

Alternative Minimum Tax

The alternative minimum tax, or AMT, is like a separate set of rules for determining your tax liability. Its purpose, as the name implies, is to ensure that taxpayers who have tax preference income, deductions, or credits pay at least a minimum tax. Tax preference items were given special treatment under the regular tax laws, so it was possible for taxpayers to take advantage of this special treatment and avoid paying any federal income tax. Congress deemed this unfair, so it implemented the concept of a second tax system to make sure that taxpayers who benefited under the regular tax laws would not escape taxation altogether. Thus, the taxpayer is to pay the greater of the regular income tax or the AMT.

The alternative minimum tax concept is not new with the most recent tax law change, but its scope is increased so that more taxpayers are now subject to this tax than was true in the past. The more common tax preferences a real estate investor will encounter, or has encountered in the past, is the excess of accelerated depreciation over the straight-line method.

Passive losses deducted against earned or portfolio income are not allowed for AMT purposes. The entire gain is considered in calculating the alternative minimum taxable income.

ASSOCIATIONS

Apartment, Landlord, and Rental Owner Associations

For a list of associations in your state, go to http://www.rentalprop.com/apt-assns .htm. These associations were organized to help landlords and property managers keep more control of their properties, providing legal guidance and support.

> Contact info for the publisher of the *Rental Property Reporter:*
> Cain Publications, Inc.
> P.O. Box 68761
> Oro Valley, AZ 85737
> 520-877-8535
> 800-654-5456
> e-mail: bobcain@rentalprop.com

Building Owners and Managers Association International (BOMA)

A source of information on costs, codes, statistics, and developments in real estate. Provides professional development, leadership, and advocacy for the commercial real estate industry.

> Contact info: http://www.boma.org
> 1201 New York Ave. NW, Suite 300
> Washington, D.C. 20005
> 202-408-2662
> e-mail: webmaster@boma.org

Institute for Professionals in Taxation

Provides education programs, resource center, and local luncheons. It's first *Sales and Use Tax* book available October 2003.

> Contact info: http://www.ipt.org
> 3350 Peachtree Road, Suite 280
> Atlanta, GA 30326
> 404-240-2300

Institute of Real Estate Management (IREM)

An affiliate of the National Association of Realtors® (NAR), IREM is an association of property and asset managers.

Contact info: http://www.irem.org
430 N. Michigan Ave.
Chicago, IL 60611-4090
800-837-0706

International Association of Assessing Officers (IAAO)

An educational and research association concerned with property taxation.

Contact info: http://www.iaao.org
130 East Randolph St., Suite 850
Chicago, IL 60601
312-819-6100

International Crime Free Association, Inc.

A nonprofit organization dedicated to crime prevention on rental properties through the partnership of local law enforcement and the community. Sponsors an annual training conference.

Contact info: http://www.crime-free-association.org
P.O. Box 31745
Mesa, AZ 85275-1745
e-mail: TimInMesa@aol.com

National Apartment Association (NAA)

Serves owners, managers, developers, and suppliers of multifamily units. Provides education and training for multisite managers and on-site staff.

Contact info: http://www.naahq.org
201 North Union St., Suite 200
Alexandria, VA 22314
703-518-6141

National Association of Realtors® (NAR)

Provides professional development and research to the public for the purpose of preserving the right to own, use, and transfer property.

Contact info: http://www.realtor.org
430 N. Michigan Ave.
Chicago, IL 60611
800-874-6500

National Association of Residential Property Managers (NARPM)

A national association for all involved in property management—owners, managers, and support staff—of single-family and small residential properties, offering education, networking, and tools.

Contact info: http://www.narpm.org
P.O. Box 140647
Austin, TX 78714-0647
800-782-3452
e-mail: Info@NARPM.org

National Multi Housing Council (NMHC)

A national association for large apartment firms.
Contact info: http://www.nmhc.org
1850 M St., NW, Suite 540
Washington, D.C. 20036-5803
202-974-2300

Self-Storage Association (SSA)

A member-based association providing support, guidance, and education to those in the self-storage business; promotes public policy related to this industry. The Web site provides links to state associations.

Contact info: http://www.selfstorage.org
SSA Headquarters Office
6506 Loisdale Road, Suite 315
Springfield, VA 22150
703-921-9105
e-mail: ssa@selfstorage.org

Society of Industrial and Office Realtors®

A commercial and industrial real estate association for Realtors and associate members involved in the commercial real estate industry.

Contact info: http://www.sior.com
1201 New York Ave. NW, Suite 350
Washington, D.C. 20005
202-449-8200
e-mail: admin@sior.com

REGIONAL ASSOCIATIONS

Arizona Multihousing Association (AMA)

Arizona's trade association for the apartment and rental housing industry, serving property owners, developers, managers, and suppliers.

Contact info: http://www.azama.org
5110 N. 44th St., Suite L160
Phoenix, AZ 85018
602-224-0657
800-326-6403

Independent Rental Owners Council (IROC)

A subgroup of the Arizona Multihousing Association (AMA), whose purpose is to educate, support, and encourage the small real estate investor (those owning fewer than 20 units).

Contact info: http://www.azama.org/iroc
IROC chairman Jeff Young Jyoung@ffec.com
AMA office: 5110 N. 44th St., Suite L160
Phoenix, AZ 85018
602-224-0135
800-326-6403

South East Valley Real Estate Investors Group (SEVREIG)

An association in the southeast Phoenix, AZ, area geared to networking between landlords and real estate investors, and learning about acquisition and management of properties.

Contact info: http://www.AZProp.com
Chris Durham
Arizona Properties
P.O. Box 11248
602-617-1492
e-mail: Chris@AZProp.com

BOOKS

The Absentee Landlord's Survival Guide, 2nd ed., by Jack Rower, Mellwood Publishing, 1997

Buy Low, Rent Smart, Sell High, by Andy Heller and Scott Frank, Dearborn Trade Publishing, 2003

Complete Idiot's Guide to Being a Smart Landlord, by Brian F. Edwards, Casey Edwards, and Susannah Craig, Alpha Books, 2000

Dictionary of Real Estate Terms, 5th ed., by Jack Friedman, Jack Harris, and Bruce Lindeman, Barron's Educational Services, 2000

Down to Earth Landlording: A Guide to Successful Part-time Property Management, by Donald Beck, Skyward Publishing Company, 2004

Every Landlord's Legal Guide, 6th ed., by Marcia Stewart, Ralph E. Warner, and Janet Portman, Nolo Press, 2003

The Landlord, by Ken Merrell, KayDee Books L.C., 2001

Landlord and Tenant (Ask a Lawyer), by Steven D. Strauss, W.W. Norton & Company, 1998

Landlording: A Handy Manual for Scrupulous Landlords and Landladies Who Do It Themselves, 9th ed., by Leigh Robinson, Express, 2001

Landlording as a Second Income: The Survival Handbook, by Lawrence London, Madison Books, 1998

The Landlord's Kit: A Complete Set of Ready-to-Use Forms, Letters, and Notices to Increase Profits, Take Control, and Eliminate the Hassles of Property Management, by Jeffrey Taylor, Dearborn Trade Publishing, 2002

The Landlord's Troubleshooter, 2nd ed., by Robert Irwin, Dearborn Trade Publishing, 1999

Making Big Money Investing in Real Estate without Tenants, Banks, or Rehab Projects, by Peter Conti and David Finkel, Dearborn Trade Publishing, 2002

Making Big Money Investing in Foreclosures without Cash or Credit, by Peter Conti and David Finkel, Dearborn Trade Publishing, 2003

The New No-Nonsense Landlord: Building Wealth with Rental Properties, 2nd ed., by Richard H. Jorgensen, McGraw-Hill Trade, 1994

Rental Houses for the Successful Small Investor, by Suzanne P. Thomas, Gemstone House Publishing, 1999

Profitable Real Estate Investing, by Roger Woodson, Dearborn Trade Publishing, 1999

Property Management for Dummies, by Robert S. Griswold, For Dummies, 2002

Property Management Forms and Products, free catalog, Peachtree Business Products, 800-241-4623

Secrets of a Millionaire Landlord: Maximize Profits and Minimize Hassles, by Robert Shemin, Dearborn Trade Publishing, 2001

Shakespeare's Landlord, by Charlaine Harris, Dell Publishing Co., 1997

FORMS AND SUPPLIES

Peachtree Business Products

Offers forms and products for property management companies, apartments, condominiums, etc.

Contact info: http://www.pbp1.com
               800-241-4623
               800-231-7150 (fax)
               P.O. Box 13290 Atlanta, GA 30324

LANDLORD CONSULTANTS/COACHES

Scott Henderson

Contact info: http://www.persmgt.com
               Property Manager/Consultant
               303-998-0754
               e-mail: info@persmgt.com

Kent Mitchel, M.A., CPCC

Contact info: Property Investor and Certified Coach
510-548-2554
e-mail: kent.mitchell@sbcglobal.net

Nancy Spivey

Contact info: http://www.transformit.net
Transformation Consultants, Inc.
P.O. Box 190075
Atlanta, GA 31119
770-377-1847
e-mail: nspivey@transformit.net

MAGAZINES

Apartments for Rent

An apartment-listing magazine with separate editions for over 40 cities.

Contact info: http://www.forrent.com
e-mail: customerservice@forrent.com

Journal of Property Management

Published bimonthly by the Institute of Real Estate Management (IREM). Caters to property managers of large apartment communities but is also useful for small-scale owners and/or landlords.

Contact info: http://www.irem.org
Editorial Offices
Amanda Drucker
430 N. Michigan Ave.
Chicago, IL 60610-4090
312-329-6056
e-mail: adrucker@irem.org

Multifamily Executive

Targets senior-level executives responsible for owning, managing, developing, and investing in multifamily housing units. Published monthly, it covers sales and marketing, finance, legal issues, and property management.

> Contact info: http://www.multifamilyexecutive.com
> One Thomas Circle NW, Suite 600
> Washington, D.C. 20005
> 202-452-0800
> 800-422-2681

MultiHousing News

Caters to property managers for large apartment communities but has many articles for owners and/or landlords as well.

> Contact info: http://www.multi-housingnews.com
> 770 Broadway
> New York, NY 10003
> 800-250-2430

RealEstate.com

Real estate listing Web site for apartments, homes, and new construction. RealEstate.com's parent company is publishing company PRIMEDIA, Inc. It offers listings through:

ApartmentGuide.com – listings in 20,000 communities
NewHomeonline.com – new home communities
MovingResourceGuide.com – source of moving and relocation services

> Contact info: http://www.realestate.com

Units

From the National Apartment Association. Covers affordable housing, maintenance, design and development, fair housing, marketing, legal, and leasing.

> Contact info: http://www.naahq.org
> 201 N. Union Street, Suite 200
> Alexandria, VA 22314
> 703-518-6141
> e-mail: webmaster@naahq.org

SOFTWARE

The Complete Real Estate Software Catalog

Selections evaluated by real estate professionals. Includes a wide variety of software programs.

Contact info: http://www.z-law.com
Z-Law Software, Inc.
80 Upton Ave.
P.O. Box 40602
Providence, RI 02940-0602
800-526-5588
e-mail: info@z-law.com

Management Plus™

Property management software for Windows. Assists in managing any company size or type of property.

Contact info: http://www.acsoftware.com
American Computer Software
2829 Royal Ave.
Madison, WI 53713
608-221-9449
800-527-9449

PROMAS—Property Management Accounting Software

Integrated accounting and management reporting that accommodates start-up and small-scale operations. Cost for 50 units is $395; unlimited unit version is $1,995.

Contact info: http://www.promas.com
CMS Inc.
311D Maple Ave. West
Vienna, VA 22180
West Coast: 888-591-5179
East Coast: 800-397-1499
e-mail: sales@promas.com

Rent Manager

Software combining property management features with a fully integrated accounting system.

Contact info: http://www.rentmanager.com
London Computer Systems, Inc.
1007 Cottonwood Dr.
Loveland, OH 45140
800-669-0871

RentRight Property Management Software

Windows-based software that works for a few rental units or extensive property management. Web site offers free demo.

Contact info: http://www.rent-right.com
Dayton, OH 45475
800-RENT-065
e-mail: sales@rent-right.com

Tenant File

Property management software that creates automatic vendor payments and does not require a monthly closing.

Contact info: http://www.tenantfile.com
W.G. Software, Inc.
P.O. Box 3829
Austin, TX 78764
800-398-3904
e-mail: sales@tenantfile.com

Tenant Pro

A Windows-based property management software that tracks information about your owners, properties, units, tenants, and vendors.

Contact info: http://www.tenantpro.com
Property Automation Software Corporation
800-964-2792

TENANT SCREENING COMPANIES

Landlord Portal.Com

Discussion forums, tenant screening, forms and agreements, do-it-yourself tips, and free rental postings.

Contact info: http://www.landlordportal.com

Rental Housing On-Line

A comprehensive landlord-tenant Web site, containing forms and agreements, state laws, housing acts and agencies, vacancy listings, e-courses, tenant screening, and member support.

Contact info: http://www.rhol.org
RHOL (United States)
2887 Krafft Road, Suite 1500
Port Huron, MI 48060

RHOL (Canada)
855 Ross Ave., Suite 1
Sarnia, ON N7T 7R1
810-984-1263
e-mail: membersupport@cses.com

RentGrow

Provides applicant screening, generating a recommendation within minutes.

Contact info: http://www.rentgrow.com
800-736-8476
e-mail: support@rentgrow.com

RentPort, Inc.

Makes accurate leasing recommendations in seconds. Also provides reports that give insight into the leasing process, helping property managers manage their credit risk.

Contact info: http://www.rentport.com
888-387-1750

Tenant Screening Center, Inc.

Runs a comprehensive national credit reporting business. Fees range from $20 for a minireport to $45 for a full report.

> Contact info: http://www.tsci.com
> 800-523-2381
> e-mail: info@tsci.com

WEB SITES

Environmental Protection Agency (EPA)

A federal government agency whose mission is to protect human health and safeguard the natural environment. Features databases of information about environmental laws and conditions in your community.

> Contact info: http://www.epa.gov

Landlord Association.Org (LLA)

Teaching the "tricks of the trade" through business peers.

> Contact info: http://www.landlordassociation.org
> 1218 French Street, Suite 103
> Erie, PA 16501
> 814-452-1700
> e-mail: contact@landlordassociation.org

Landlord Portal.Com

Discussion forums, tenant screening, forms and agreements, do-it-yourself tips, and free rental postings.

> Contact info: http://www.landlordportal.com

Landlord-Tenant Laws at mrlandlord.com

Mrlandlord.com provides links to the laws for almost all 50 states. To check out your state's landlord laws, go to http://www.mrlandlord.com/laws.

Landlords Web

Part of Rental Housing On-Line (see below). Answers to hundreds of landlord questions.

Contact info: http://www.landlords.com

'Lectric Law Library

Uniform Residential Landlord and Tenant Act—this act represents the latest legal views on what a landlord-tenant relationship should be.

Contact info: http://www.lectlaw.com/files/lat03.htm

Mrlandlord.com

Provides a wealth of industry-related information, advisors, chat rooms, e-newsletters, legal references, and much more.

Contact info: http://www.mrlandlord.com

MobileHomeNews.com

Features news, discussion forums, free classifieds, and industry voices.

Contact info: http://www.mobilehomenews.com
              http://www.mfdhousing.com

RentGrow.com

Provides credit reporting services. Specializes in fair housing compliance, and the rules and regulations surrounding fair housing in each state.

Contact info: http://www.rentgrow.com
              800-736-8476
              e-mail: support@rentgrow.com

Rental Housing On-Line

A comprehensive landlord-tenant Web site containing forms and agreements, state laws, housing acts and agencies, vacancy listings, e-courses, tenant screening, and member support.

> Contact info: http://www.rhol.org
> RHOL (United States)
> 2887 Krafft Road, Suite 1500
> Port Huron, MI 48060
>
> RHOL (Canada)
> 855 Ross Ave., Suite 1
> Sarnia, ON N7T 7R1
> 810-984-1263
> e-mail: membersupport@cses.com

Sheminrealestate.com

Member-based Web site that offers proven programs for building real estate wealth.

> Contact info: http://www.sheminrealestate.com

US Legal Forms.com

All types of landlord and tenant forms for commercial or residential use.

> Contact info: http://www.uslegalforms.com/landlordtenant
> P.O. Box 406
> 203 Mary Ann Drive
> Brandon, MS 39043
> 601-825-0382
> e-mail: lawnetco@uslegalforms.com

abandonment Refers to tenants leaving a property they are leasing without notice. *Abandonment* is a term that has a technical meaning in the law, and some states have specific statutes defining it.

advertising A means of making something known. For landlords, it's a means of making it known that a property is available for rent.

amenities Facilities or features of a property that make renting more attractive or valuable, such as community pools or laundry rooms; in a single residence, items such as air-conditioning or hardwood floors.

appreciation in value An increase in price or worth over time.

arbitration The process by which the parties to a dispute submit their differences to the judgment of an impartial person or group appointed by mutual consent or statutory provision.

asset A valuable item (such as property) that is owned.

background check An inquiry into an applicant's record—including credit, criminal, and employer information.

clause/rider Additions to a lease. Clauses are typed into the lease; riders are separate sheets that are attached to the lease.

collection agency A business that collects outstanding bills, usually on a contingency basis, charging a percentage of the amount collected as the fee.

covenant A binding agreement, a compact; can refer to rules set by homeowners associations and other real estate applications.

constructive eviction A form of eviction that occurs when a tenant voluntarily vacates the premises because of a defect in the condition of the unit (e.g., a leaking roof). See *eviction.*

credit check An inquiry into an applicant's credit history, (i.e., late payments, debt obligations, and recent applications for credit).

delinquent Failing to do what law or duty requires.

demographics The characteristics of human populations and population segments, especially when used to identify consumer markets.

depreciation in value A decrease in price or worth of a property over time because of wear or market conditions.

discrimination Denying consideration on the basis of race, color, religion, sex, or national origin. To avoid discrimination, criteria must be applied equally to all applicants, with the process well documented.

express warranty A promise to a tenant about the condition of a specific unit, overall premises, services, repairs, or replacements. This promise is binding, whether oral or written.

eviction A last resort to force a tenant out of the property by legal process.

fair housing laws Antidiscrimination laws legislated and enforced at the state level.

forcible detainer A form of behavior in which the owner may initiate eviction proceedings if tenants fail to vacate the unit or return the keys.

foreclosure The legal proceedings initiated by a creditor to repossess the property on a defaulted loan.

insurance See "The Language of Insurance" in Chapter 9 for various insurance terms.

Internet An interconnected system of networks that connects computers around the world via the TCP/IP protocol.

judgment (in court) A determination of a court of law; a judicial decision.

landlord/landlady One who owns property, which he or she leases to tenants.

lease agreement A contract granting occupation of property during a specified period in exchange for a specified rent. Can include terms beyond period and price, such as clauses concerning pets, maintenance and repairs, parking, and so on. All clauses must follow local landlord-tenant relation laws. The lease should be reviewed by a lawyer.

lease with option to purchase A lease that gives the lessee the option to purchase the home before the end of the lease term. Often the rent is slightly higher, with a portion going toward a down payment.

multiple listing service (MLS) Real estate sales listings distributed to all brokers; some also contain rental listings.

notice of termination A form used for different types of lease violations other than nonpayment of rent, including unauthorized pets, overoccupancy, or excessive noise. Serving this notice is the first step in the eviction process.

notice to vacate A notice sent to tenants at least 30 days before the end of the lease stating the rental property must be vacated.

ordinance A statute or regulation, especially one enacted by a city government.

passive income According to tax laws, most income from real estate holdings is classified as passive income. See Chapter 12 on taxes.

premises The complete address of the property being leased.

property manager Person responsible for accounting and reporting of all payables and receivables. The manager is responsible to owners, the management company, and to residents/tenants.

prorated Lease dates generally start on the first of the month, but if tenants cannot move in then, they pay a prorated amount of a full month's rent. The amount depends on the date they move in.

rent (n) Payment made by a tenant in exchange for the use of property.

rent (v) To grant temporary occupancy of property in return for regular payments.

return on investment (ROI) The yield an investor receives from an investment.

rider/clause Addition to the lease. Riders are separate sheets of paper attached to the lease; clauses are typed into the lease.

security deposit A refundable sum of money paid by the lessee to assure the lease conditions will be fulfilled. It helps cover the owner against any losses in the event of damage, early vacating by a tenant, or unpaid utility bills. The amount that can be charged is often set by state law but is limited by the local market.

statute An act of the legislature of a state or country.

sublease agreement A lease from one lessee to another. The management has a right to require the replacement meets the criteria all residents do. The original lessee is still legally liable for all rental payments and conditions of the lease, including damages that may occur under the sublessee.

TYPES OF PROPERTIES

apartment A building with several households renting separate residences.

condominium A building in which the units are individually owned, and common areas and structures are jointly owned.

duplex, triplex, etc. Detached homes that are split into parts, usually with separate entrances. A duplex is split into two complete residences, a triplex into three, and so on.

industrial complex A group of manufacturing-related businesses in one or more buildings designed for manufacturers.

megamall A collection of stores, businesses, and restaurants connected by walkways, usually enclosed. Only a few businesses have entrances from the parking lot; most are accessed from the common walkways.

mobile home community A neighborhood consisting of manufactured homes placed on concrete pads. The spaces can be rented, as can individual mobile home units. Some communities offer such amenities as a community swimming pool.

office complex A group of offices in one or more buildings occupied by white-collar businesses.

self-storage units Commercial warehouse units that consumers rent to store, lock, and access items.

single-family home Detached house intended for occupancy by one family.

strip mall A collection of businesses lining a busy street with parking in front. Each business has an entrance from the parking lot.

For additional real estate terms, refer to: *Dictionary of Real Estate Terms,* 5th edition, by Jack Friedman, Jack Harris, and Bruce Lindeman, Barron's Educational Services, 2000